IMAGES
of America

PLUMSTEAD TOWNSHIP

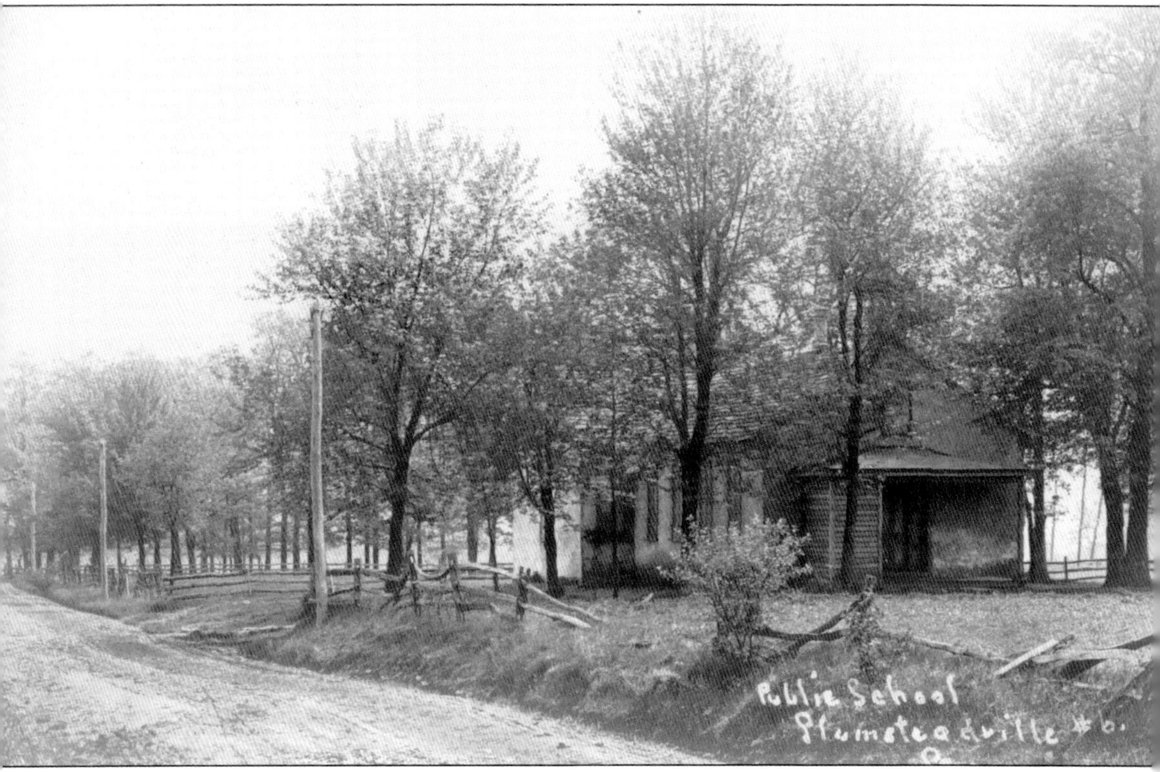

PLUMSTEADVILLE SCHOOL, C. 1900. The Plumsteadville School was built in 1858 and served as one of 12 one- or two-room schoolhouses in the township. The structure is now part of the township municipal building. Records indicate that the school was also used for community meetings, including an 1873 discussion on women's suffrage.

On the cover: **ALONG THE CANAL, C. 1900.** An empty barge makes its way through the canal at Point Pleasant.

IMAGES
of America

PLUMSTEAD TOWNSHIP

Plumstead Township Historic Advisory Committee

ARCADIA
PUBLISHING

ISBN 978-0-7385-3649-1

Published by Arcadia Publishing
Charleston, South Carolina

Printed in the United States of America

Library of Congress Catalog Card Number: 2004107284

For all general information, contact Arcadia Publishing:
Telephone 843-853-2070
Fax 843-853-0044
E-mail sales@arcadiapublishing.com
For customer service and orders:
Toll-Free 1-888-313-2665

Visit us on the Internet at www.arcadiapublishing.com

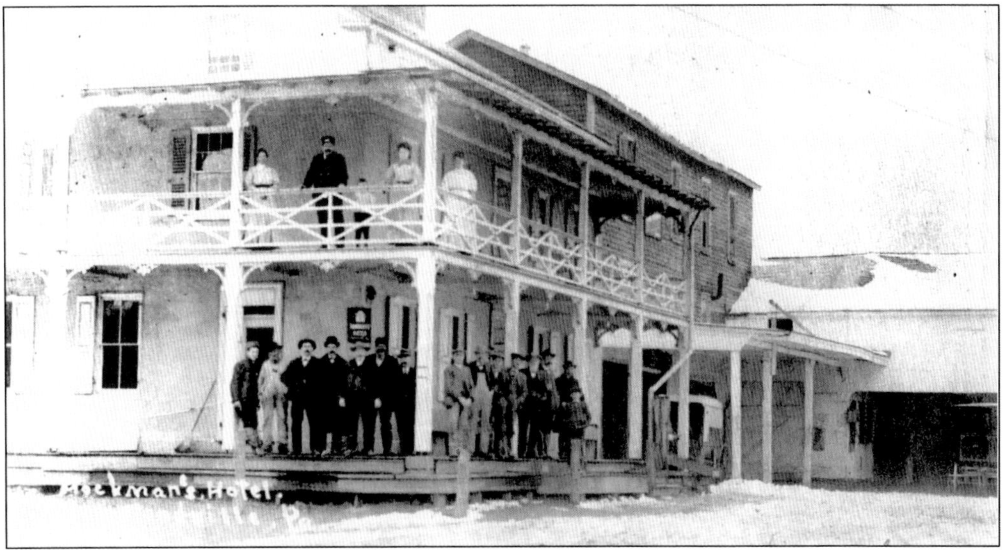

HOCKMAN'S TAVERN, C. 1890. The old tavern, now the Plumsteadville Inn, located at the corner of Stump and Easton Roads, has been expanded and rebuilt over the years, but has remained an important landmark and meeting place. Records suggest a tavern was located here prior to the Revolutionary War. The present building dates to the mid-19th century.

Contents

Acknowledgments		6
Introduction		7
1.	Early Homes and Families	9
2.	Farms	31
3.	Villages	47
4.	Schools	77
5.	Leisure	89
6.	Service	109
7.	Changing Times	119

ACKNOWLEDGMENTS

On behalf of the Plumstead Township Board of Supervisors—Frank Froio, chairman; Karen E. Helsel, vice chairman; Vince Formica, secretary-treasurer; and Housley Carr and Stacey Mulholland—the Historic Advisory Committee would like to thank residents and former residents and their family members from across the country who assisted us in this effort. Many individuals supplied cherished family photographs as well as information that made this glimpse of our past much more interesting than the committee had ever anticipated. Special thanks are extended to Tim Adamsky, Esther and Barbara Althouse, Verna Angeny, Dan Bender, Walter H. Bishop, Doris A. Bleam, Anna Booz, Rosemary Carroll, the Crooke family, Anna Detweiler, Neil Ellenoff, Peggy Feiler, Chester Fluck, the Gayman family, Ina M. Harmath, William Heacock, Bruce Hellerick, Peter Hunsberger, Evelyn Kuller, Budd Mann, Alice H. Marshall, Clarence Myers, Clayton Myers, Doris Myers, Stanley B. Myers, Helen A. Neppes, Joyce Overpeck, Jane Roman, Mildred N. Roman, Richard Rush, Milton Rutherford, the Sabath family, Edith Sames, Helen Sassaman, Ray Shull, Roy and Lillian Shull, Herman and Ann Silverman, Victoria M. Smith, Jeffrey and Colleen Trauger, Anthony Ventresca, Cynthia D. Wilson, and William Worthington. We also want to thank area organizations and businesses, including the Bucks County Extension Office, Fisher Hardware, the *Intelligencer*, and Central Bucks School District. We are especially grateful for the assistance of the Bucks County Historical Society for their encouragement and for allowing us to use historic photographs from Spruance Library.

I personally want to thank the volunteers and the township's Historic Advisory Committee members who spent hours contacting area residents and encouraging them to dig through their attics for lost treasures. These volunteers—many lifelong residents—include Donald and Barbara Morris, Carol Norwood, Annette Rosanelli, and Florence Cook, who never missed a meeting and who helped spur the project with her donation of an early map of the township. All of the volunteers shared their extensive collections of personal photographs and provided excellent advice, and also shared their knowledge of the township. I also want to thank Historic Advisory Committee members Helen Mitchell, Maris Langford, and Glenn Burd for their work, support, and guidance throughout the project. The entire township staff has also been extremely helpful to me during this project, but I would especially like to thank Linda Barratt, Alan Bleam, and Duane Hasenauer, who assisted with locating photographs and contacts, and Charleen Hard, who assisted me with layout and editing.

The number of photographs collected for this project was overwhelming, making it extremely difficult to decide which images to use. However, even those photographs not selected for this book have become part of a new project to archive and permanently identify pictures associated with Plumstead's early history. All photographs will be copied and, we believe, will be extremely important to researchers, residents, and future property owners who are interested in learning more about their homes and community.

Like any worthwhile project, this endeavor brought back old stories and memories, and provided hours of enjoyment for those involved. It provided many newcomers, including myself, with a better idea of our past and a sense of community. We hope the publication and the enthusiasm it has generated will be the first step in a series of history- and community-building projects.

—Michael May
Project Director

INTRODUCTION

European settlement in what is now Plumstead Township began in the early 1700s. Because of the township's location at the northernmost edge of 17th-century development, it became an area settled by both new immigrants and second-generation Americans searching for new land and resources. Among the first to build here were English Quakers who migrated from the more-established communities to the south. Most early inhabitants pursued farming and cleared large tracts of land. In 1725, the area was populated enough that a petition to form Plumstead Township was granted. By the mid-1700s, the area was no longer frontier territory and the typical log homes were replaced by more substantial stone buildings. Most early farmsteads were centered on the tracts in the English fashion, containing a house, barn, and associated outbuildings. A large German population was also found in Plumstead by the middle of the 18th century. For the most part, the German settlers constructed their farmsteads close to the roads and brought new architectural traditions.

Life in early Plumstead was dominated politically by English settlers, mostly members from the Quaker community. However, the Federal Direct Tax of 1798 suggests that residents of German descent made up the majority of families by the end of the 18th century. Over the years, the blend of English, German, and to a lesser extent the Scotch-Irish, helped create a variety of civic, religious, and educational institutions. However, daily life for most families continued to center around their meetinghouses, including the Quaker meeting at Gardenville, the German Mennonite meeting at nearby Deep Run, and later at Groveland Road.

During the Revolutionary War, many Plumstead residents fought with the patriots, supplied Continental troops with provisions, and cared for the sick and wounded. The old tavern at present-day Gardenville served as a forage station, and the Quaker meetinghouse was converted into a hospital for soldiers wounded in the New Jersey campaign. Revolutionary War records suggest that both the pacifist German Mennonites and English Quakers stayed clear of the conflict, even though they sympathized with the cause. The war often caused friction in the religious communities when members were sanctioned for donating supplies to the Continental Army, or when young men enlisted for service.

Among the most notorious Plumstead residents of the Revolutionary War era were members of the Doan gang. These outlaws and loyalists terrorized the community during the war. Folklore about the gang, including stories of their hideouts, raids, and treasures, has dominated oral and written history of the township. Much of the folklore is associated with the Doan Cave, which is believed to be the group's hideout, and the Doan graves outside the Quaker meeting.

By the early 19th century, the township's agricultural community had prospered, helping to develop villages that provided services and housed institutions. Crossroad communities and hamlets emerged around the early mills, taverns, ferry crossings, and crossroads where homes, general stores, blacksmith shops, and inns were built. Many of these villages expanded over the years, including the communities of Danboro, Fountainville, Plumsteadville, Gardenville, and Point Pleasant, while others such as Kendigtown, Grier's Corner, and Hinkletown were overshadowed by other towns and are now largely forgotten.

Plumstead's population in the 19th century grew steadily. Farming continued to be the dominant occupation, but farming practices changed by the mid-19th century, and most subsistence farms developed into specialized operations. The dairy industry emerged as the leading industry, and creameries were organized in various areas of the township to make production and marketing easier. Most farms, small and large, raised poultry with egg hatcheries and grew vegetables and fruits that were used locally and sold to the Philadelphia market. By the late 1800s, Plumstead also became known for its cattle and horse auctions. New technologies, including tractors, silos, and improved milking equipment, revolutionized farm life.

Although most families remained in agricultural pursuits, other industries developed in Plumstead during the 19th century and early 20th century. In addition to village service industries, a handful of highly successful businesses developed. The Schwartz Factory in Point Pleasant, for example, manufactured carriages, caskets, and furniture. In Plumsteadville, Aaron Kratz's carriage works became one of the largest manufacturers of horseless carriages and wagons on the East Coast. The Keller Glove Factory, established in the early 20th century, was also a major employer in Plumstead for many years. As the 19th century turned into the 20th, Kratz and Keller were the area's leading employers, and their businesses made Plumsteadville the predominant village in the township. Besides being home to important industries, Plumsteadville's location on the Easton Highway made the village an ideal location for the new Doylestown–Easton trolley line. By 1902, Plumsteadville had its own ticket office and was the site of the line's equipment and maintenance sheds.

Although Plumsteadville emerged as the township's largest village and the center of the community, the Delaware River was the most important transportation network. In the 18th century, several spots along the riverbank served as ferry landings, where fisheries and taverns prospered. With the construction of the Delaware Canal in 1831, shipping of coal, lumber, stone, and local farm products helped to develop river towns, including Point Pleasant. Shipping along the Delaware prospered for more than half a century, only diminishing with the construction of nearby railroad lines, and later ending when the automobile became commonplace. By the early 20th century, tourism replaced canal traffic along the river. The establishment of hotels, vacation homes, parks, and camps brought newcomers to the township, including many Philadelphians and New Yorkers who decided to stay and establish country homes. The township's unspoiled, lush rural landscape, historic homes, covered bridges, and the scenic river helped spur this vacation-related development. The river and the canal also provided recreation opportunities, such as swimming, hiking, boating, and fishing for visitors and residents alike.

As the popularity of the area increased, Plumstead became part of a national arts movement that drew artists, writers, and others associated with art and entertainment industries. Throughout the first half of the 1900s, these artists captured Plumstead in oils and watercolors or by ink and paper. Old homes were restored, an interest in history emerged, and gentleman estates began to replace the old working farms. The area's lush landscape, history, and convenience to New York made it an ideal excursion and weekend retreat well into the 20th century.

By the mid-1900s, road improvements and other new infrastructure, such as the construction of regional schools, helped pave the way for suburban growth. Still, the beauty of the river, rolling farmlands, and the township's quaint villages remain and continue to draw tourists and new residents.

One

Early Homes and Families

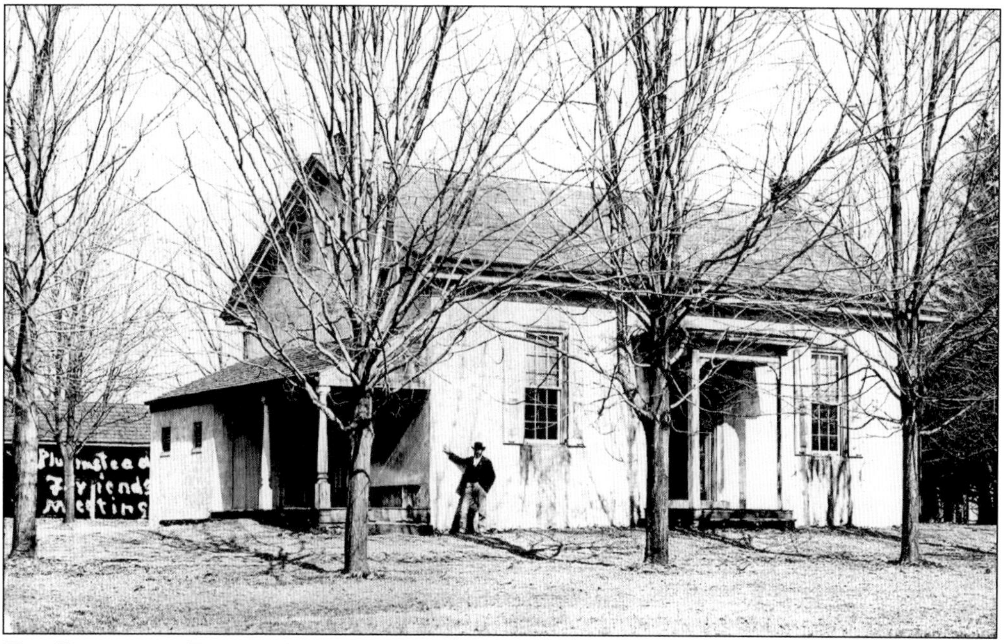

The Plumstead Friends Meetinghouse, c. 1900. English Quakers were the first to settle Plumstead in the early 1700s. Records suggest the early meetings were held in the home of Thomas Brown prior to the construction of the first meetinghouse in 1730 on land provided by the Brown family. In 1752, the original log meetinghouse was replaced with a stone structure used during the Revolutionary War as a hospital for the Continental Army. The 1752 meetinghouse was rebuilt in 1875. The meetinghouse and its walled cemetery are located west of Gardenville along Point Pleasant Pike.

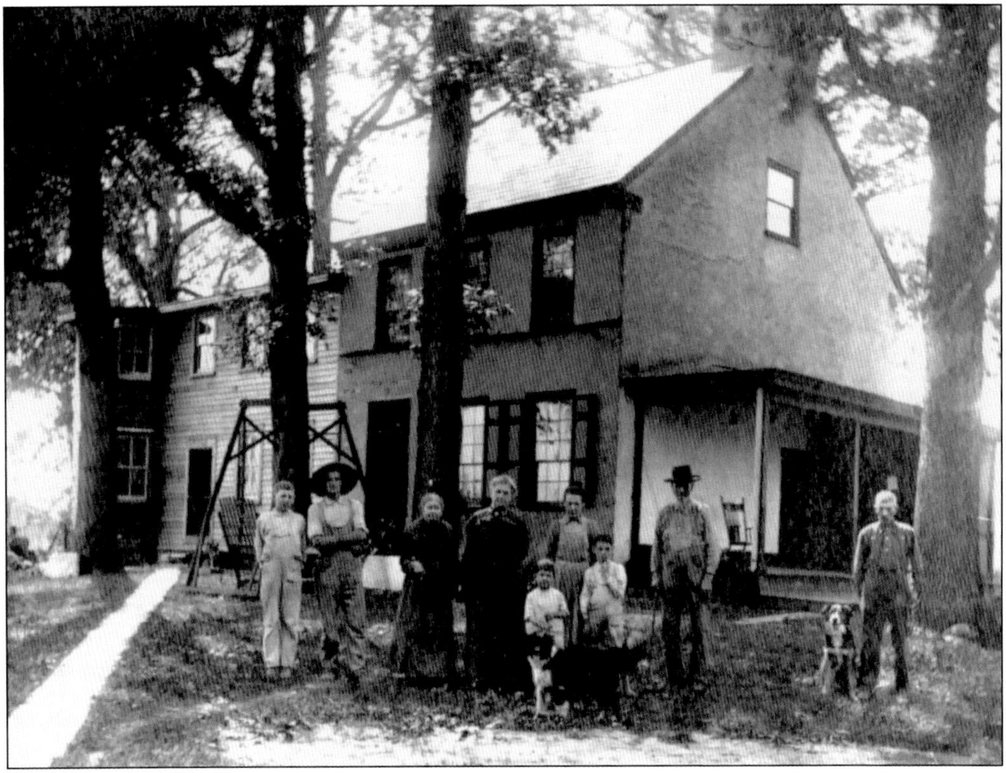

The Mill Farmstead, c. 1912. This farmhouse, located on Landisville Road, was probably built in the late 18th century by Josiah Brown, whose family held this land for many years. It later became part of a 101-acre farm held by the Smith and Harper families. In 1904 the property was sold to Linford and Irving Mills. Pictured from left to right are Floyd Mills, John Hillpot, Katie Hillpot, Emma Otteninger, Frank Mills, Nora Mills, Chester Mills, Henry Hillpot, and William Otteninger.

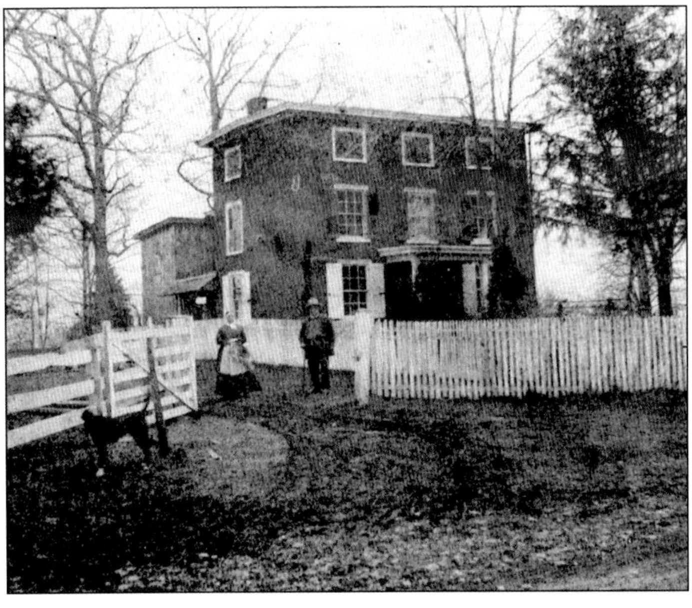

The Preston-Michener House, c. 1900. Pictured here, Sallie Stradling Preston and Nathan Preston were descendants of the township's early Quaker settlers. This home, which adjoins the meetinghouse, is typical of mid-19th-century houses built in the region. It features a low-pitched roof, third-floor eyebrow windows, and a plastered-over stone exterior. (Collection of the Spruance Library of the Bucks County Historical Society.)

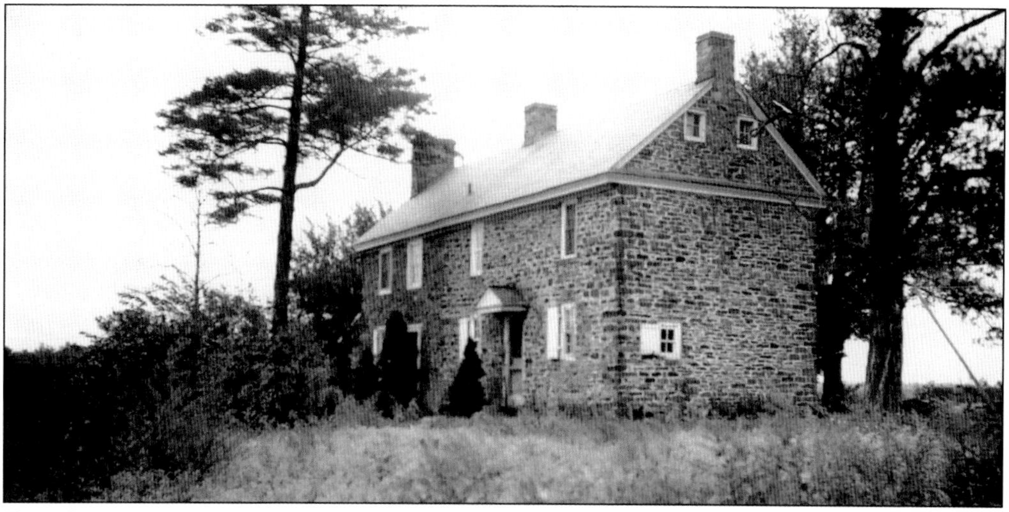

THE STRADLING-STROUSE HOUSE, C. 1949. This early stone house, situated off Point Pleasant Pike, is typical of structures built by Quaker families. The original mid-18th-century building is incorporated into the two-story section on the right side. Similar to most English farmsteads of the period, the house was located far off the road, in the middle of the farm tract. By 1752, the property was acquired by Daniel Stradling, whose family later added lateral wings. The 1798 Federal Direct Tax record indicates the house was one of only 39 stone, two-story houses in the township. Amos Strouse acquired the farm in 1872. The Strouse family held the property for more than 50 years. (Collection of the Spruance Library of the Bucks County Historical Society.)

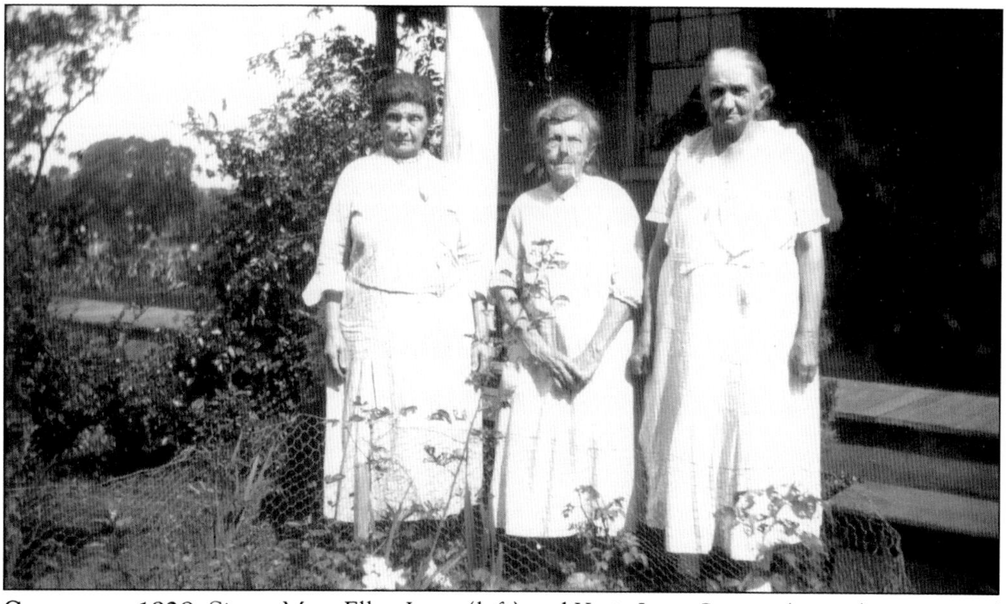

COUSINS, C. 1928. Sisters Mary Ellen Loux (left) and Katie Loux Strouse (center) are pictured with their cousin Ella Ott Michener. Katie Strouse, the widow of Elmer Strouse, lived at the old Stradling Farm at the top of Plumstead Hill. Under her husband's ownership, the property became the largest and most profitable dairy farm in the township. Katie's sister, Mary Ellen Loux, resided at her lifelong home, adjoining the Gardenville Farm, until her death in the late 1940s. The Loux house is found in the North Branch subdivision.

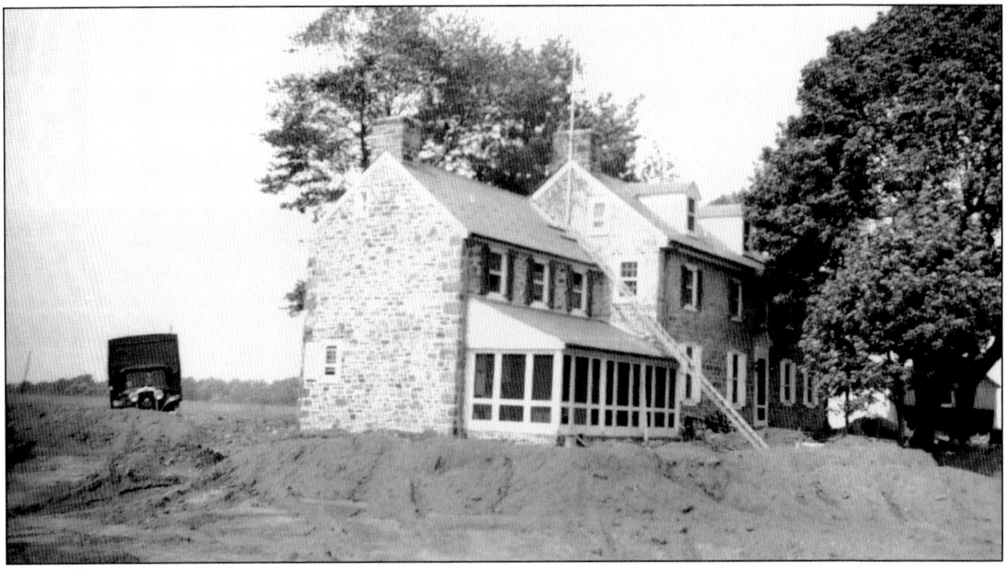

The Simpson House, c. 1930. Samuel Simpson is credited with building a portion of this early Quaker house along Twin Silo Road. Like the Stradling property, Simpson's farmhouse was built near the center of his tract. Records indicate that Simpson was active in local affairs and served as clerk of the Plumstead Meeting for more than 20 years. He resided here until 1772, when he sold the property to John Smith. The house was expanded in the Smith period (1772–1827) and also later in the 19th century. In the early 20th century, the structure was one of many restored due to the emergence of interest in Bucks County history and old stone houses. (Collection of the Spruance Library of the Bucks County Historical Society.)

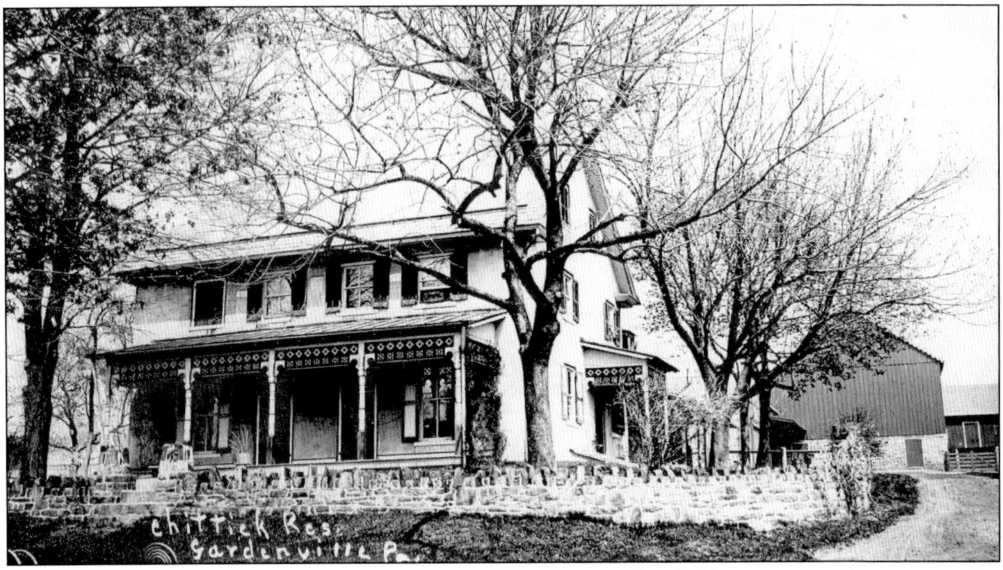

The Price-Chittick House, c. 1915. This large two-and-a-half-story stone house was the home of Smith Price, a storekeeper. It was constructed in 1794 along the Durham Road and shows Germanic influences in its large square form. Price is believed to have built the home soon after his second marriage in 1793. Records indicate he was among the few slave owners in the township. Like other area Quakers, Price emancipated his servants, including his housekeeper Esther, who was freed on May 23, 1787.

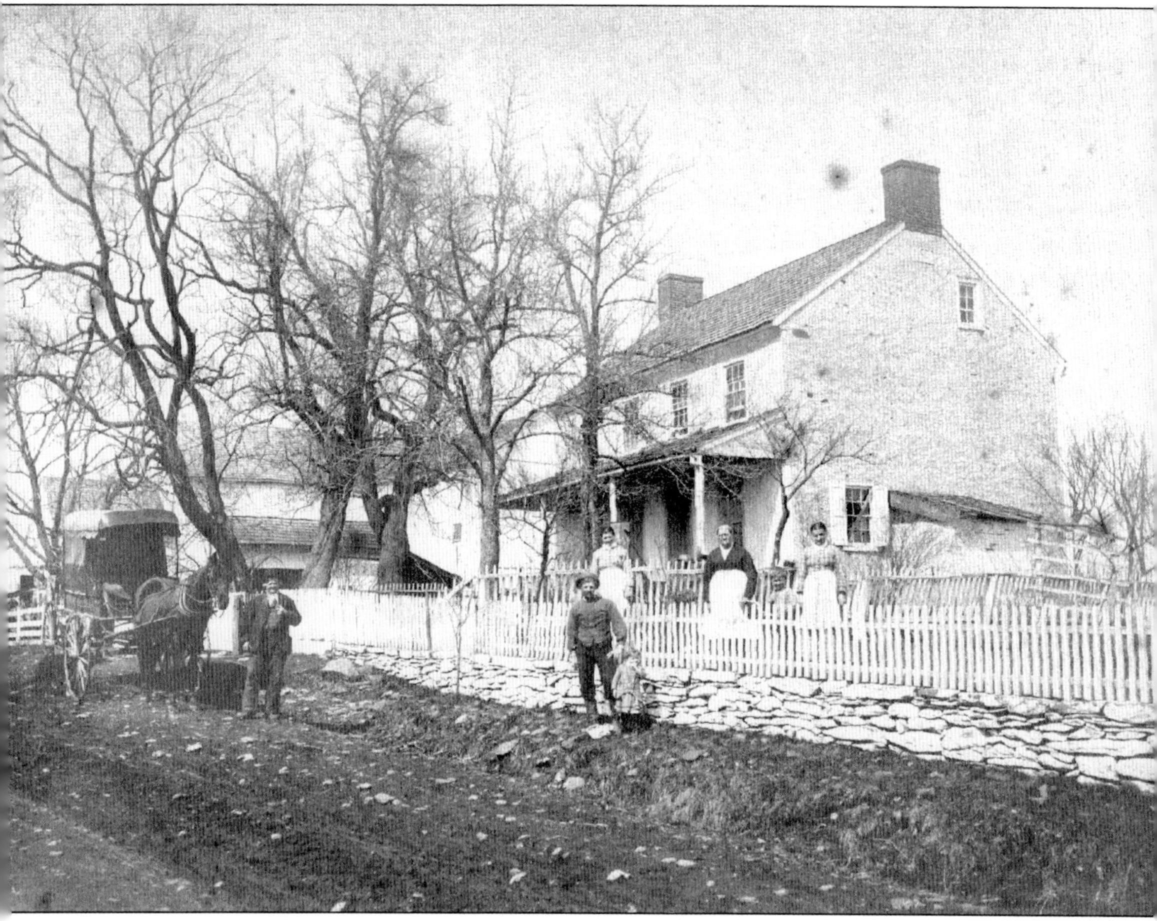

THE MICHENER HOMESTEAD, c. 1900. This style of farmhouse exemplifies a common form used in the early 1800s. Typical features include the stone construction faced with plaster, and the front porch with two central doorways. Note the bake oven on the gable end. The picket fence was another typical feature. Pictured here are unidentified members of the Hiram Michener family. The road in the foreground is Durham Road, or Route 413. The house is found near the corner of Curly Hill Road.

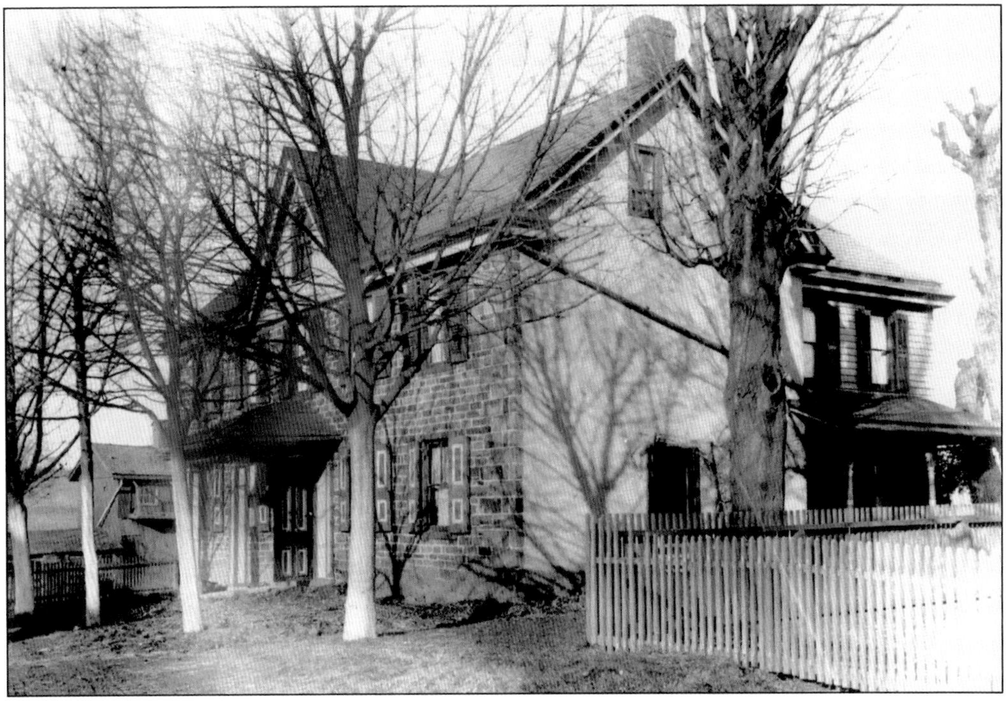

The Dyer Mansion, c. 1900. Records indicate that John Dyer purchased 51 acres for his mill and home in 1718. The original dwelling was most likely a log cabin, which was replaced by this house in the mid-18th century. Over the years, the structure was expanded to include a Victorian gable-peaked roof and other additions. John Dyer petitioned for the creation of Easton Road soon after his purchase of the property. He died in 1738 and is buried at the meetinghouse. Dyer's descendants retained the property for more than 200 years. (Collection of the Spruance Library of the Bucks County Historical Society.)

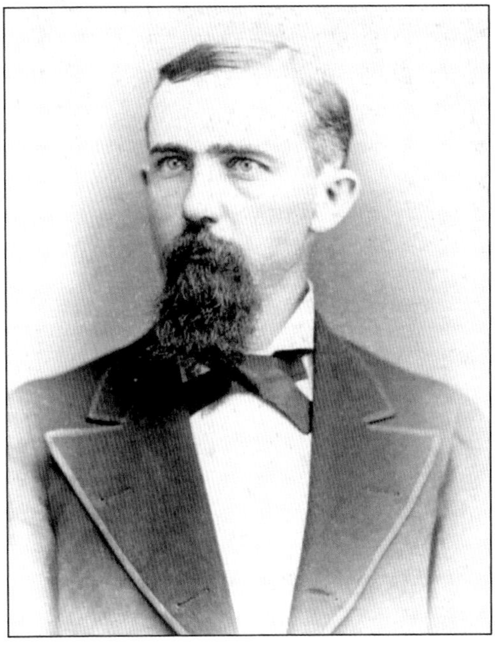

Cephas Dyer, c. 1870. Cephas W. Dyer, the son of Thomas and Jane Dyer, was born in 1838 and raised in Dyerstown. His father opened a general store in the village that same year. During the Civil War, Cephas served as a major with the 128th Pennsylvania Infantry Regiment.

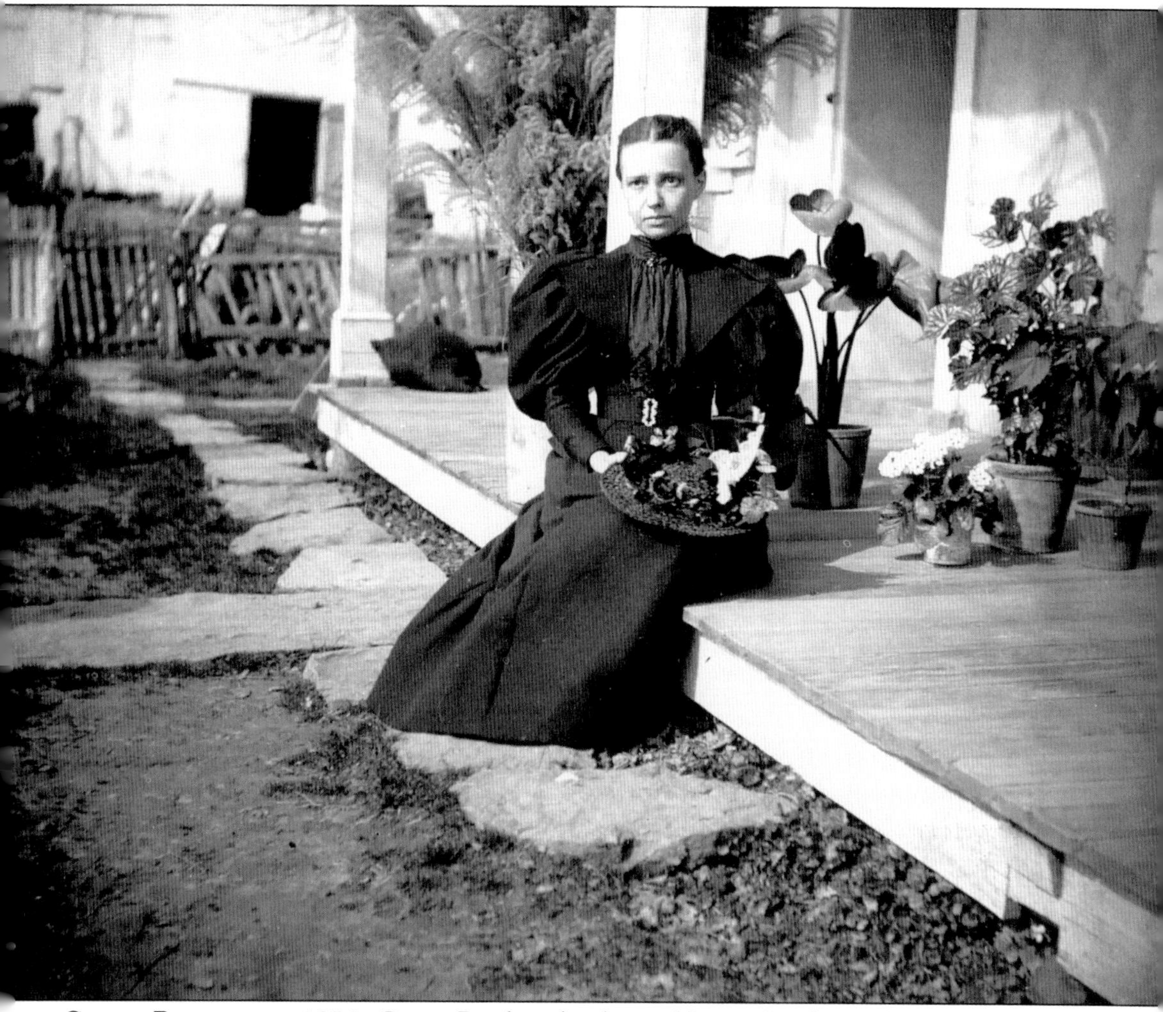

CARRIE BARCLAY, C. 1870. Carrie Barclay, daughter of James Barclay and Elizabeth Dyer Barclay, is pictured here on the Dyer House porch. Her parents inherited the old mansion and 86 acres in 1861.

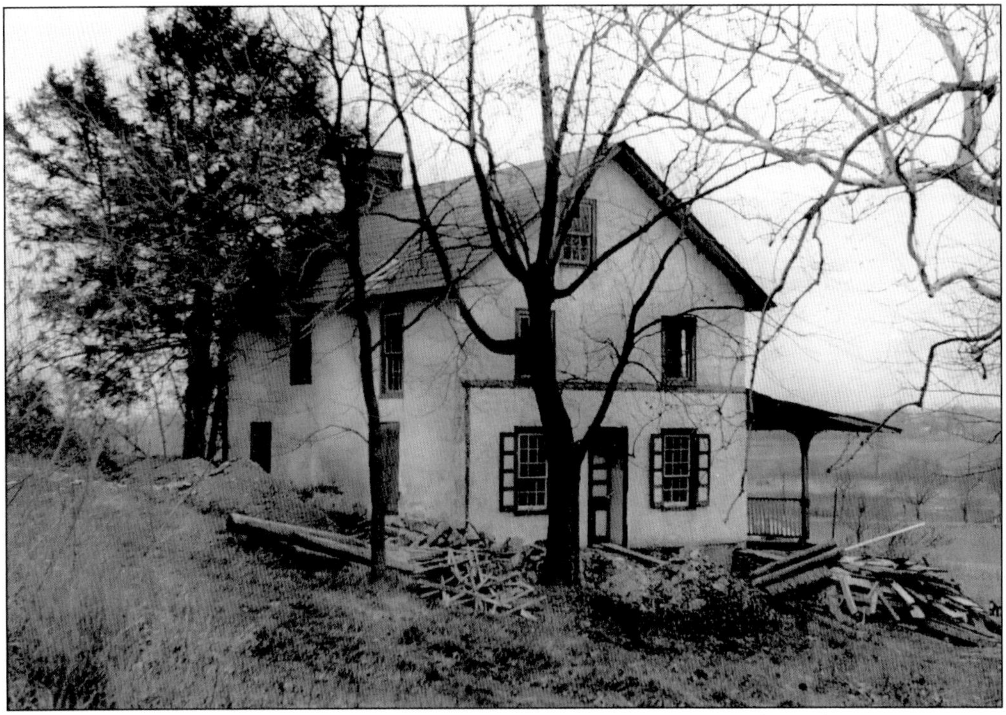

THE RICH HOMESTEAD, C. 1930. This homestead, located along Saw Mill Road near Dyerstown, was part of 75 acres that Joseph Rich purchased in the 1760s. Early records indicate that the house was originally a one-story stone structure that was expanded in the early 1800s. The above photograph shows the rear elevation and its early-1800 features intact. The property remained in the Rich family until the late 19th century, when Victorian features, including a porch and cross-gable roof, were added, as evident in the image below. In the 1930s, the historic house was restored and expanded and its Victorian elements removed.

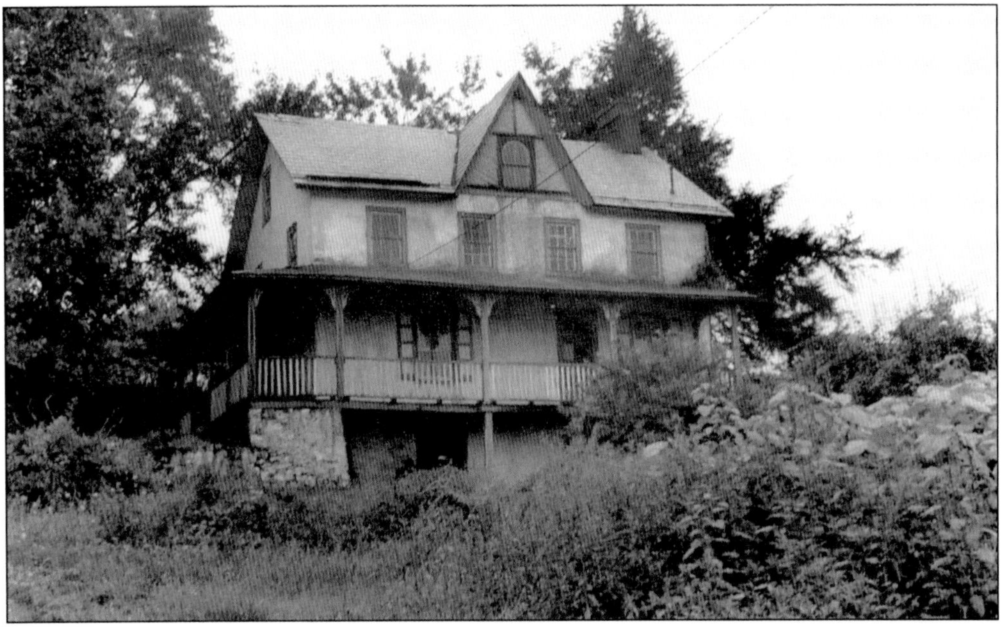

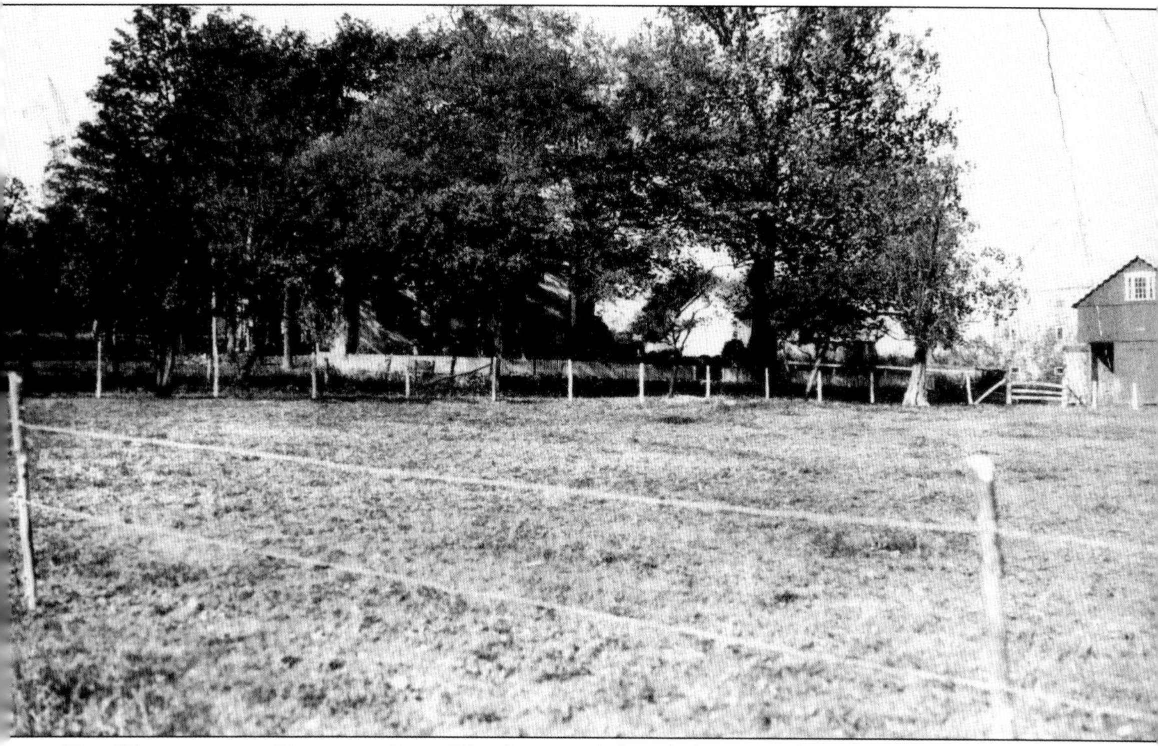

THE WORTHINGTON FARM, C. 1900. This farmstead, found along Worthington Road, was settled prior to 1759 by James Ferguson. The Ferguson family was among the large group of Scotch-Irish Presbyterians that settled here during the last half of the 18th century. In 1861, Ferguson descendants sold the farm to Aaron Worthington, whose family has continuously farmed the property ever since. The property, under conservation easement, has been permanently preserved. The large sycamore tree, planted in 1861 in front of the house, still stands.

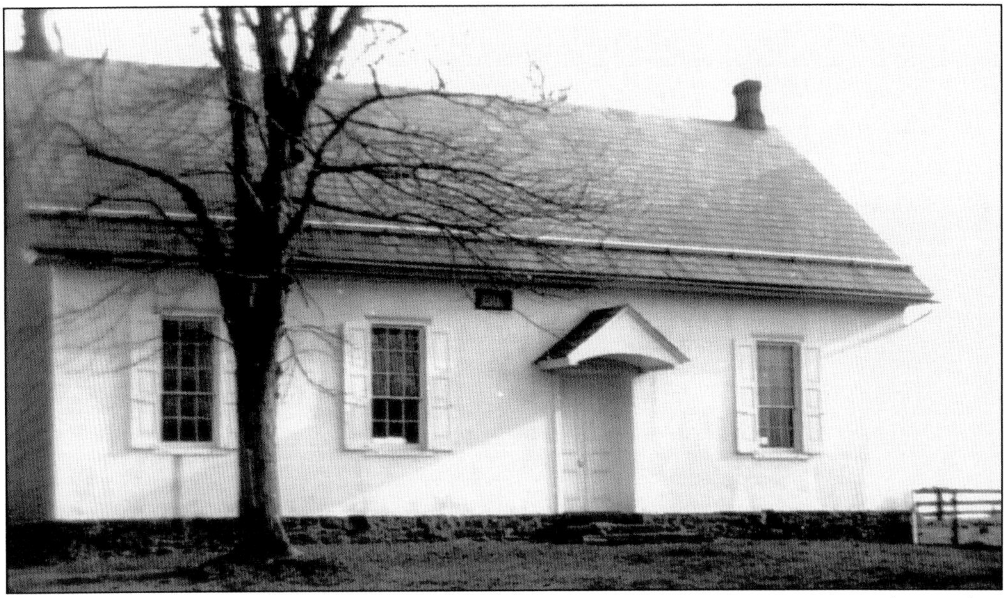

The Groveland Mennonite Meetinghouse, c. 1940. The large German population that settled among the English Quakers in the 18th century constructed their first meetinghouse in 1806 on land gifted to the church by Henry Wismer, a clockmaker. Prior to its construction, local members traveled to nearby Deep Run for religious services. The Groveland meetinghouse was enlarged in 1832 and was rebuilt in 1886. Additions were constructed in 1952 and 1963. It is now the home of the Central Bucks Christian Fellowship.

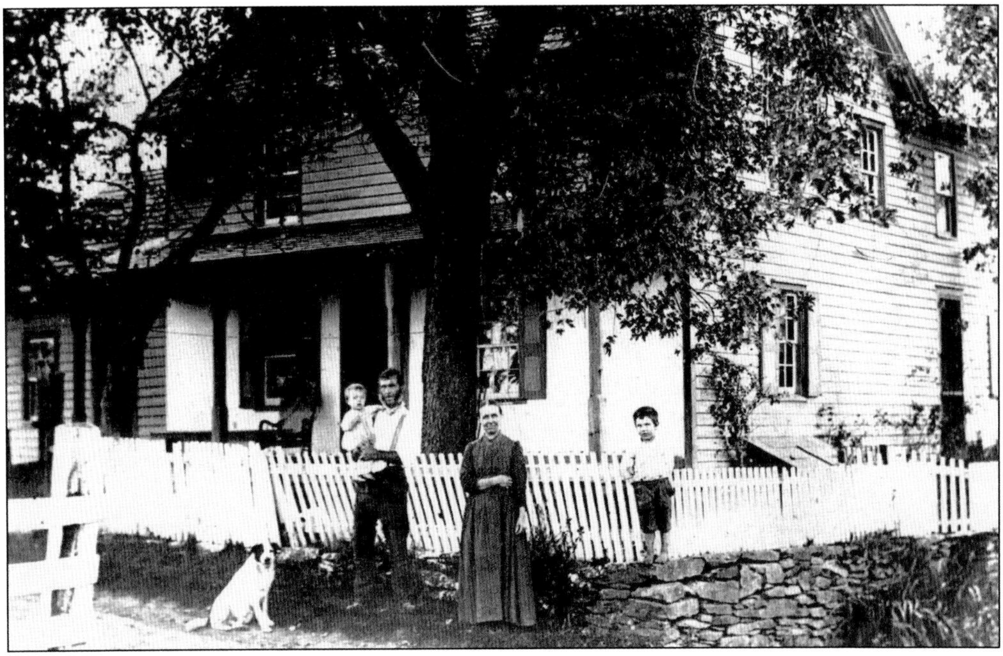

The Landes Farm, c. 1888. According to early maps, this 61-acre farm, located on Potters Lane, was held by Joseph Leatherman in the 1850s. It came into the possession of the Landes family during the last quarter of the 19th century. Pictured here are husband and wife Abraham Landes and Esther Shaddinger Landes, with their sons, Jonas (in Abraham's arms) and Reuben.

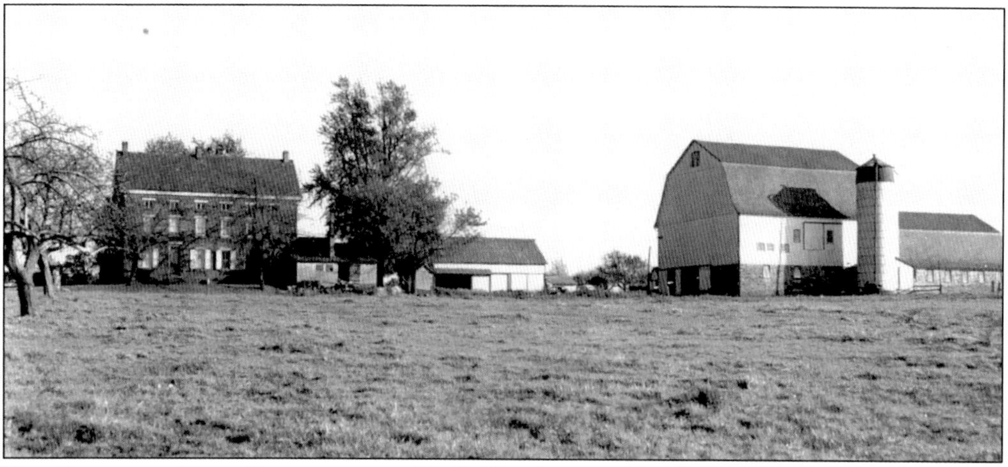

The Christian Gross Farmstead, c. 1945. This farmstead at the corner of Haring and Stump Roads has been in the Gross family for nearly 200 years. In 1810, Christian Gross acquired the property from Abraham Wismer, his father-in-law. The farmstead later passed to Christian's son Isaac, and subsequently to his son Isaac Jr. In the 1950s, Raymond Gross, who still farms the land, inherited the property. The barn pictured above replaced one that burned in 1931. Another barn fire occurred in 1957. Today this property has been permanently preserved as part of the county land conservation program. Below is Grace Gross in the home, displaying her preserves. Every farmwoman spent the summer canning produce from her garden. Cellars were filled with the winter food supply.

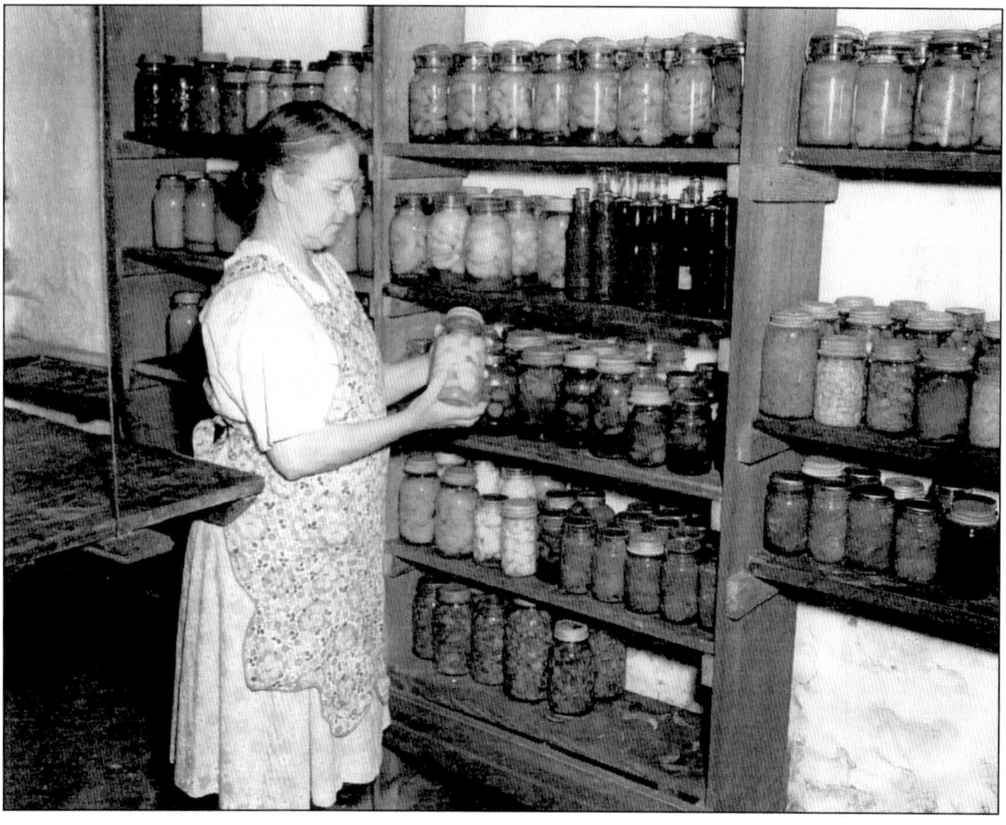

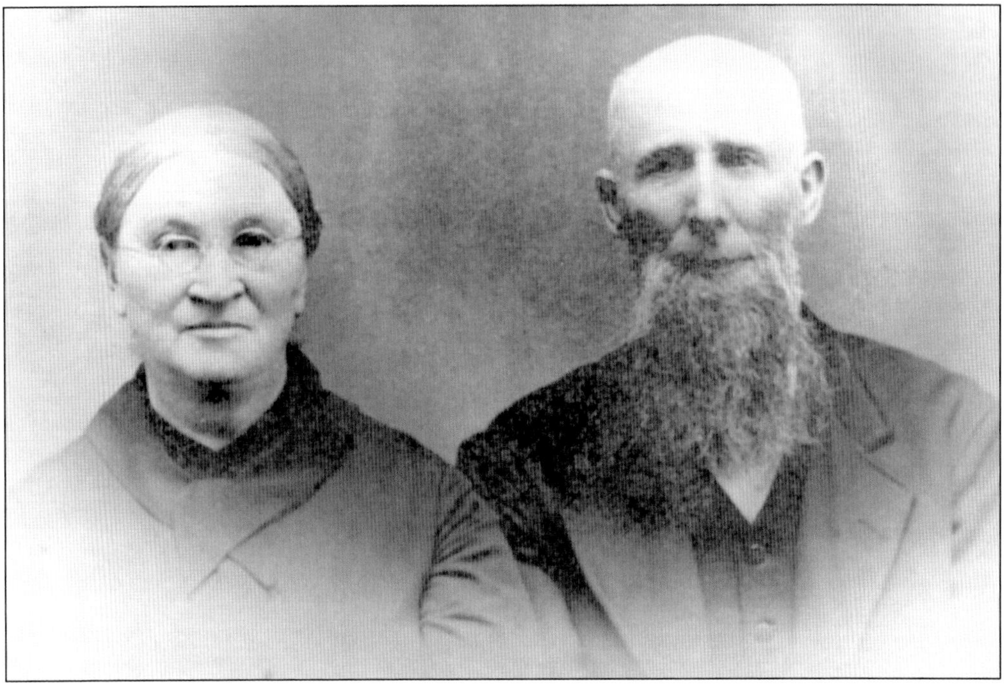

Mary Loux Hunsberger and Enos F. Hunsberger, c. 1890. Pictured here are Mary Loux Hunsberger and her husband, Enos F. Hunsberger. Their farm was located at the corner of Stump and Haring Roads. The family was a member of the Deep Run Mennonite Church in nearby Bedminster Township. German traditions continued for generations—according to her obituary, Mary Hunsberger's funeral service was conducted in German. Today, the Hunsberger property has been permanently preserved.

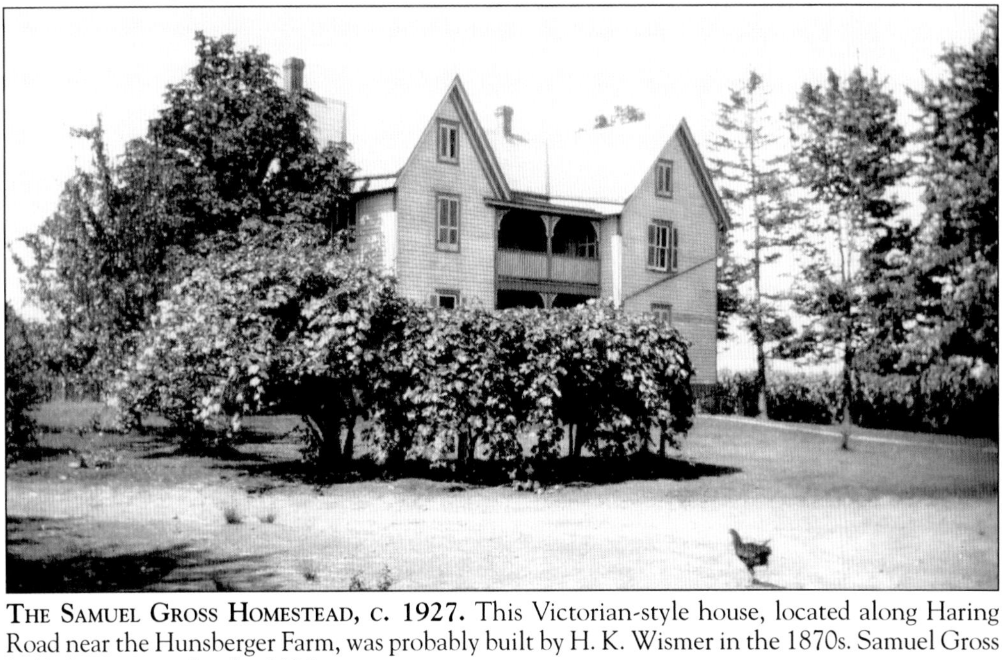

The Samuel Gross Homestead, c. 1927. This Victorian-style house, located along Haring Road near the Hunsberger Farm, was probably built by H. K. Wismer in the 1870s. Samuel Gross held the property by the 1890s.

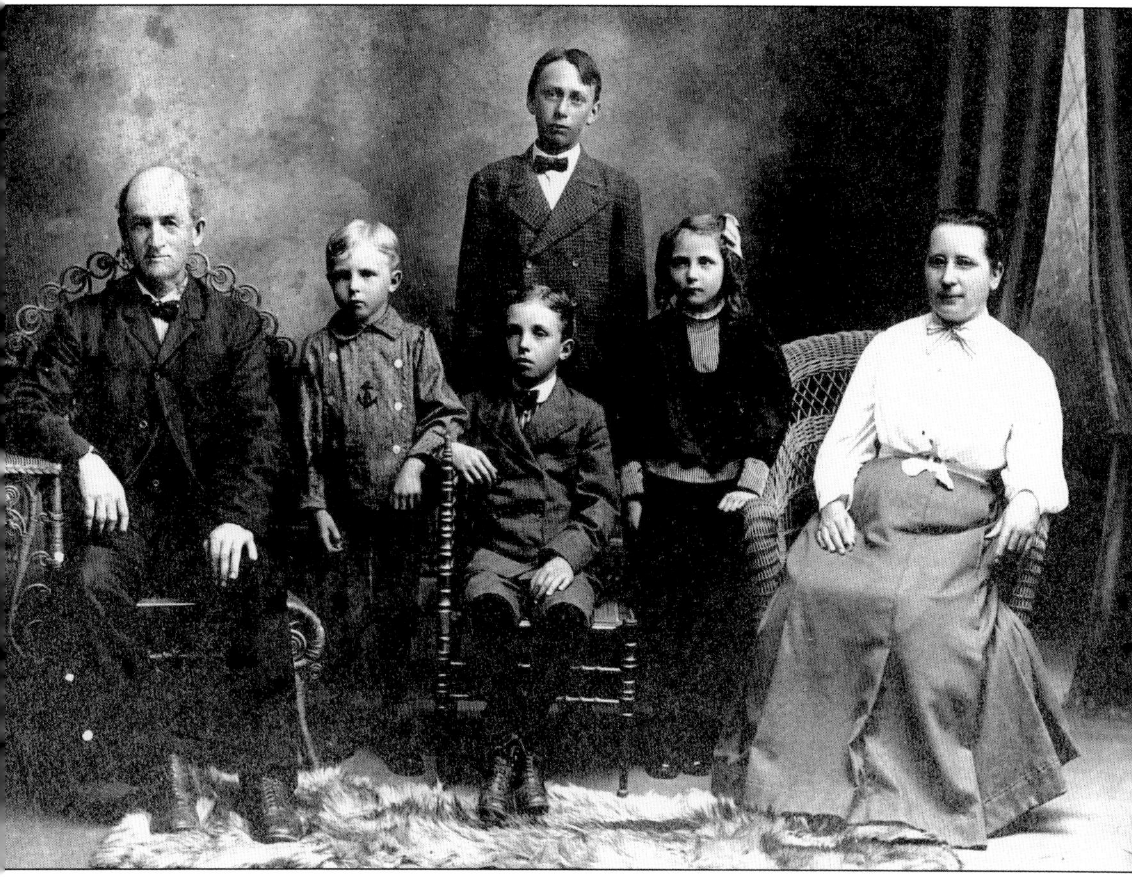

The Gross Family, c. 1890. Shown are Samuel Gross and Emma Hunsberger Gross with their adopted children. From left to right are Samuel, Eli, Paul, Mary Emma, and Emma. Joseph Mountenay is standing at center.

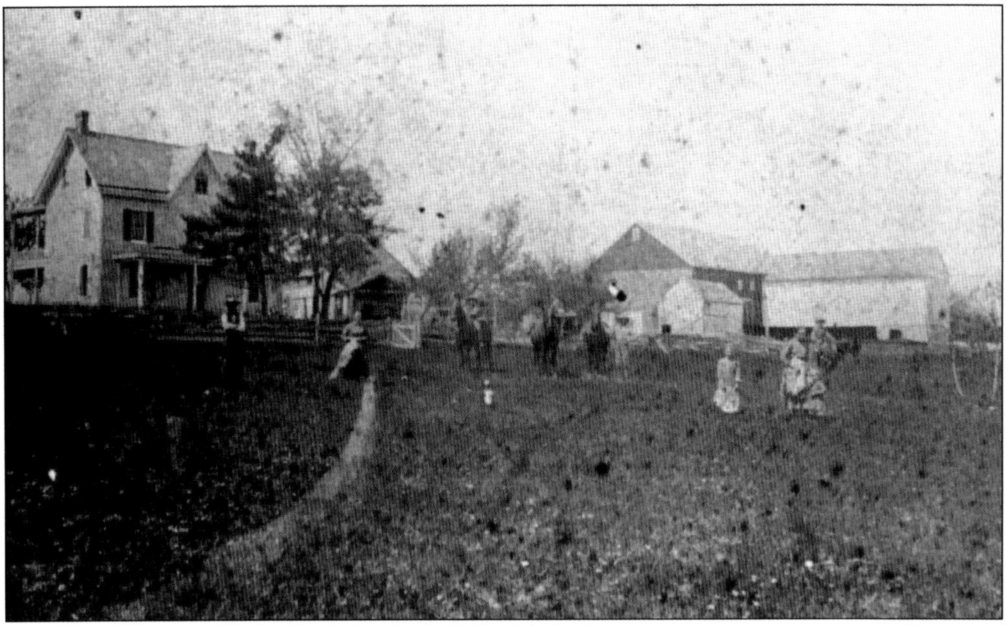

The Myers Farmstead, c. 1890. The Myers family had numerous representatives in Plumstead by the early 1800s. This farm, located along Potters Lane, was owned by the Myers family for more than 100 years. Like many early buildings, the original farmstead was probably a log structure, replaced in the mid-19th century with the Gothic Revival–style home. Shown below are Huldah and Amos Myers, early owners of this property, sitting outside the home.

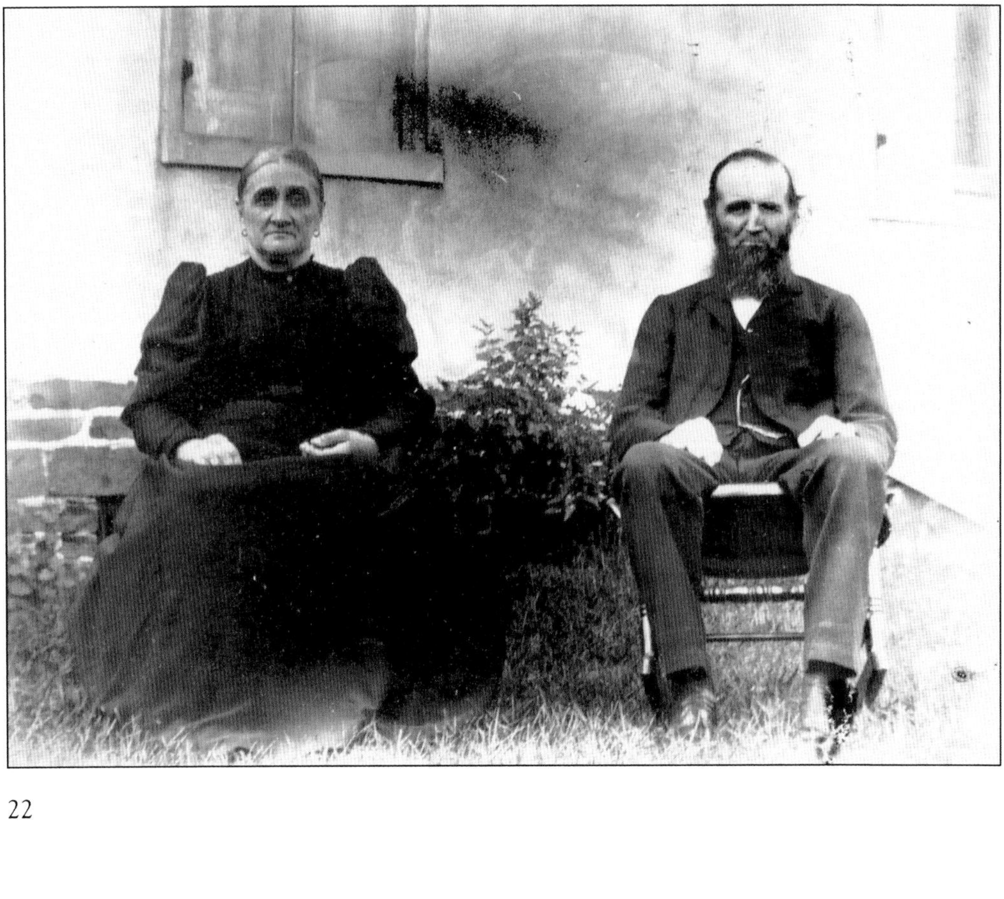

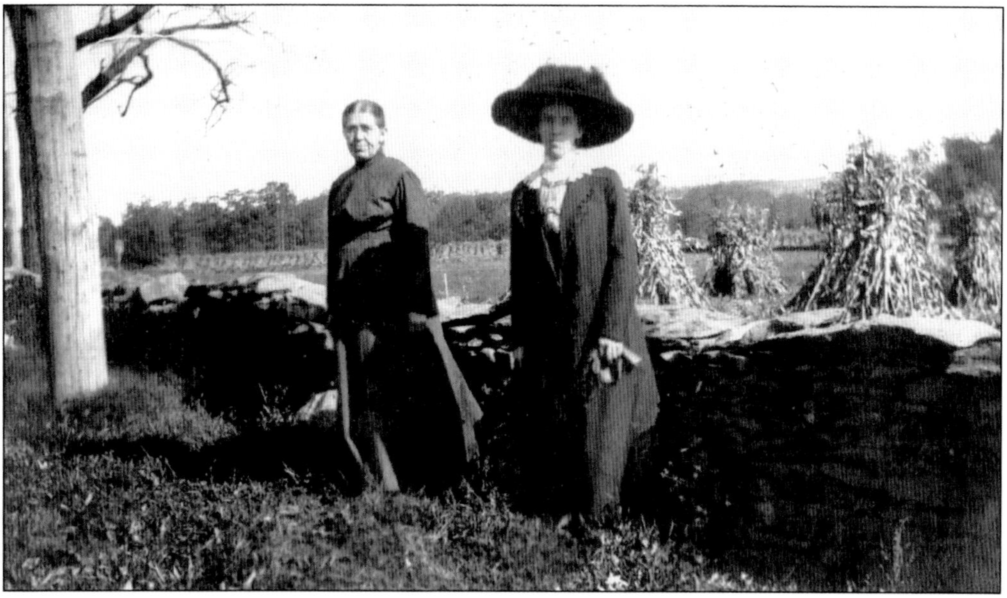

EMMA BEIDLER MYERS AND GRANDMOTHER BEIDLER, C. 1900. Emma (right) and her grandmother pose in front of a stone wall along Curly Hill Road. Similar stone walls can still be seen along many country lanes in the area.

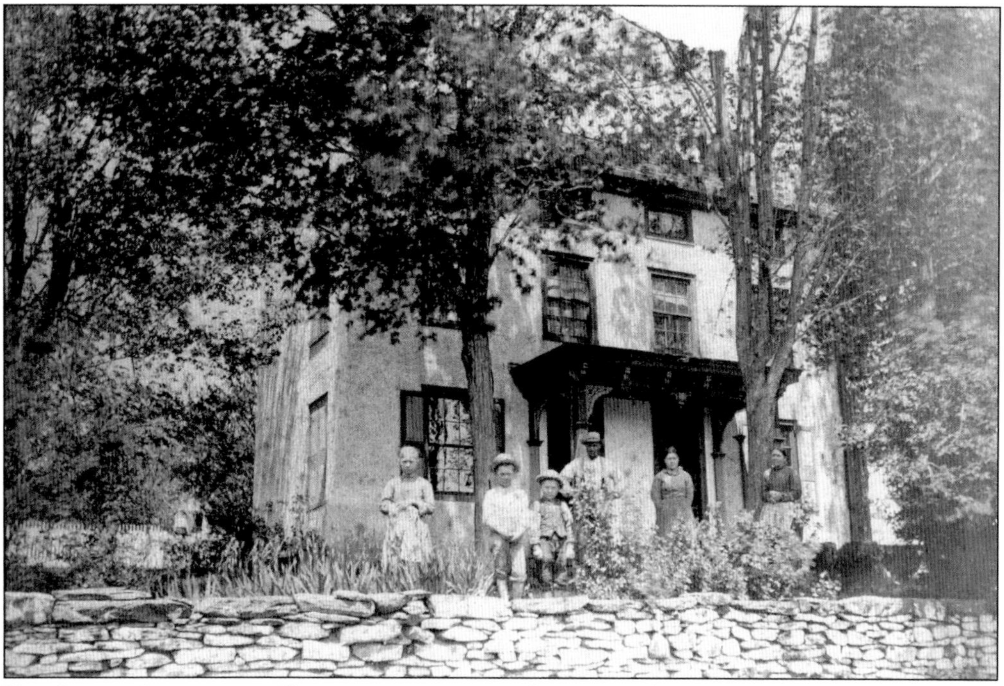

THE GIBSON-SHADDINGER HOMESTEAD, C. 1890. The 1859 and 1876 maps of Plumstead indicate that Andrew Gibson owned this homestead along Curly Hill Road. The Gibson family acquired the land in the 18th century, and constructed the house and its early outbuildings by the mid-19th century. By 1890, the property was owned by the Shaddinger family. This early view shows, from left to right, Mary Shaddinger, Harvey Landis, John Landis, Samuel Shaddinger, Suzanne Landis, and Rachel Lapp Shaddinger in front of the house.

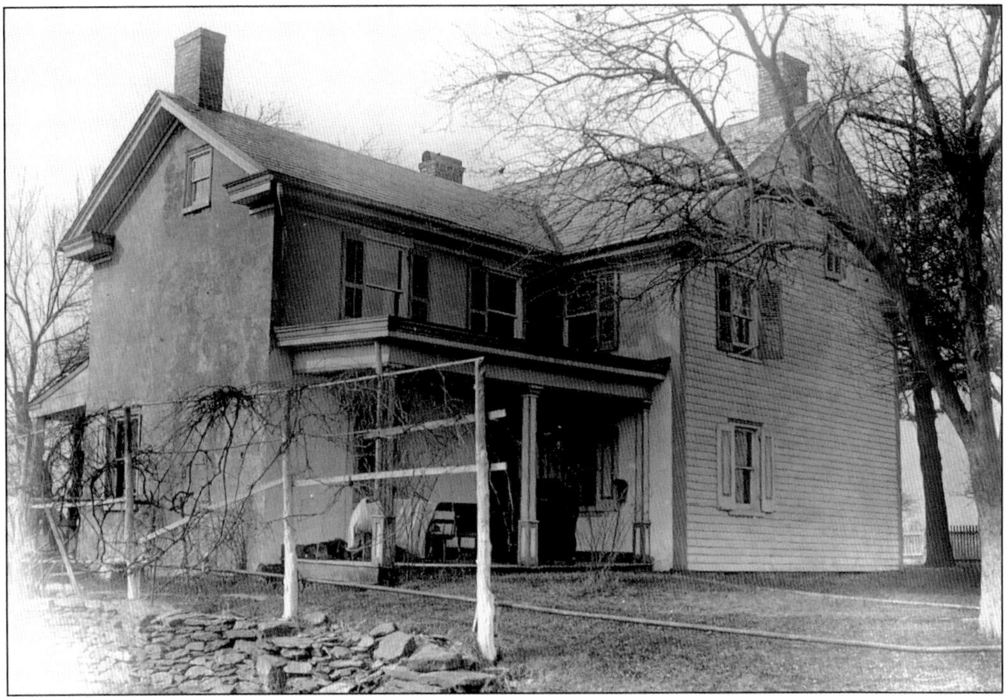

THE SHULL FARM, C. 1923. This farmhouse on Groveland Road was built in 1851 by E. K. and Mary Myers. The property was sold to Henry Fulmer in 1861 and has been in the same family since then. The farm eventually passed to Fulmer's daughter and son-in-law Ida May and Albert Yerger, and was subsequently purchased in 1938 by their daughter and son-in-law Minnie and Arthur Shull. Today, the property remains in the Leroy and Lillian Shull family and has been preserved as part of the county land preservation program.

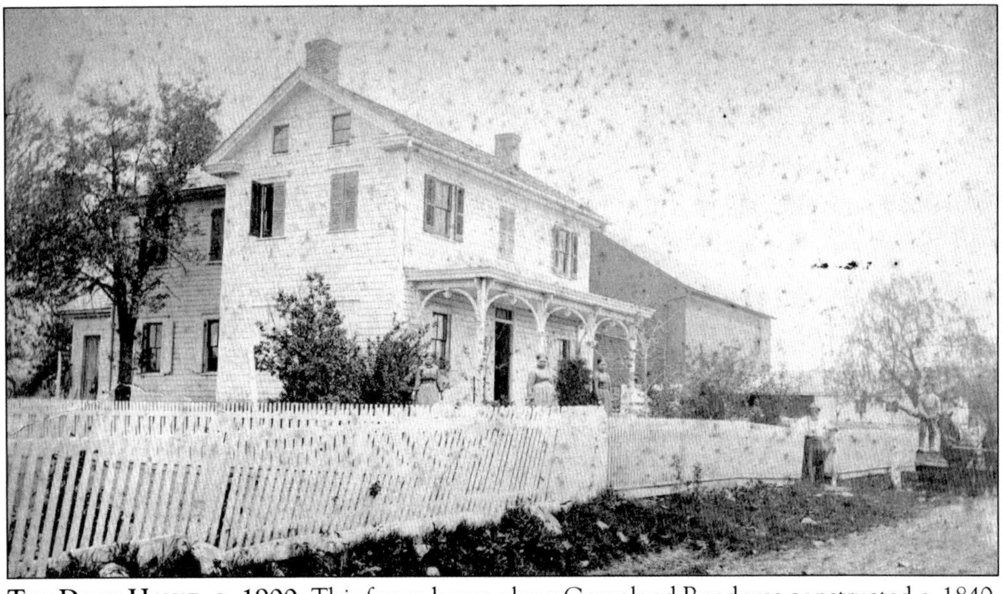

THE DAVIS HOUSE, C. 1900. This frame house along Groveland Road was constructed c. 1840. The 1859 map of Plumstead indicates the owner as Enoch Davis. For most of the last two centuries the house has been associated with the Shull Farm.

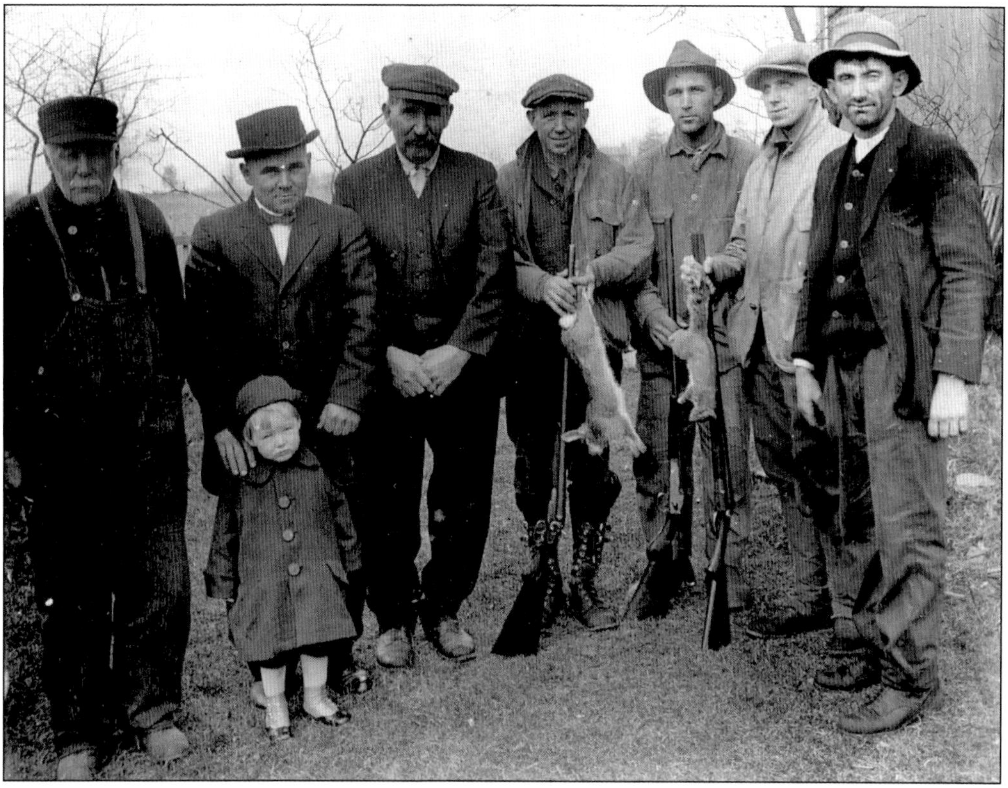

A Gunning Party, c. 1923. Members of the Shull family and friends pose after a day of squirrel and rabbit hunting on the farm. Pictured here are Urius Fulmer, Wilson Yerger with son Albert Yerger, Arthur Shull, Arthur Lear, Milton E. Miller, and Calvin E. Miller.

The Constantine House, c. 1900. This building is found along Point Pleasant Pike at the top of Bergstrom Road. Like many early houses, it was shaded by trees and separated from the road and fields by a white picket fence. Pictured here are two unidentified members of the Constantine family.

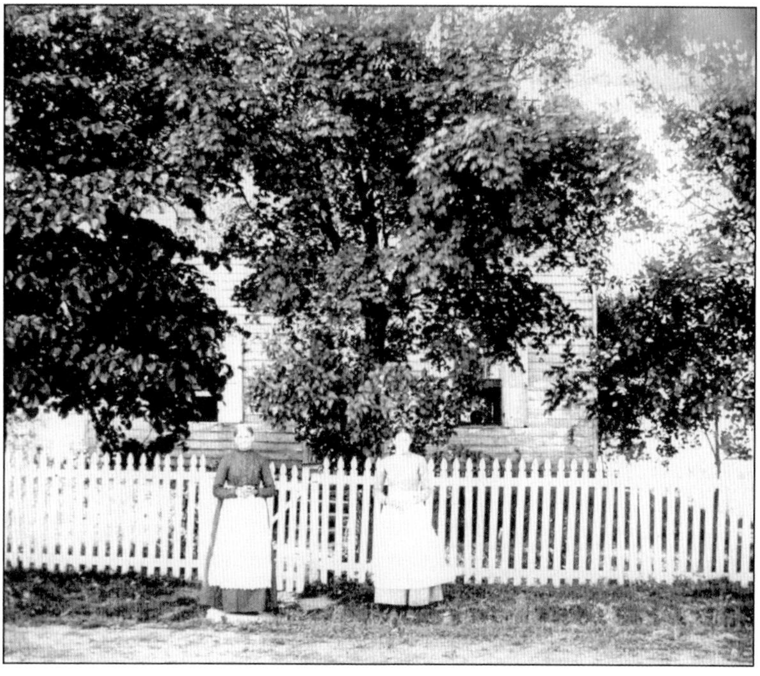

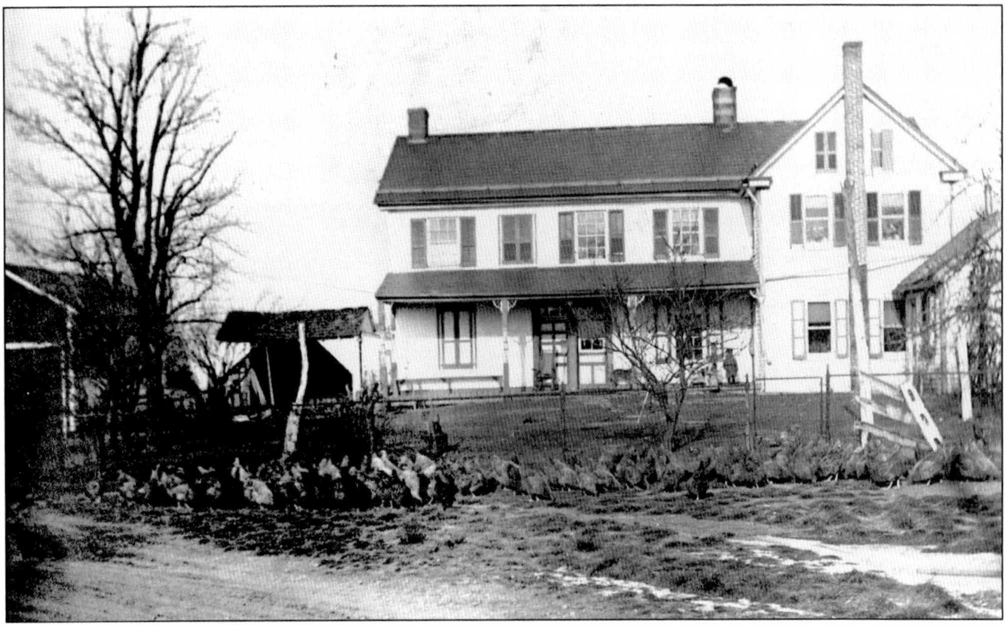

The Old Abram Myers Homestead, c. 1930. This *c.* 1840 house was owned by the Schwartz and Garis families for most of the 19th century. Abram Myers came into possession of the 114-acre farm by the 1890s. The small addition to the right was moved to the site and originally served as a tollhouse for the nearby Point Pleasant Turnpike. To the left of the house is the woodshed.

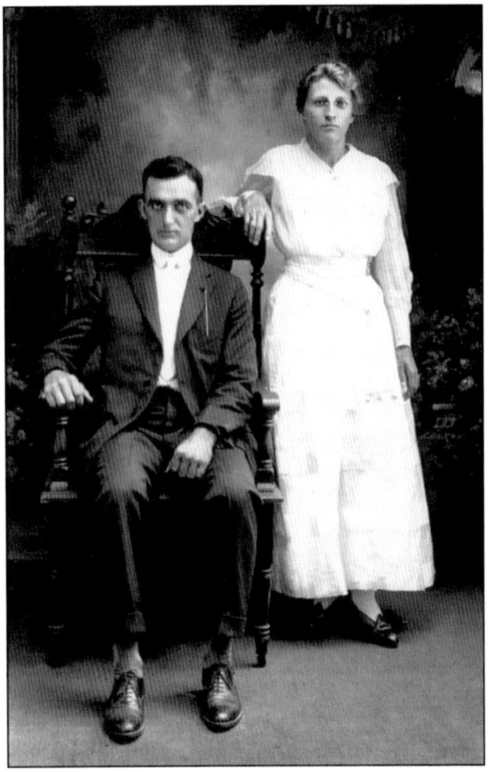

A Myers Wedding Picture, c. 1918. Harrison Myers and his bride, Annie Rice, held the farm for many years.

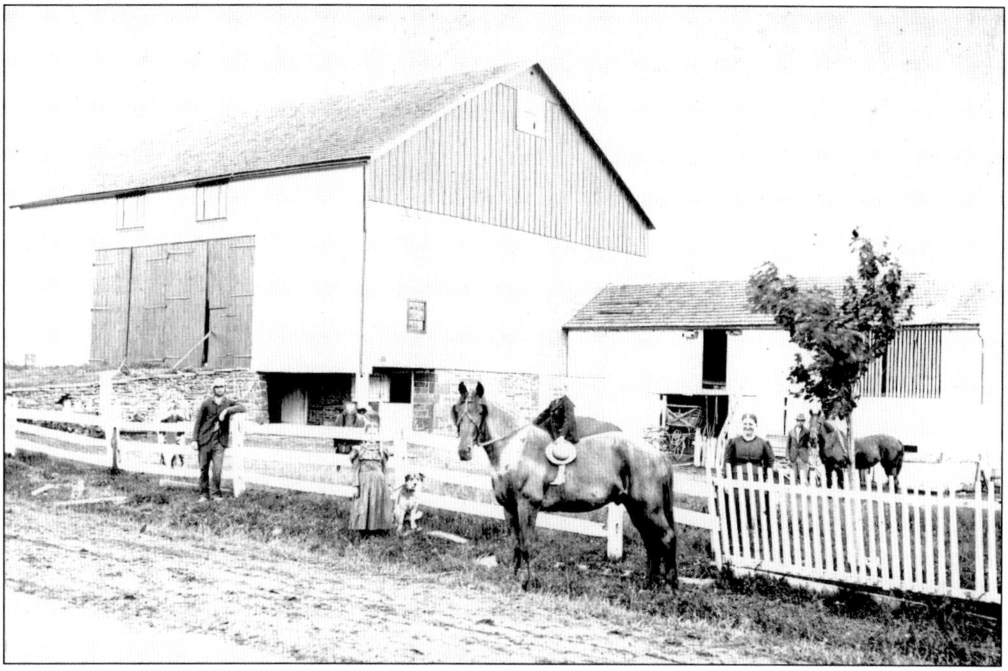

The Myers Family in front of Their Barn, c. 1897. Located at the east end of Bradshaw Road, the farm remains in the Myers family. The barn is no longer standing but its ramp and stone stabling remain. Shown in this image are, from left to right, Abram L. Myers (January 1, 1859–July 7, 1925), Laura Myers (August 8, 1885–March 26, 1950), Harrison M. Myers, on horse (February 8, 1890–December 13, 1971), Lizzie M. Myers (August 10, 1859–December 29, 1944), and an unidentified man.

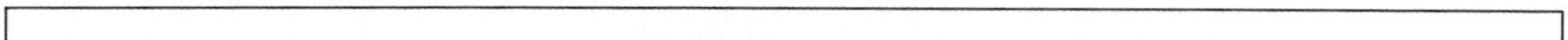

The Myers House, Durham Road, c. 1920. This delivery truck is stopped in what is now the old Durham Road near Hinkletown. The house, associated with a branch of the Myers family, was built in two sections. The west end of the house stood prior to 1859. A new front section, facing the road, was added in the last quarter of the 19th century. Note the open farm field beyond the house; today this land is mostly wooded.

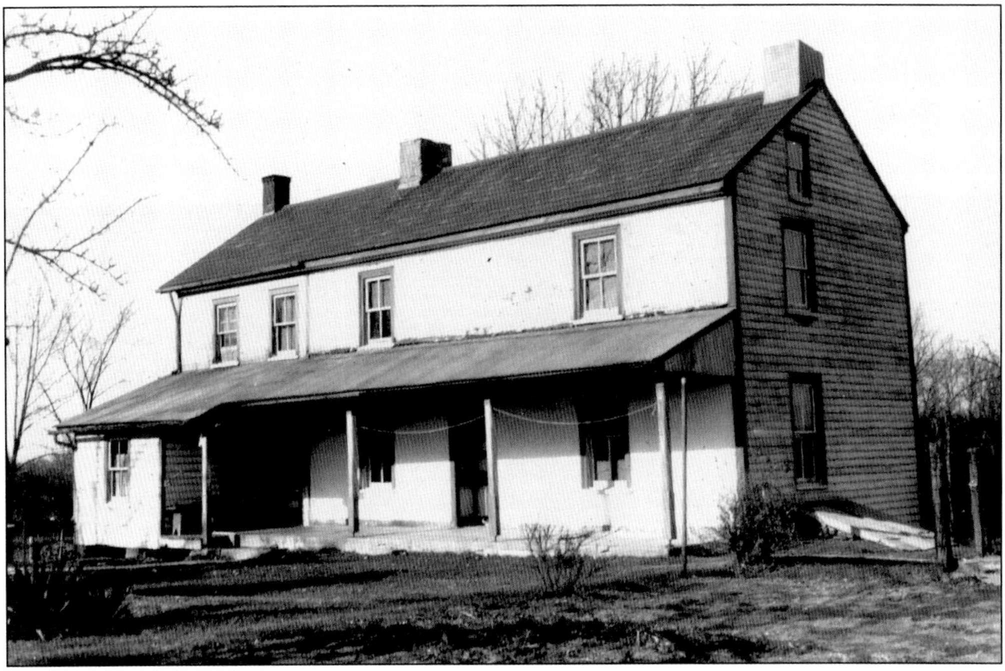

The Mergenthaler House, c. 1938. This farm was purchased by Daniel Mergenthaler in 1895. John Henry Mergenthaler, his son, continued to farm the land until 1954. The building is located far off the road, near the intersection of Stump and Schlentz Hill Roads.

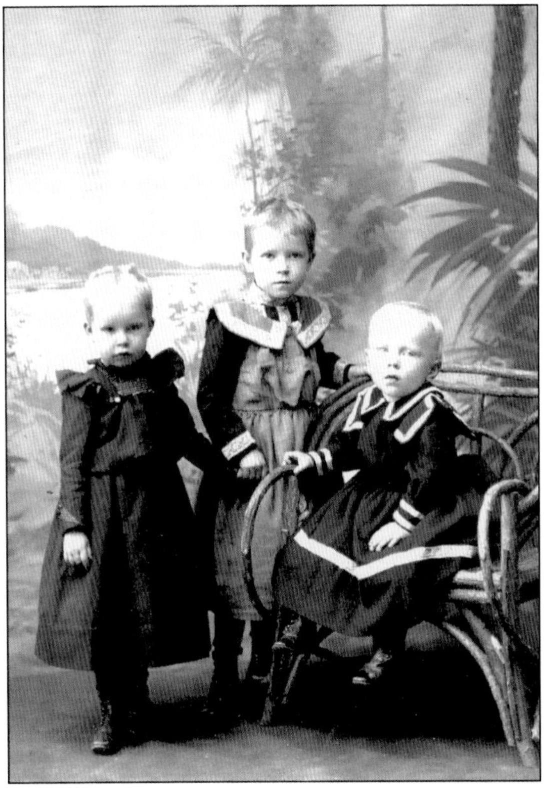

The Mergenthaler Children, c. 1900. The children of Daniel F. and Mary Mergenthaler included Mary Magdalena, age 3, Catherine, age 4, and John Henry, age 18 months.

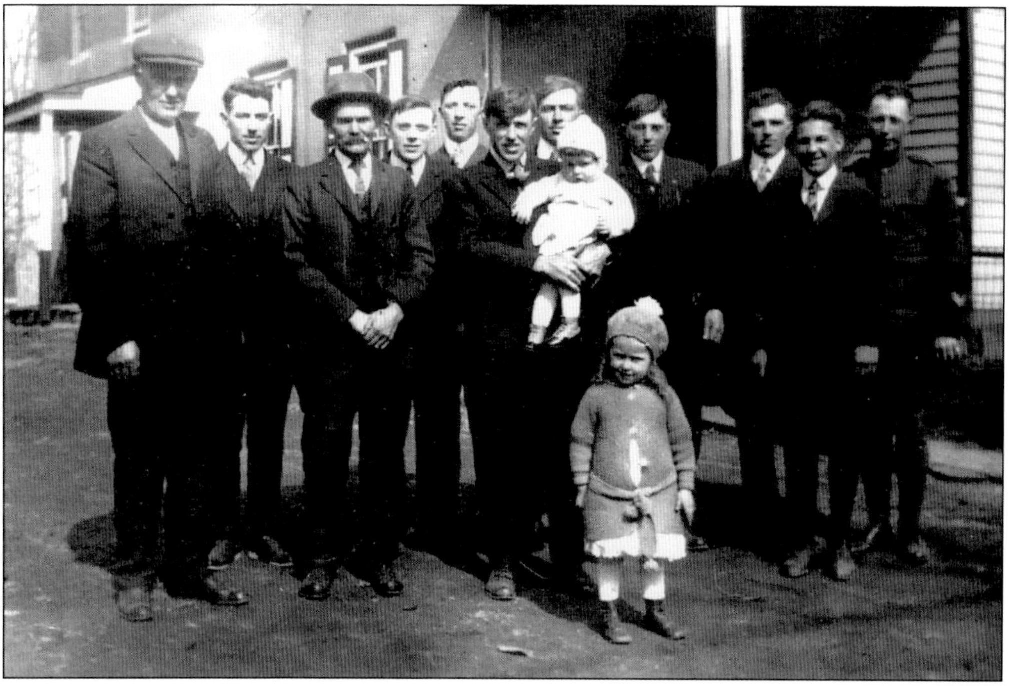

The Wolfinger Family and Friends, c. 1918. Pearson Wolfinger poses in front of the family homestead with his sons, grandchildren, and neighbors. Pictured from left to right are Pearson Wolfinger, Henry Wolfinger, Fred Long, George Wolfinger, Winfield Wolfinger with infant Chester, Ira Wolfinger, Horace Wolfinger, Warren Wolfinger, Fred Long Jr., and Grover Chittick. Young Doris Wolfinger stands in front of the group.

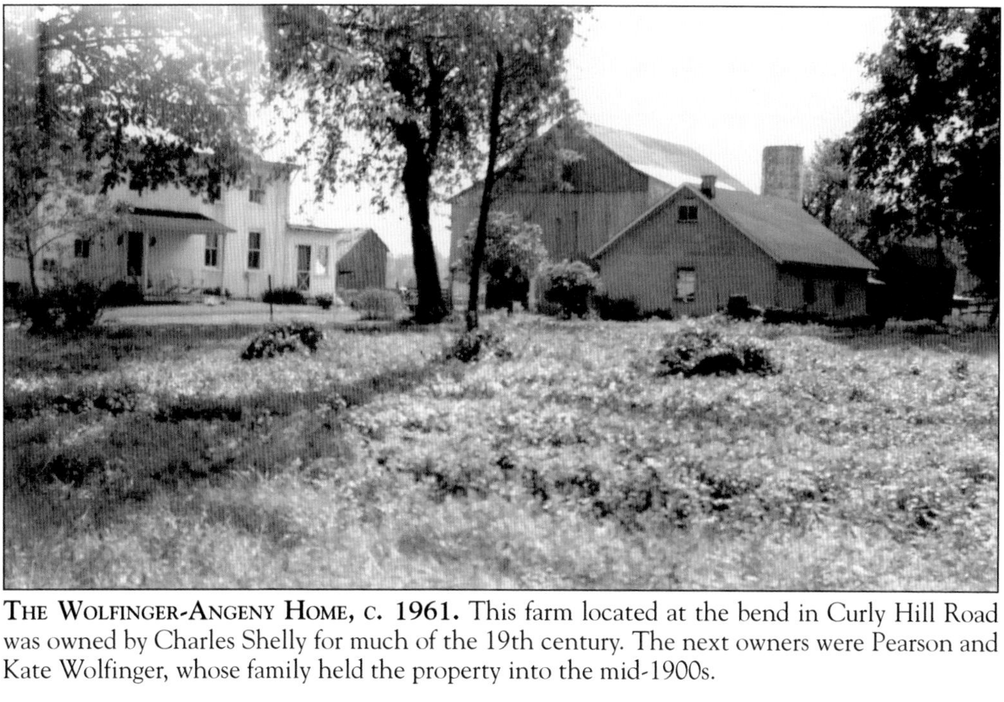

The Wolfinger-Angeny Home, c. 1961. This farm located at the bend in Curly Hill Road was owned by Charles Shelly for much of the 19th century. The next owners were Pearson and Kate Wolfinger, whose family held the property into the mid-1900s.

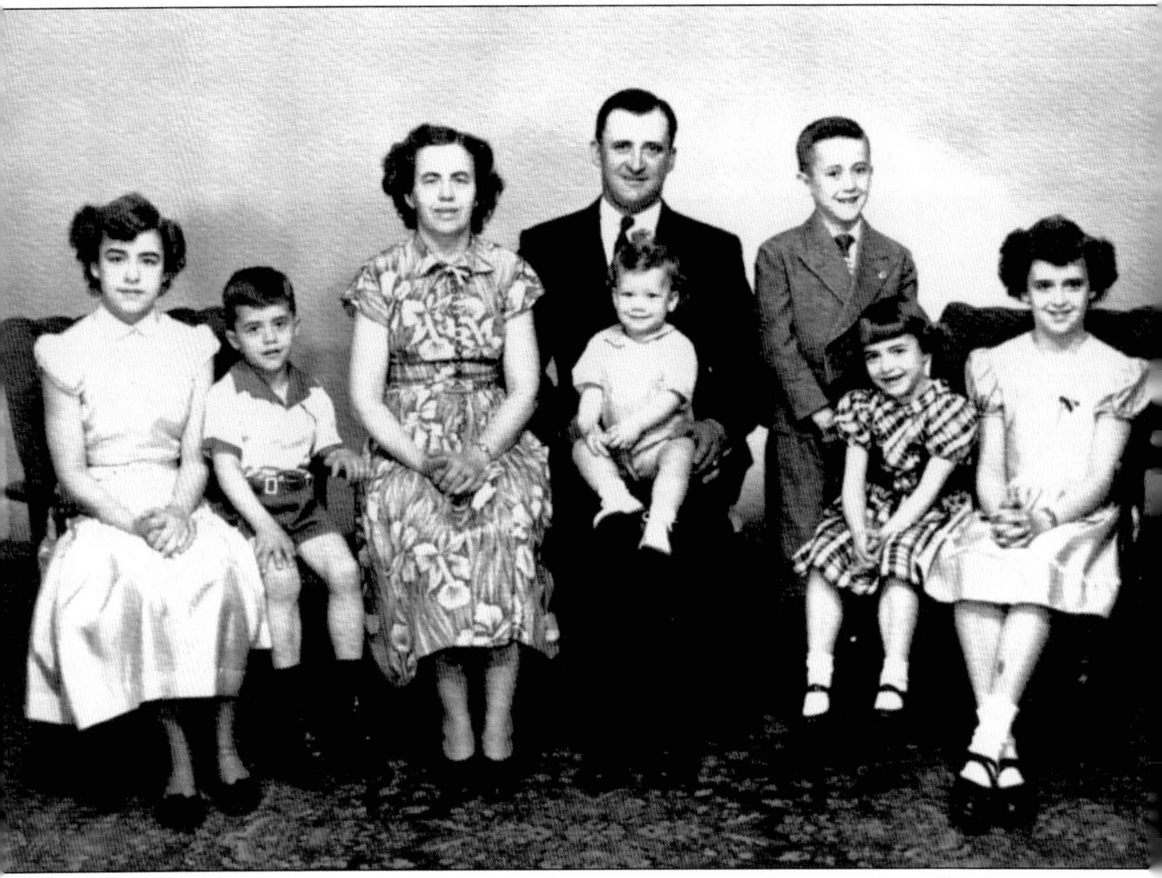

The Bishop Family, c. 1950. The Bishops were among the many farm families in the township. Their farm was located on Swamp Road, now the Brookside subdivision. Pictured here from left to right are Margaret, Herman, Ida, Herman with Walter on his lap, Clyde, Mary Jane, and Lois.

Two

FARMS

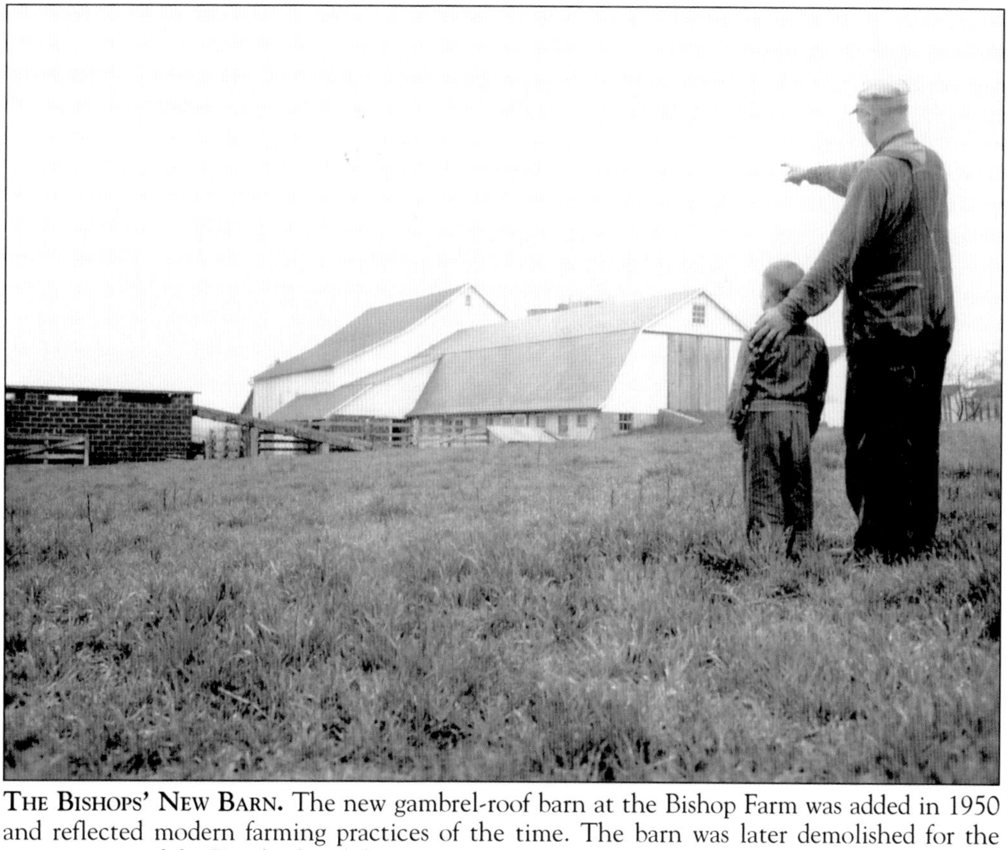

THE BISHOPS' NEW BARN. The new gambrel-roof barn at the Bishop Farm was added in 1950 and reflected modern farming practices of the time. The barn was later demolished for the construction of the Brookside subdivision.

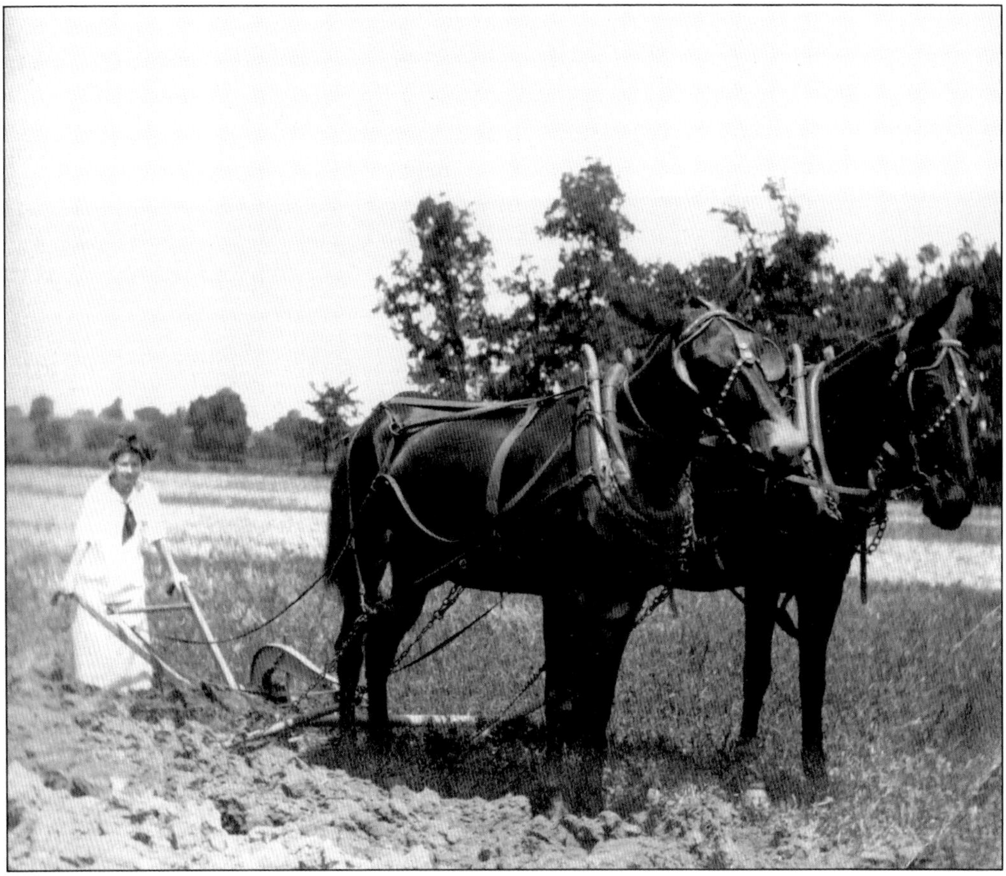

Plowing, c. 1920. Woman's work was not confined to the house. Here a woman plows the fields at the old Beidler Farm, along Curly Hill Road.

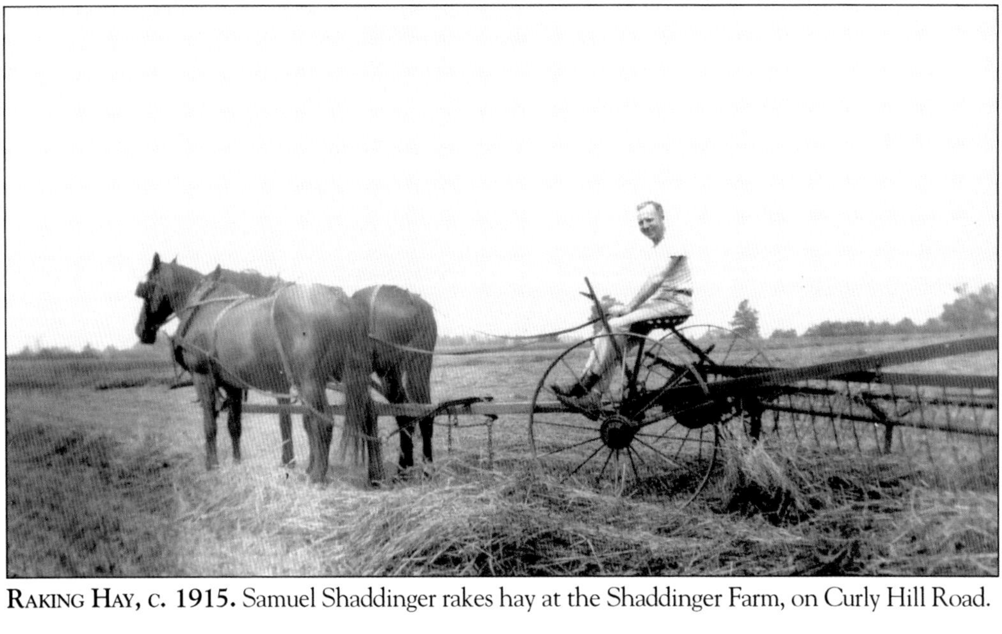

Raking Hay, c. 1915. Samuel Shaddinger rakes hay at the Shaddinger Farm, on Curly Hill Road.

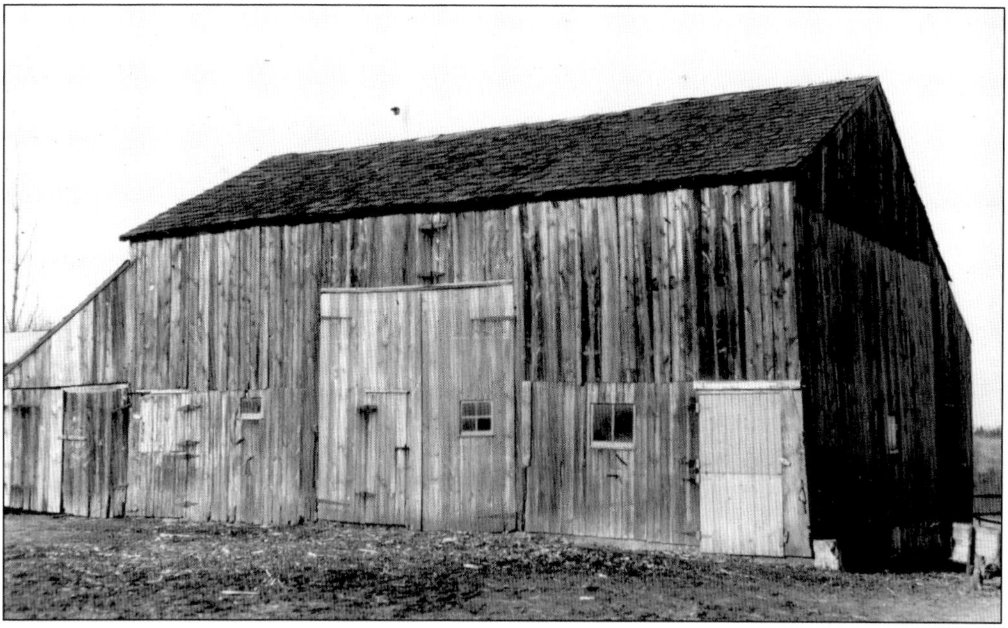

THE MERGENTHALER BARN, C. 1938. The barn at the Mergenthaler property on Stump Road was typical of low barns found on many small farms. The barn was destroyed by fire after being struck by lightning in 1941.

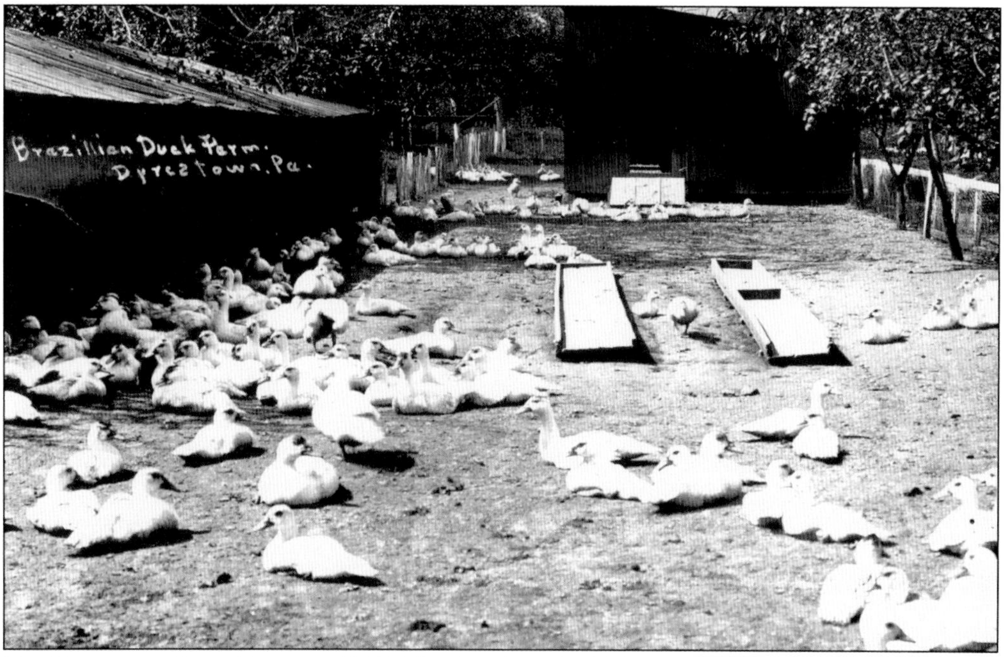

THE BRAZILIAN DUCK FARM, C. 1915. The Brazilian Duck Farm, owned by Charles F. Beaumont, was located in the heart of Dyerstown. Beaumont moved to Plumstead in 1883, where he operated the Dyer mill and began breeding fancy stock. His specialty was the Brazilian duck, which he raised for markets in Philadelphia and Atlantic City. Specialized farming, including dairy, egg, and poultry farms, predominated agriculture in Plumstead from the 1860s into the early 20th century.

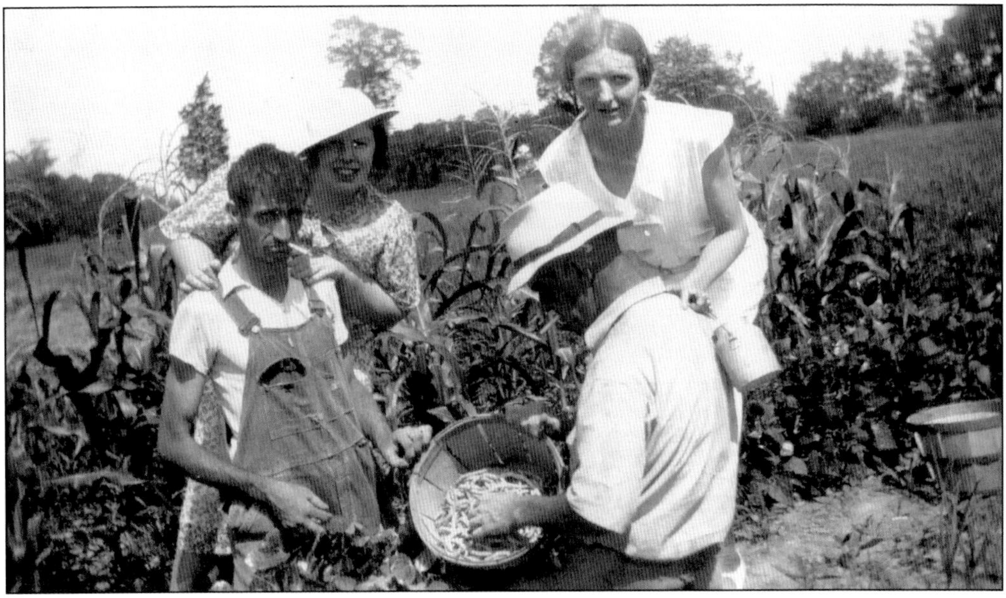

In the Garden Patch, c. 1937. An important part of agricultural pursuits was the family vegetable garden. Small gardens helped stretch food for the family and were also used to produce income for other expenses. Often residents sold fruits and vegetables at the Philadelphia market as city vendors. This truck patch was found in Gardenville. Pictured here are Clarence and Edna Ott Michener (on left) and William and Helen Michener Jacobs.

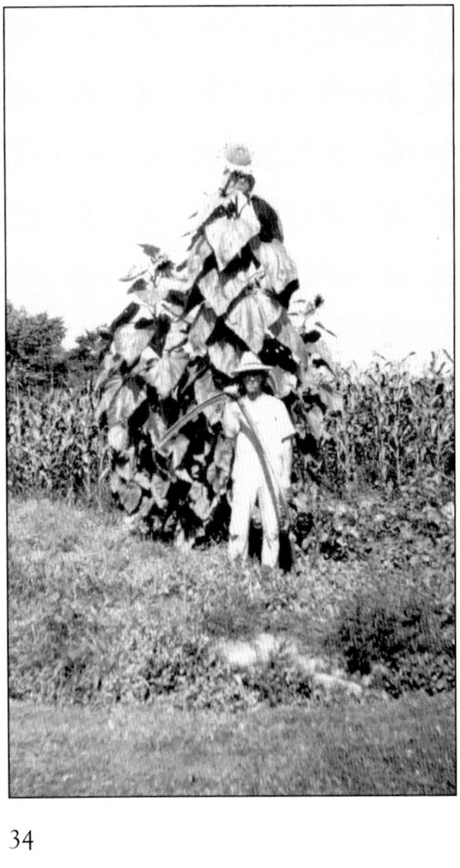

Sunflowers, c. 1946. John Mergenthaler stands in front of his giant sunflowers.

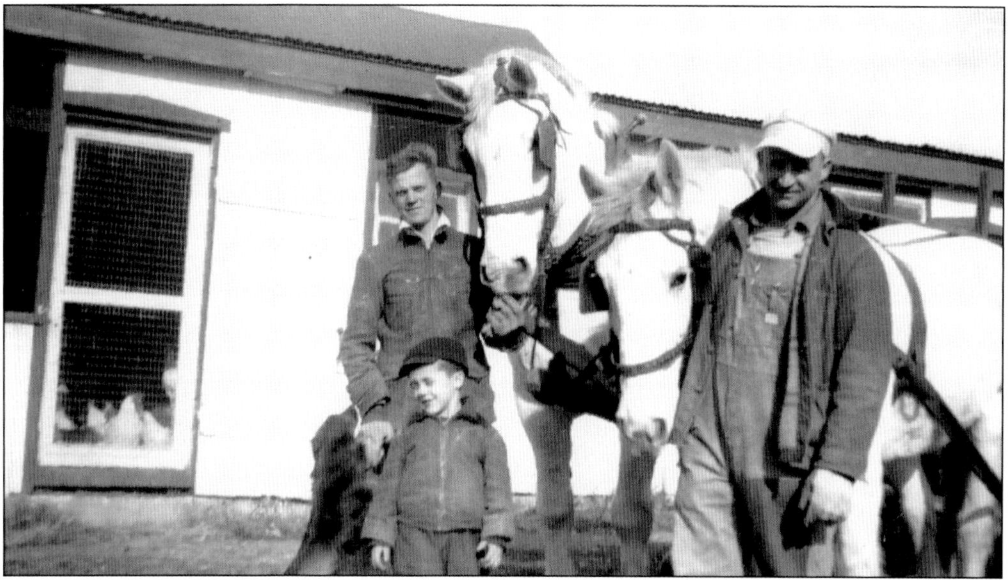

The Bishop Farm, c. 1950. Herman Bishop Jr. is pictured here with a team of horses, along with his father, Herman Sr. (left), and hired man Ray Dueckuewitz. Note the chickens in the chicken house window. Egg production remained an important business through the first half of the 20th century and most farms, big and small, produced eggs.

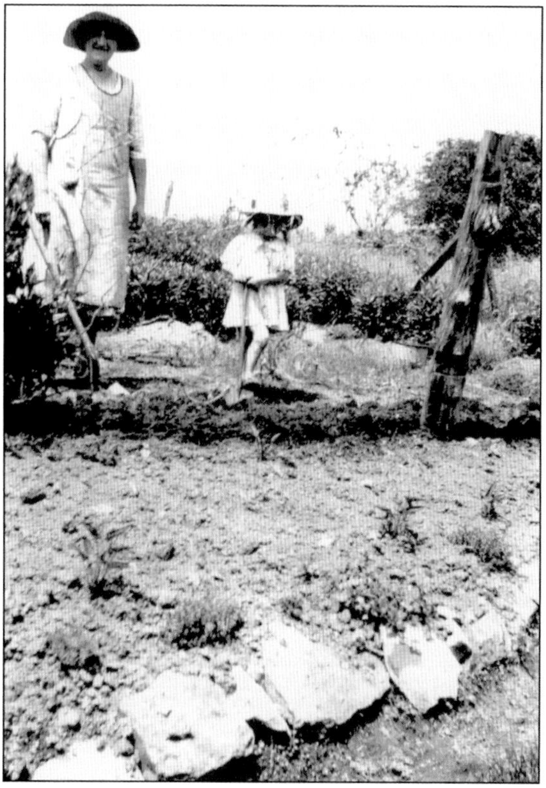

In the Garden, c. 1937. Ina Harmath and her great-aunt Alice Myers tend the family garden at the old Myers place on Potters Lane.

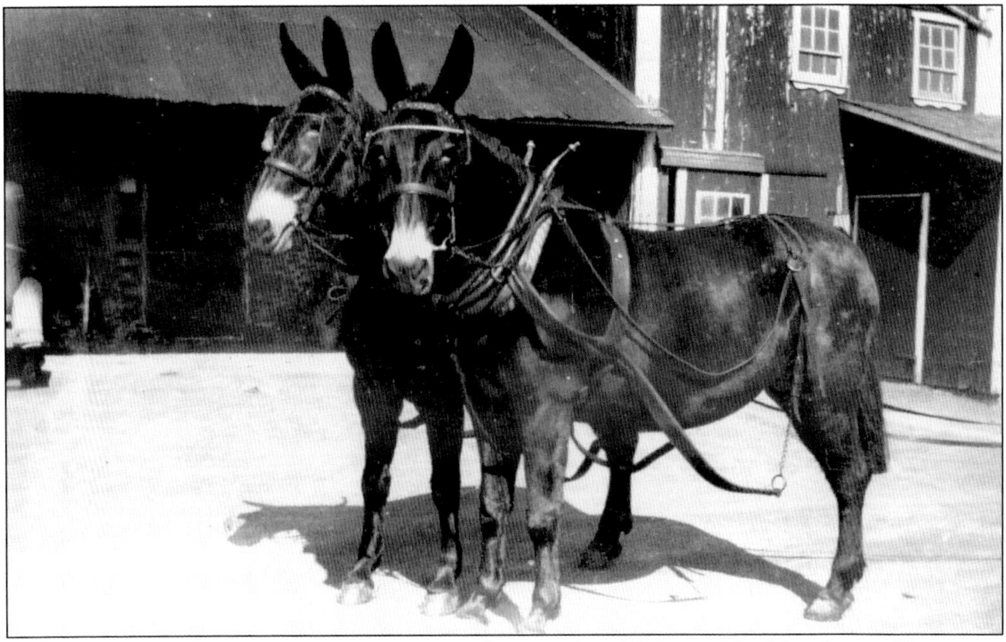

MULES, C. 1930. Shown in this image are mules Maud and Jenny at the Hunsberger Farm.

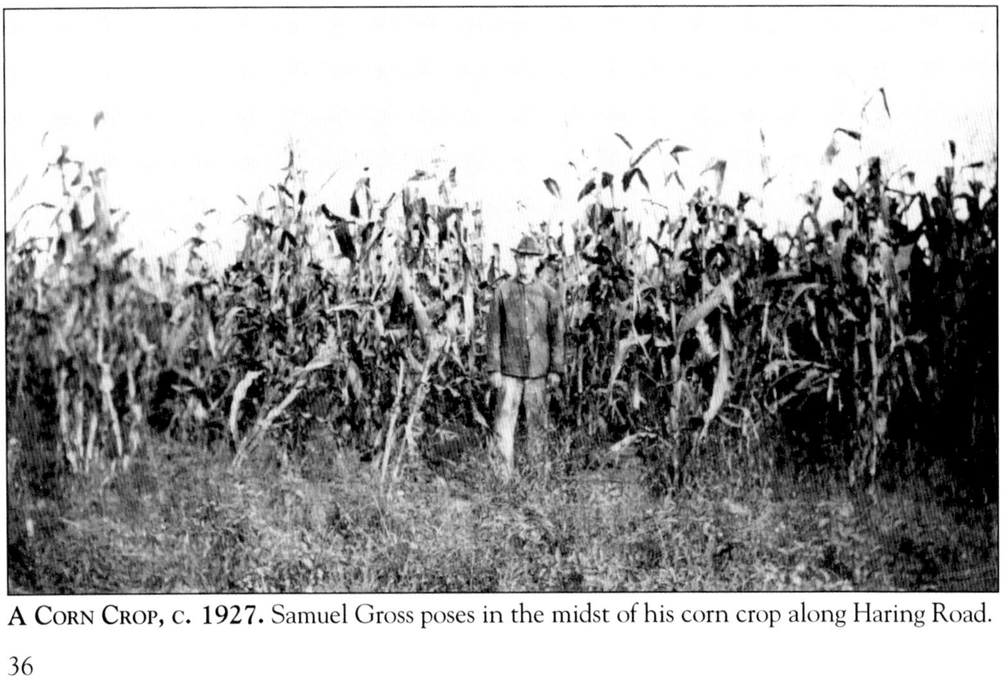

A CORN CROP, C. 1927. Samuel Gross poses in the midst of his corn crop along Haring Road.

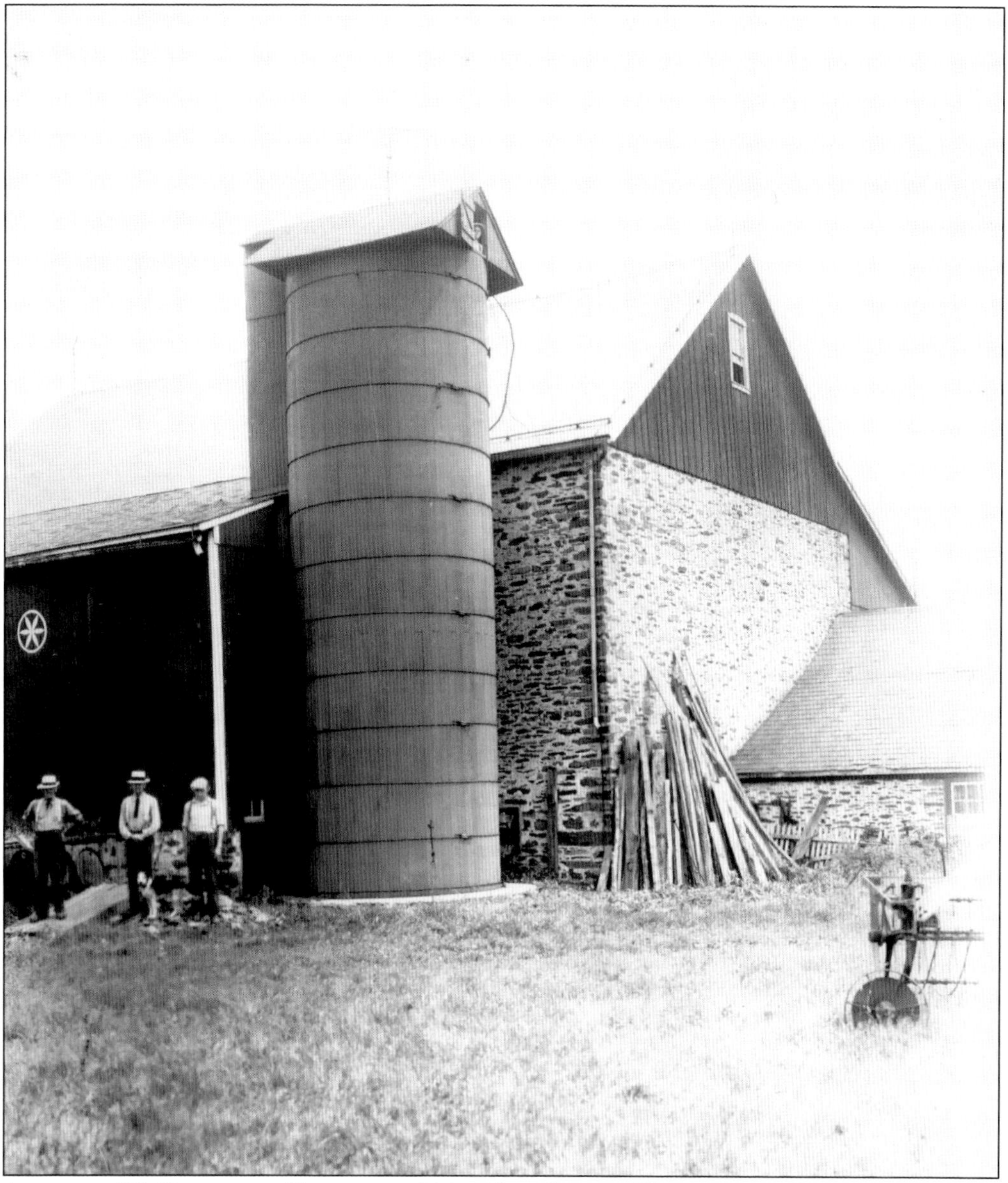

Abraham W. Detweiler Farm, c. 1930. Silo salesman Eli Myers Sr. (left), Joseph Tyson (center), and Eli Myers Jr. stand in front of the newly erected silo on the Detweiler Farm. This silo was the first of its kind in the area and may be the reason for the road's name, Silo Hill Road. The barn was built in 1855 by Joseph Myers. Abraham Detweiler purchased the farm in 1915 and operated a dairy there. Today, the farm remains in the Detweiler family and has been preserved by a conservation easement.

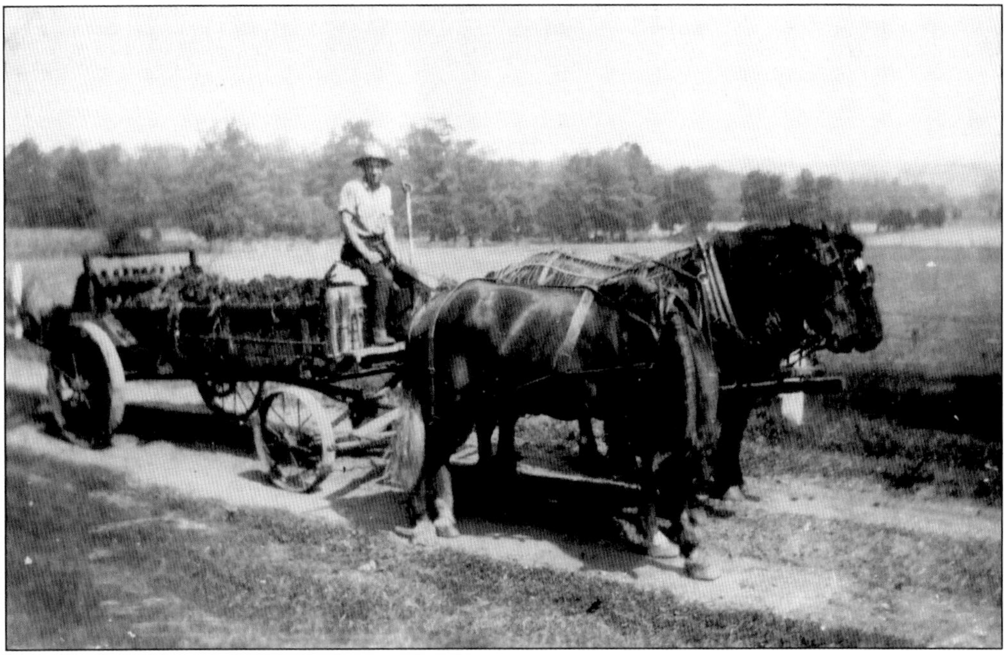

A Manure Spreader, c. 1915. Richard Shaddinger drives a manure spreader along Curly Hill Road.

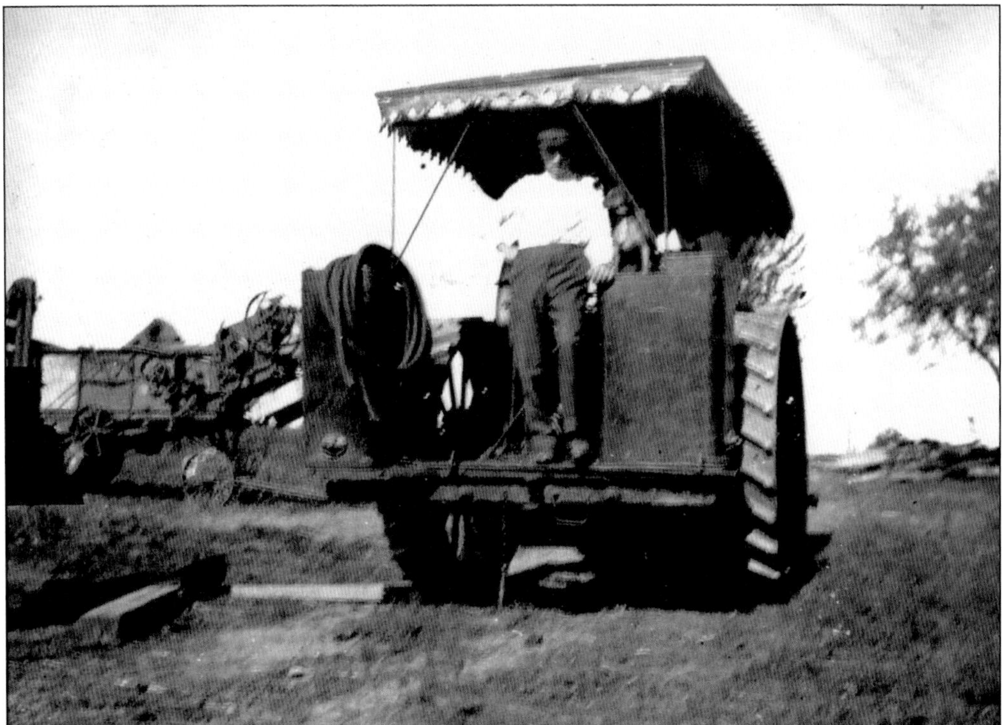

An Oil-Fired Tractor, c. 1915. An oil-fired tractor is shown on the Beidler Farm, along Curly Hill Road. In the background is a Doylestown thresher, invented in nearby Doylestown. Due to their cost, threshers were shared between farms.

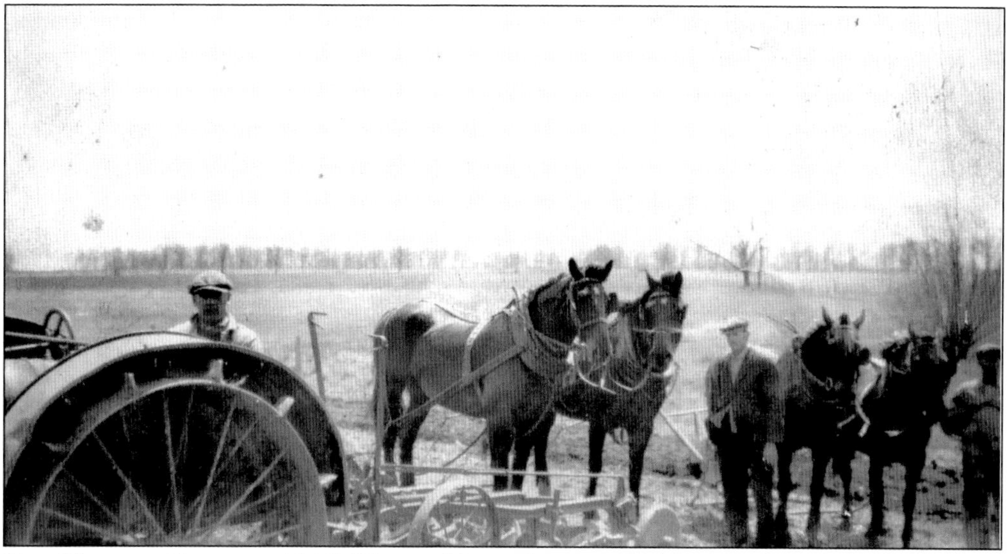

THE HEACOCK FARM, C. 1915. Warren Heacock is pictured here with unidentified men at his farm along Ferry Road. Today, the property is one of 23 permanently preserved farms in the township.

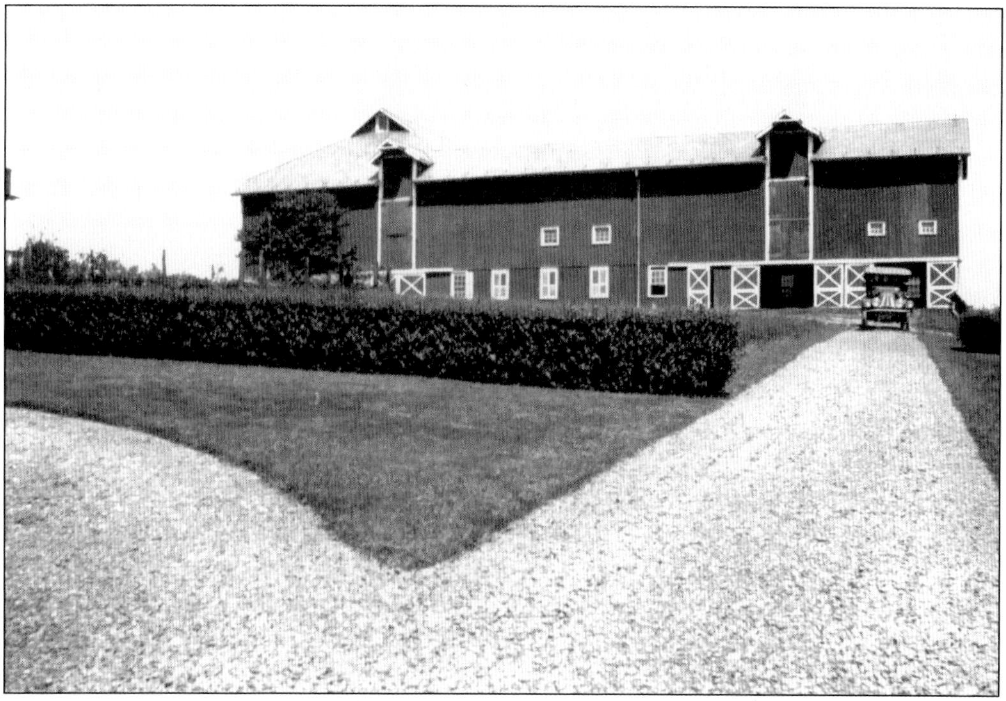

DILLON ROAD BARN, C. 1920. The Dillon Farm was considered one of the finest farms in the area in the early 20th century. The large red barn was one of many improvements built by James Dillon, who acquired the property in 1901. The barn was considered the largest in Bucks County at the time and was known throughout the area. Material for its construction came by railroad to Doylestown. The barn was demolished in later years. Today, the Summer Meadow development occupies this site.

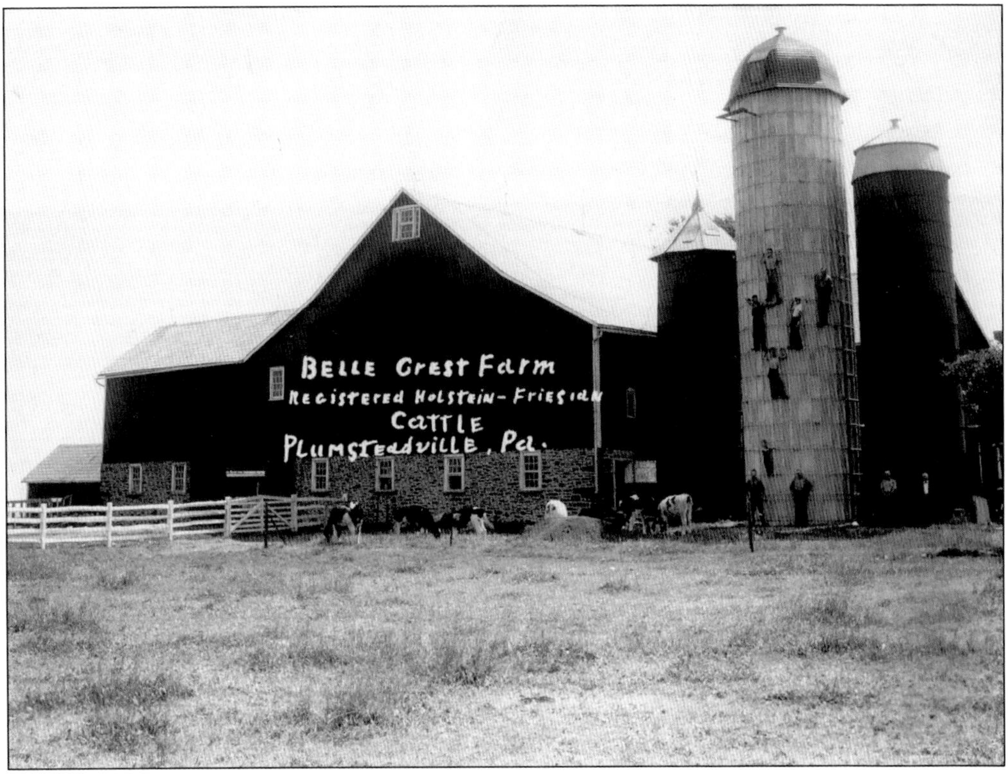

THE BELLE CREST FARM, C. 1935. The silo was an important part of the dairy farm. Belle Crest, also known as the Hunsberger Farm, was a Holstein cattle operation. Here, a new silo was constructed. This picture was most likely taken as a promotional piece for the silo salesman. Note the boys climbing the silo.

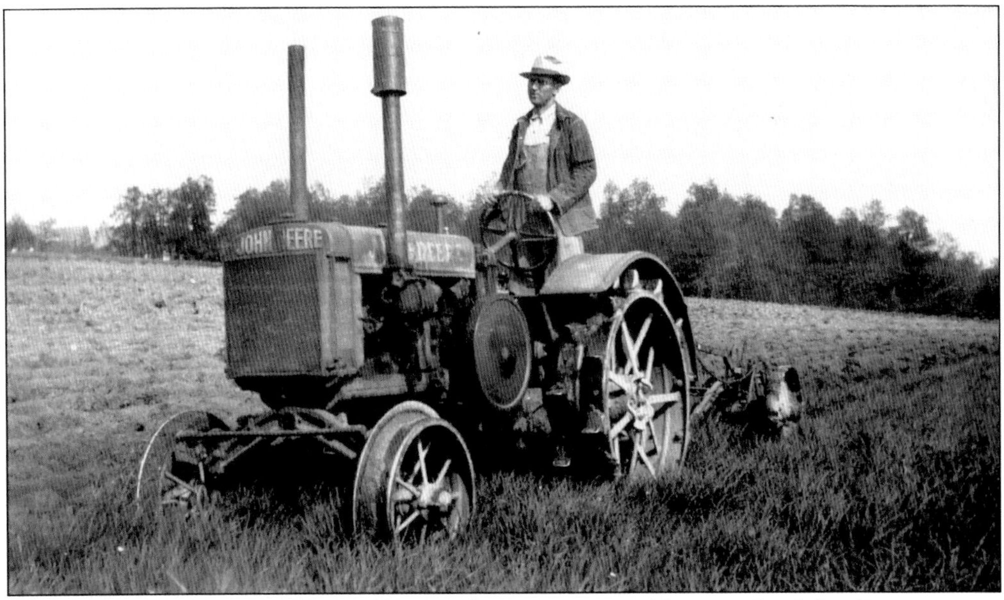

AN EARLY TRACTOR, C. 1920. Willis Hunsberger is pictured here on his John Deere tractor. The tractor revolutionized farming practices. Note the tireless wheels.

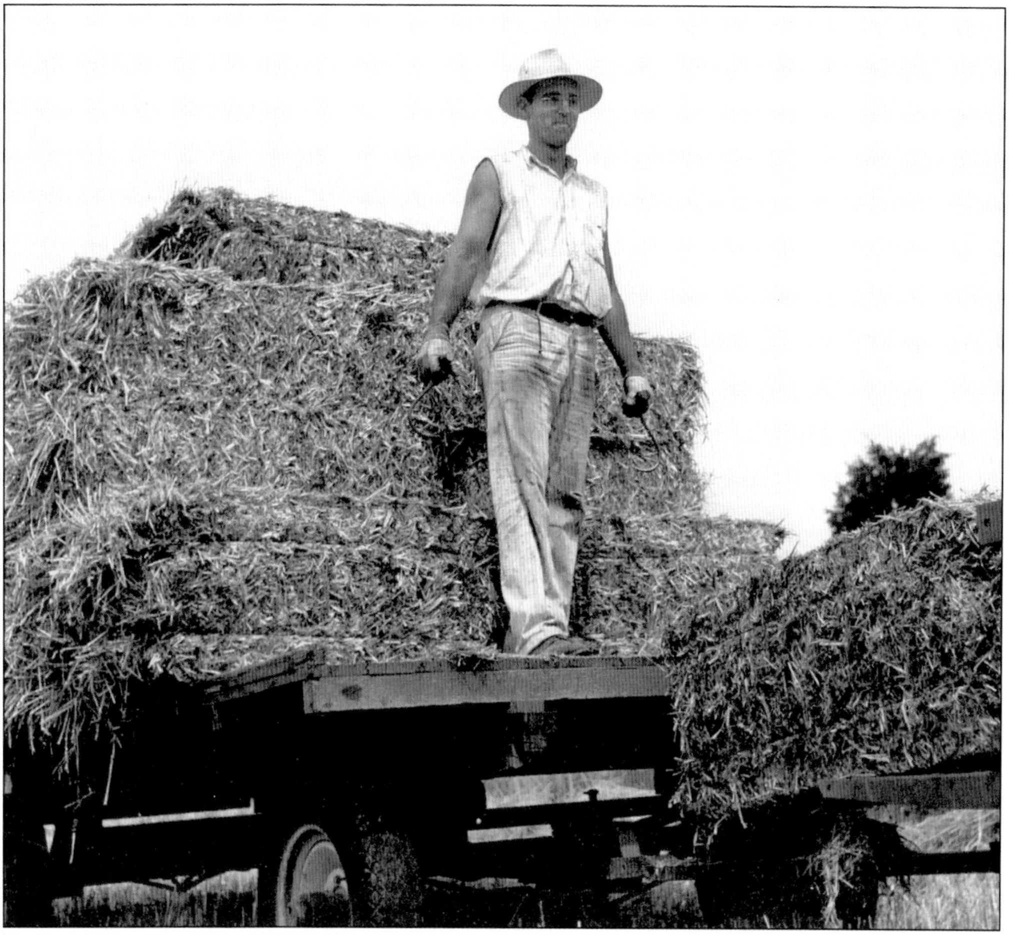

Baling Hay, c. 1930. George Hunsberger stands on top of his hay crop.

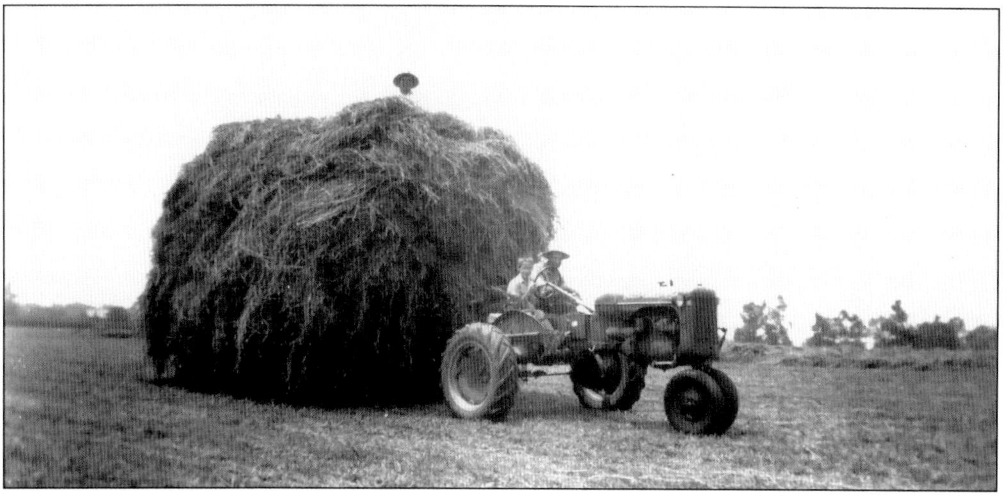

The Hay Wagon, c. 1945. Moving hay prior to baling was sometimes a tricky business.

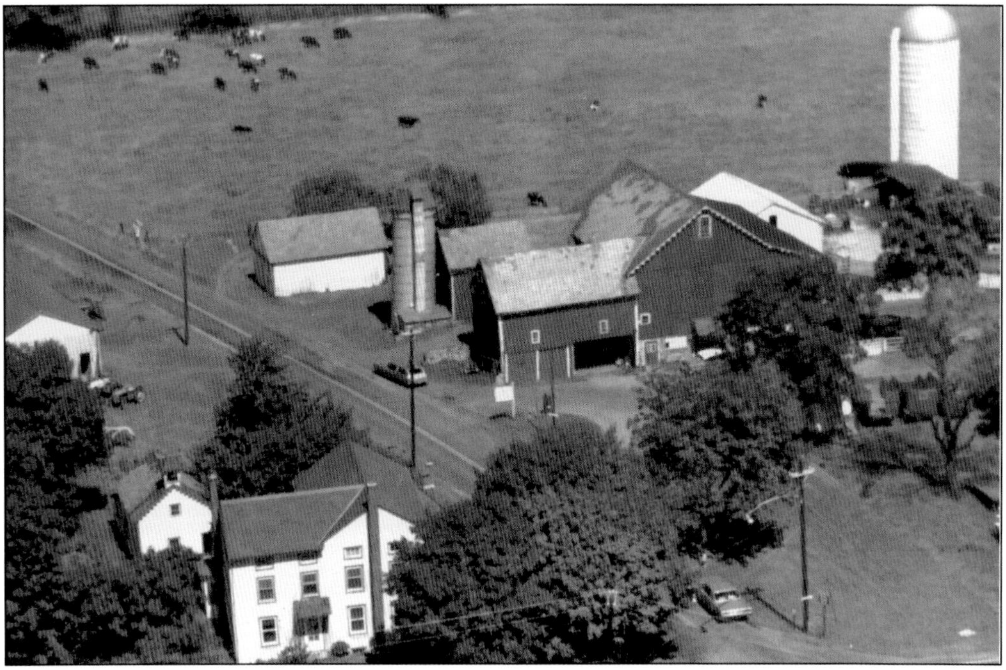

THE SAMES FARM, C. 1960. This aerial view of the Sames Farm shows the collection of outbuildings associated with most farmsteads in the 19th century and early 20th century. The barns and silos on the opposite side of Stump Road are no longer standing. Adjoining the house is a Victorian-era wash house with gingerbread trim and cupola. The site, owned by the Hinkle family between 1805 and 1877, was at one time an important crossroads known as Hinkletown. Hinkletown included a store and tavern.

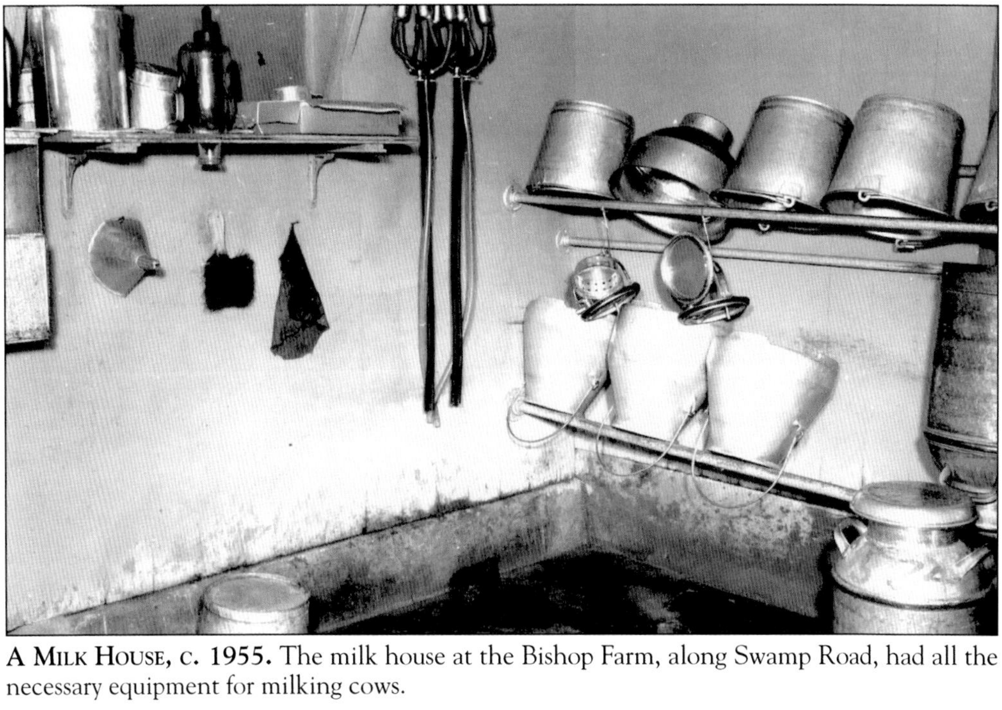

A MILK HOUSE, C. 1955. The milk house at the Bishop Farm, along Swamp Road, had all the necessary equipment for milking cows.

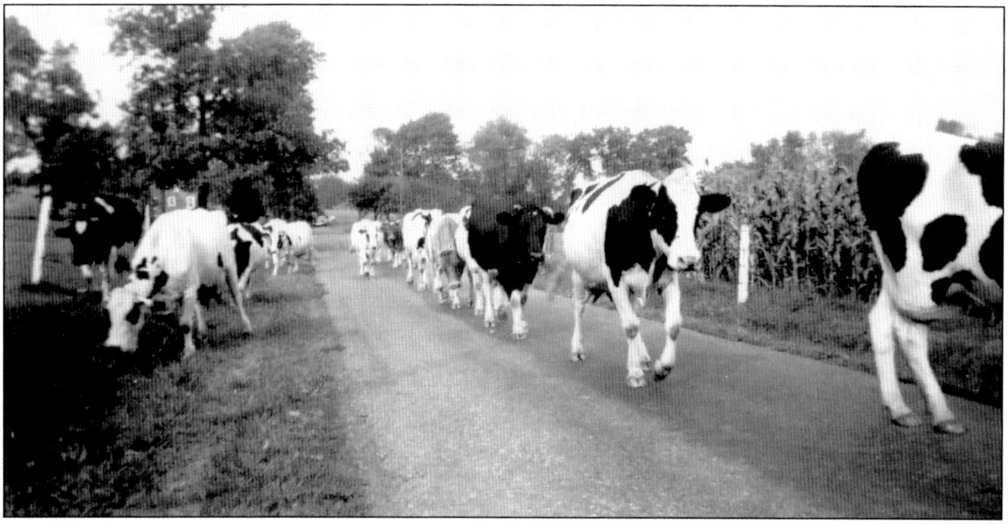

Roaming Cattle, c. 1945. Cattle moving from field to field, or to and from the barn, were frequent fixtures on township roadways into the mid-20th century. Here, cattle roam along Curly Hill Road.

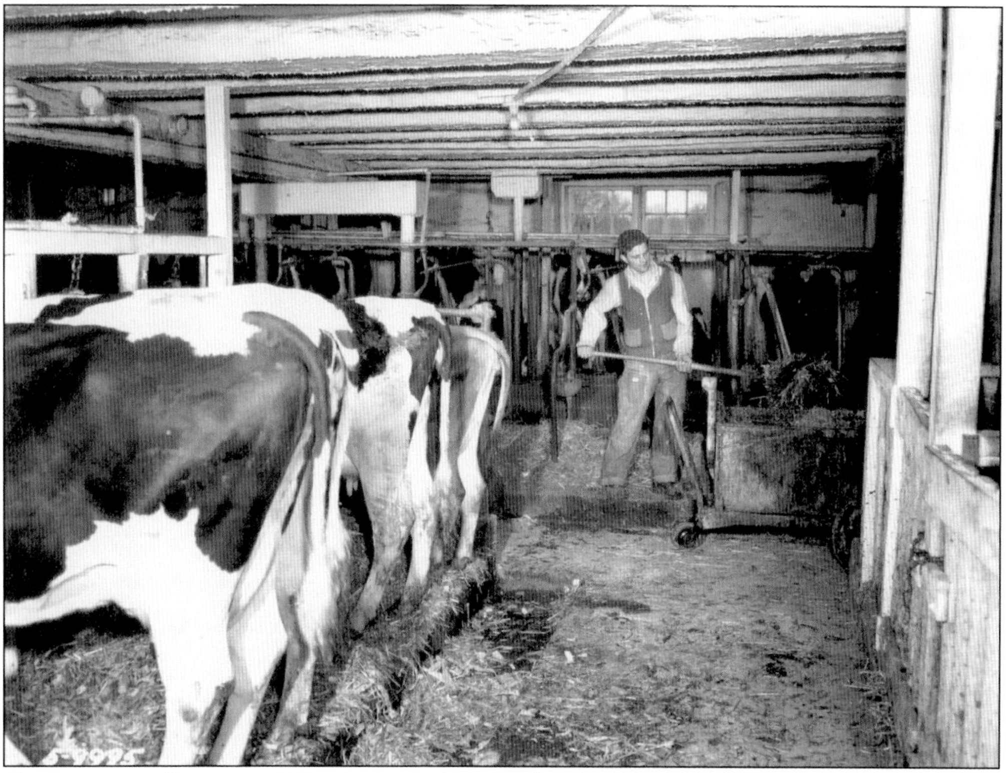

Cleaning the Barn, c. 1950. Prior to the installation of modern barn cleaners, manure was manually shoveled from the old barns. The barn pictured here was located at the Bishop Farm.

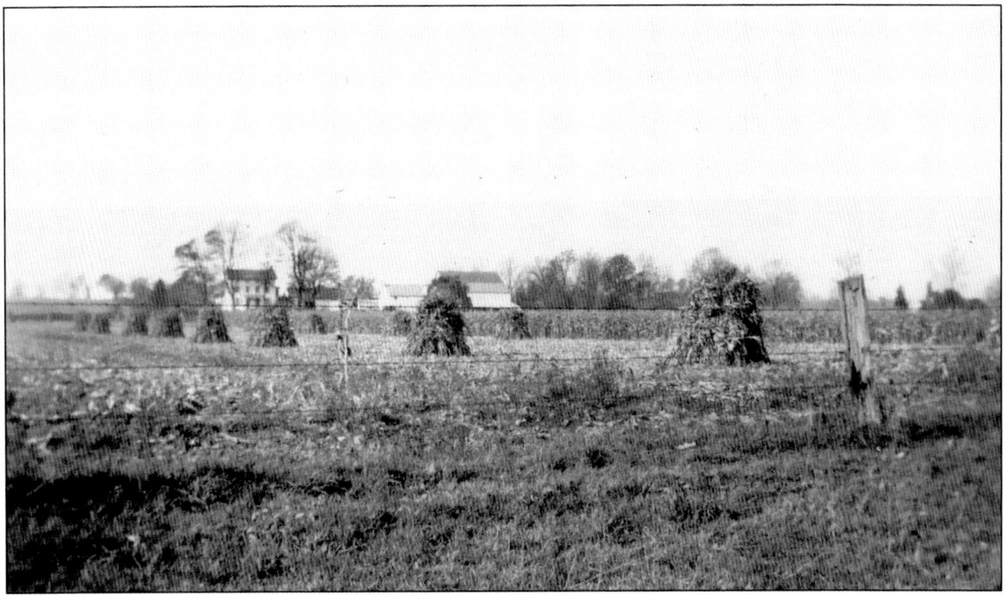

CORNSTALKS, C. 1920. A common sight during the fall were cornstalks bound in this fashion. In the background is the old Shaddinger residence along Curly Hill Road.

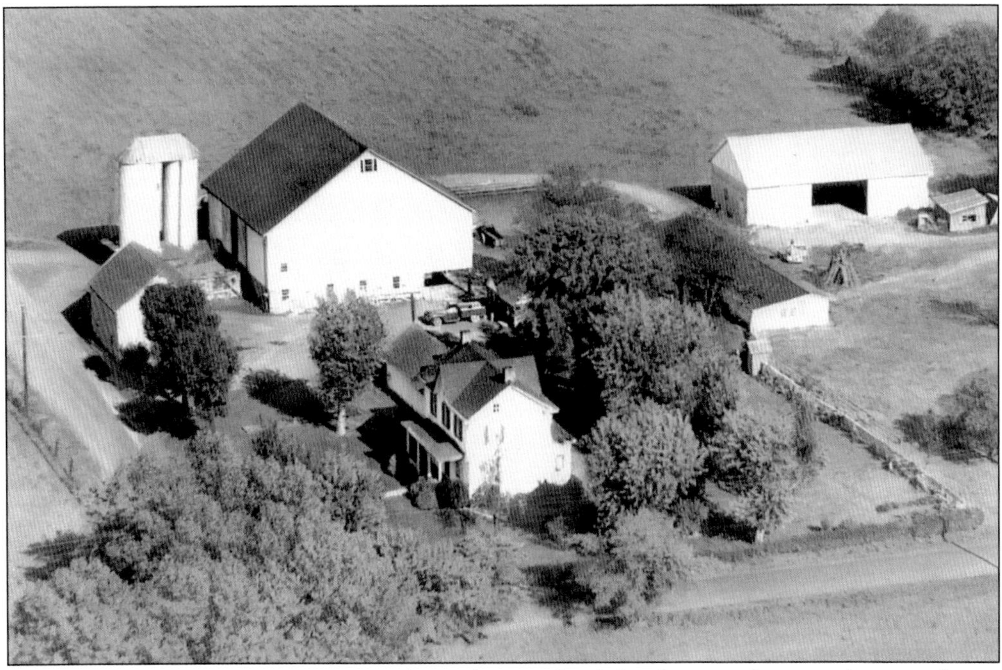

THE SAMUEL MYERS FARM, C. 1950. A good example of the thriving farms in the township is the Samuel Myers Farm, at the intersection of Groveland and Wismer Roads. The barn dates to 1922, when Samuel Myers purchased the property. To the left of the farmhouse are the woodshed, smokehouse, and wash house. The privy in the backyard is one of the last outhouses left in the township.

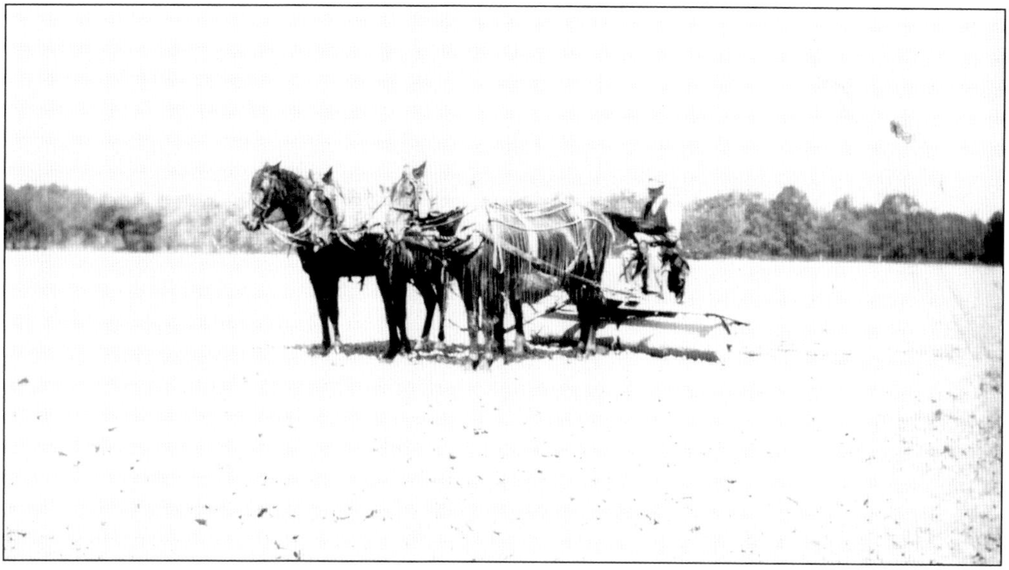

Rolling the Fields, c. 1924. Rolling the fields was a practice on every farm. Here, Samuel Gross rolls the fields along Haring Road. Note the fringed harness—called a fly net—thrown over the animal's back to keep flies off.

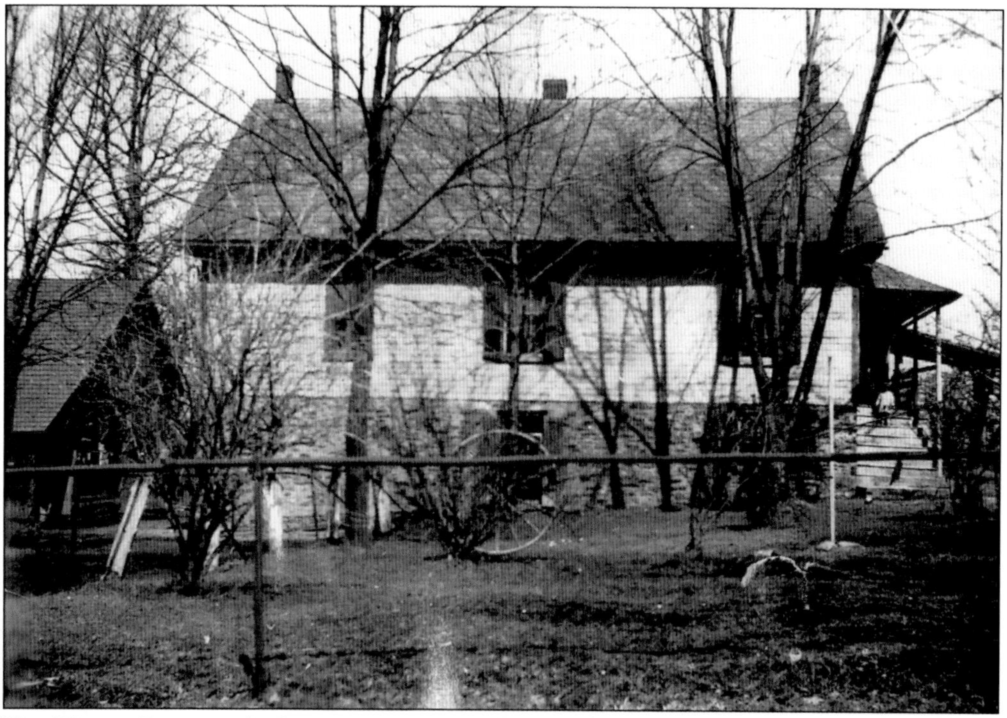

The Union Dairymen's Creamery, c. 1922. During the late 19th century, dairy associations were formed, creating collection centers where farmers could deliver their milk. The Union (or Wismer) Creamery was built prior to 1876. Henry Shull operated the creamery from 1922 to 1928. Later operators included Harry Myers in the 1930s and David Burd in the 1940s. At this creamery, the living quarters were found upstairs, and milk was accepted along the porch overhang. Milk was lowered to the basement, where three large vats produced cottage cheese.

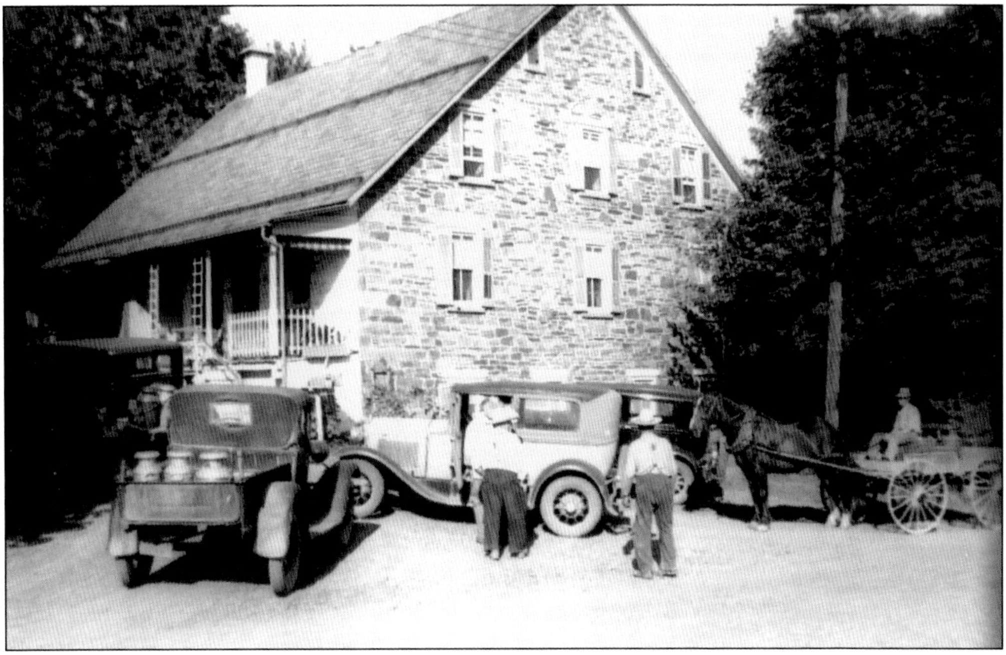

The Plumsteadville Creamery, c. 1930. The Plumsteadville Creamery on Kellers Church Road was established in 1888 and operated until 1945. By the late 1940s, the building was used as a frozen food factory by Myers Frozen Foods Company and later by Hanover Foods. There were at least two other creameries in the township, including the Gardenville Creamery on Durham Road, and a creamery along Curly Hill Road near Route 611.

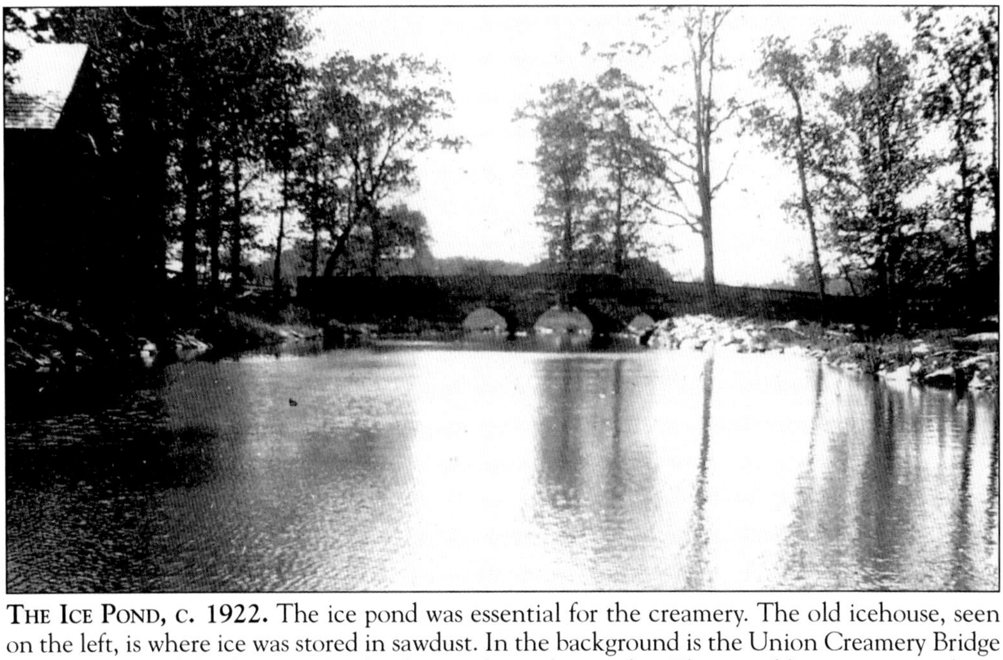

The Ice Pond, c. 1922. The ice pond was essential for the creamery. The old icehouse, seen on the left, is where ice was stored in sawdust. In the background is the Union Creamery Bridge on Wismer Road, built in 1885. The dairy industry boomed in Plumstead but was not without problems. Many dairymen lost their herds due to the foot-and-mouth epidemic of 1913. During the Depression, many dairy farms changed hands because of the hard times.

Three

VILLAGES

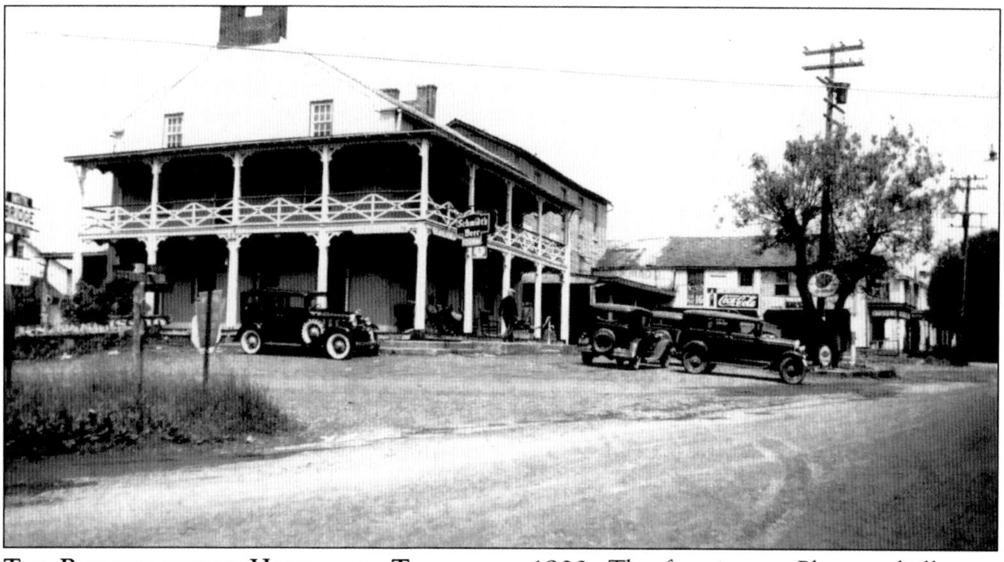

THE PLUMSTEADVILLE HOTEL AND TAVERN, C. 1900. The first inn at Plumsteadville was established c. 1751 and was known as Hart's Tavern; it was later known as Rodrock's. The inn was the heart of the village, occupying the northwest corner of Stump and Easton Roads. A post office was established here in 1832, and the tavern and village became known as Fisherville. By 1840, the name was changed to Plumstead, and in 1846, Plumsteadville. Henry Shisler rebuilt the old tavern in 1863. Later owners included the Hockman and Hellerick families.

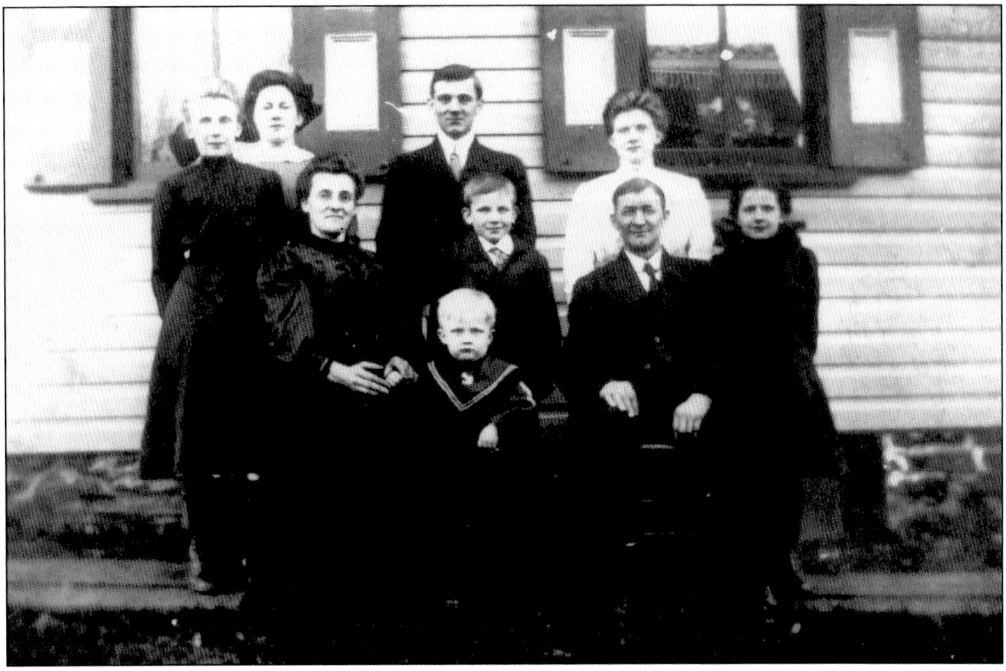

The Hellerick Family, c. 1915. The Hellerick family is pictured in front of the hotel. Shown sitting in this image are Flora Sames Hellerick, holding the hand of William, and George Sr. Shown standing are, from left to right, Mary, Marie, George Jr., Irwin, Carrie, and Flora.

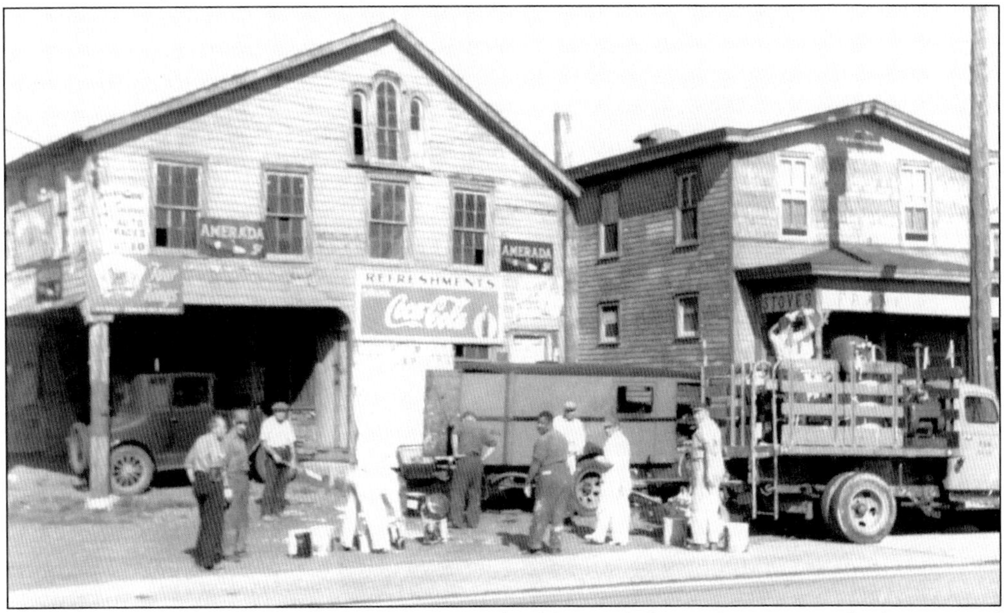

A Carriage House, c. 1939. The large frame building at left was the carriage shed associated with the hotel. The first floor was used for carriage storage, and the second and third floors served as community meeting space. A stage was found on the second floor, where musicals, plays, and other performances were held. George Hellerick, the hotel proprietor, raised pigs behind this building and used the area along the road for butchering. The building stood until the 1950s.

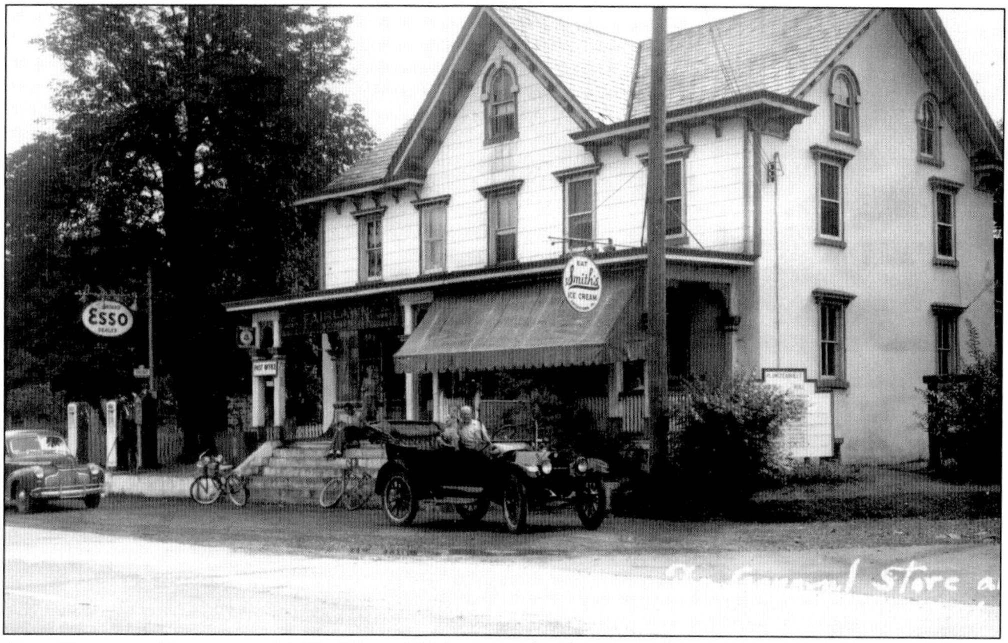

The General Store, c. 1945. The old Plumsteadville post office and general store, located at the southeast corner of Stump and Easton Roads, was built by J. B. Snyder c. 1858.

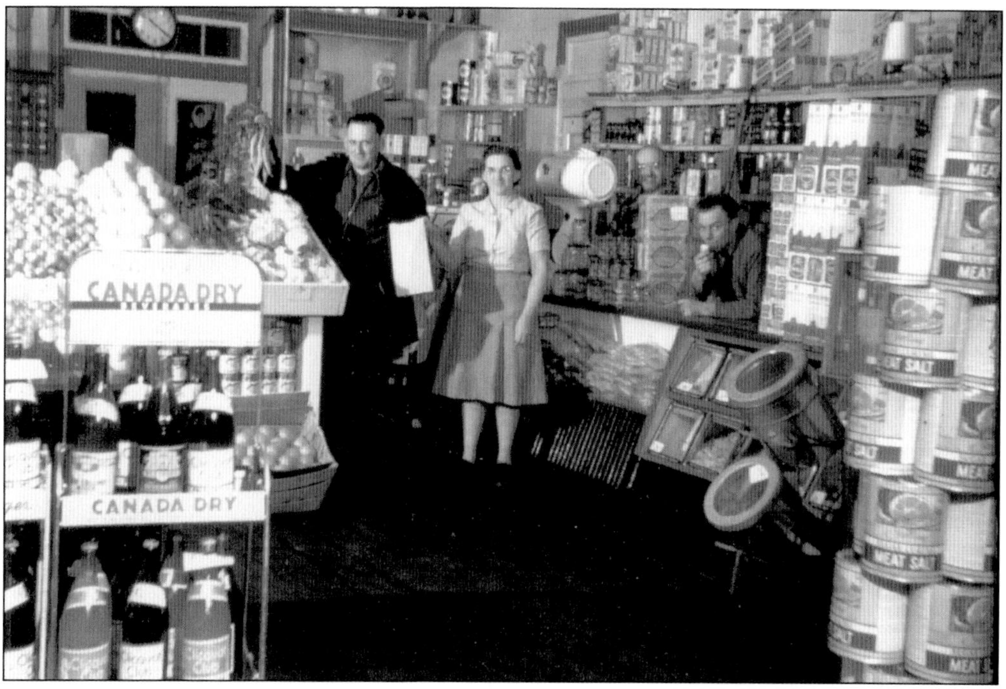

The Plumsteadville General Store, c. 1950. Shown inside the Bishops' general store are, from left to right, Lloyd Crouthamel, Jane Bishop, Paxson Bishop, and Harold (Pat) Leatherman. Post office boxes are visible at the upper left. The Bishops were the fourth and final operators of the general store. Previous operators were Snyder, Yost, and Weingold.

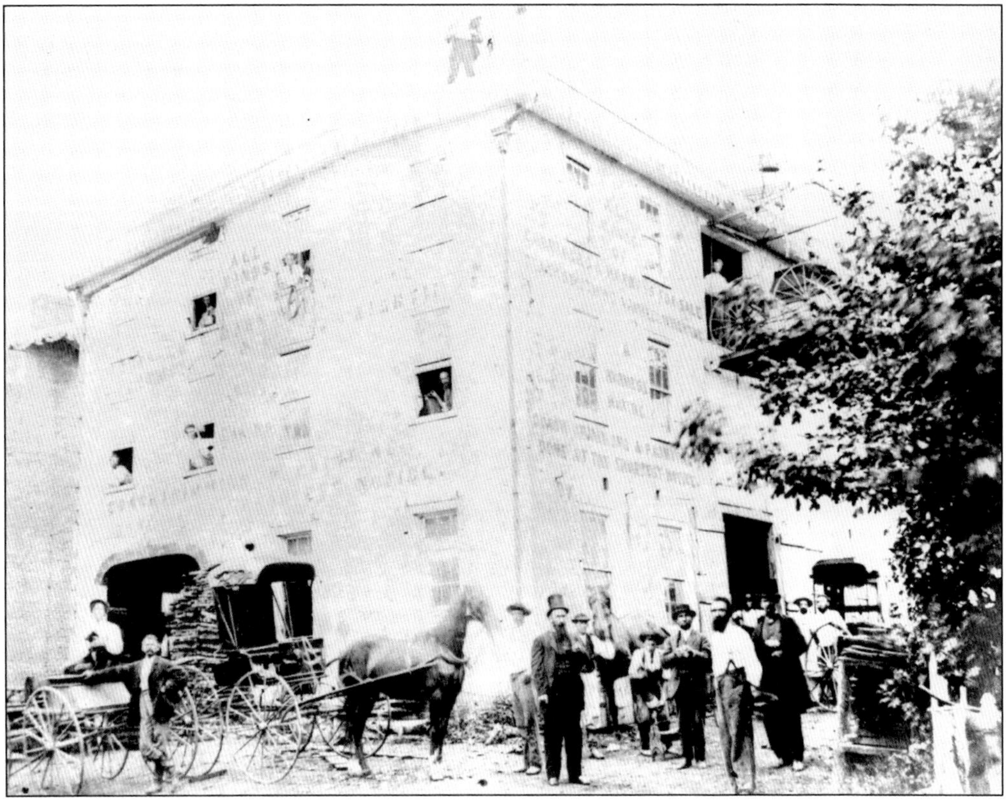

THE COACH AND WAGON FACTORY, C. 1880. This coach and wagon factory was established by Aaron Kratz in 1857. In 1900, the factory was described as the oldest and largest manufacturer of carriages in the state, with more than 500 in stock. The company boasted that carriages were made and sold to markets as far away as Canada. The development of the village echoed the growth and success of Kratz's business. Between 1860 and 1890, dozens of buildings were constructed to house factory workers and other residents who provided everyday services. (Collection of the Spruance Library of the Bucks County Historical Society.)

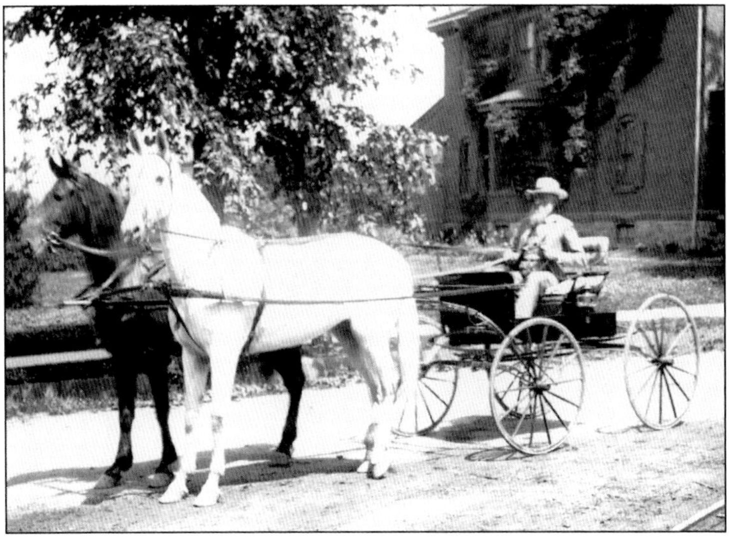

AARON KRATZ, C. 1900. Aaron Kratz, born in Plumstead on July 9, 1832, was the most prominent citizen in the region in the 19th century. He is pictured here in one of his wagons in Doylestown. (Collection of the Spruance Library of the Bucks County Historical Society.)

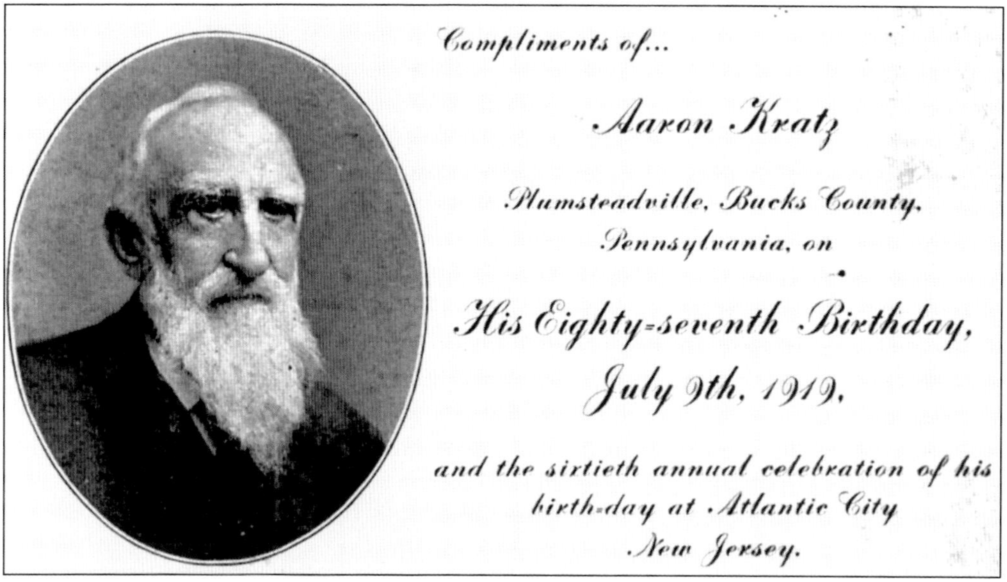
Compliments of...

Aaron Kratz

Plumsteadville, Bucks County,
Pennsylvania, on

His Eighty-seventh Birthday,
July 9th, 1919,

and the sixtieth annual celebration of his
birth-day at Atlantic City
New Jersey.

AARON KRATZ BIRTHDAY PASS, C. 1914. Among his many contributions to the community was Kratz's annual birthday celebration. On his birthday, Kratz was known to give out free passes to fellow residents for travel to and from Atlantic City.

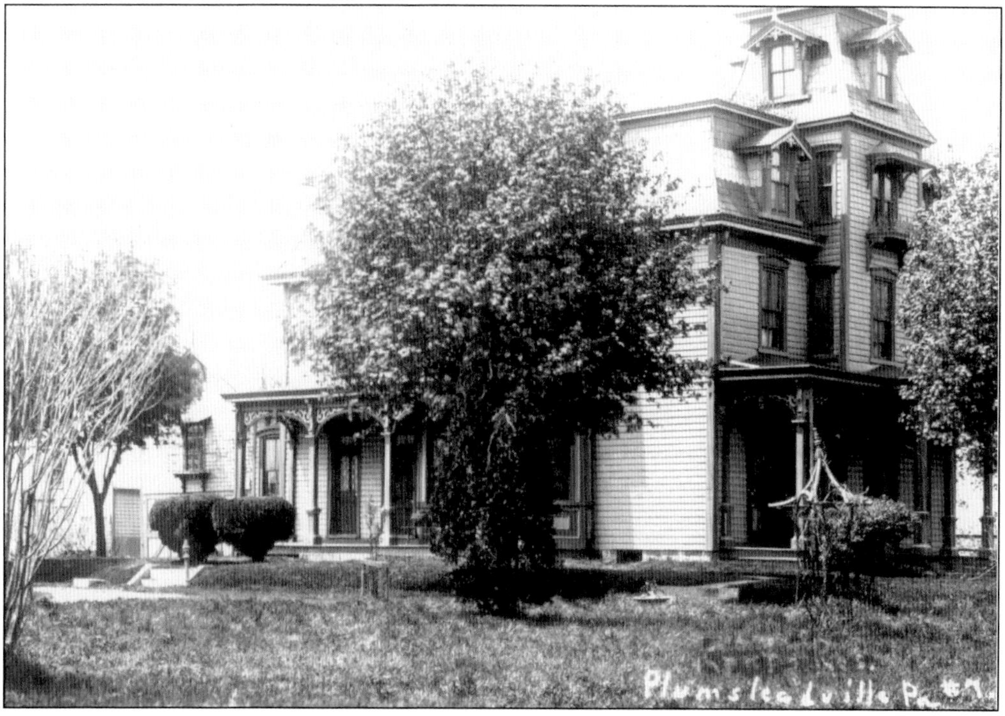

THE LINCOLN KRATZ HOUSE, 1900. Fine Victorian mansions were constructed along Stump Road for the Kratz family and families of other local businessmen. Lincoln Kratz, son of Aaron, was the company's bookkeeper. He built this house, once found just west of the village, on Stump Road.

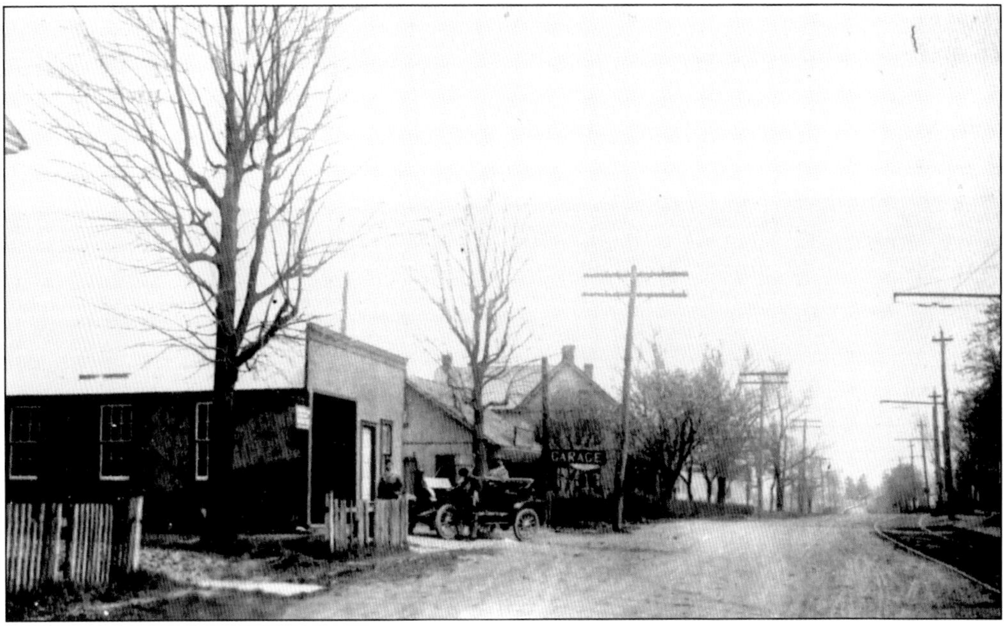

Easton Road Looking South, c. 1910. Easton Road, the main road through the village, remained a narrow roadway into the 20th century. This view shows Jake Gilbert's garage at left, with the Metzger Barbershop and the Rush property beyond.

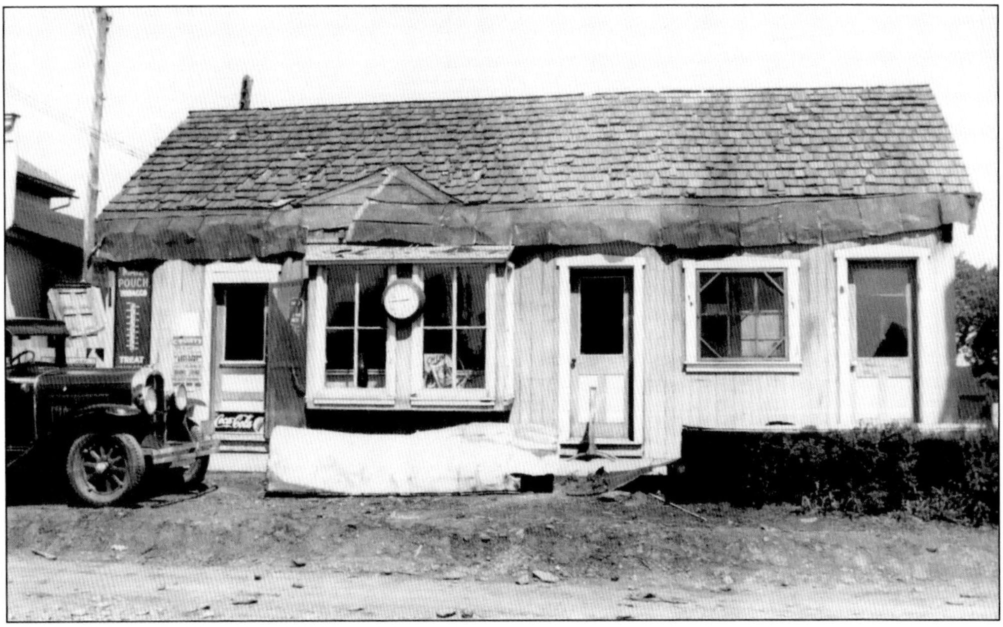

J. W. Metzger Barbershop, c. 1939. The local barber operated out of the one-story building on the east side of Easton Road. The structure originally had a porch that was taken down to make room for road widening in 1939. Metzger also sold ice cream, sodas, candy, and newspapers at this location. The building still stands along the highway.

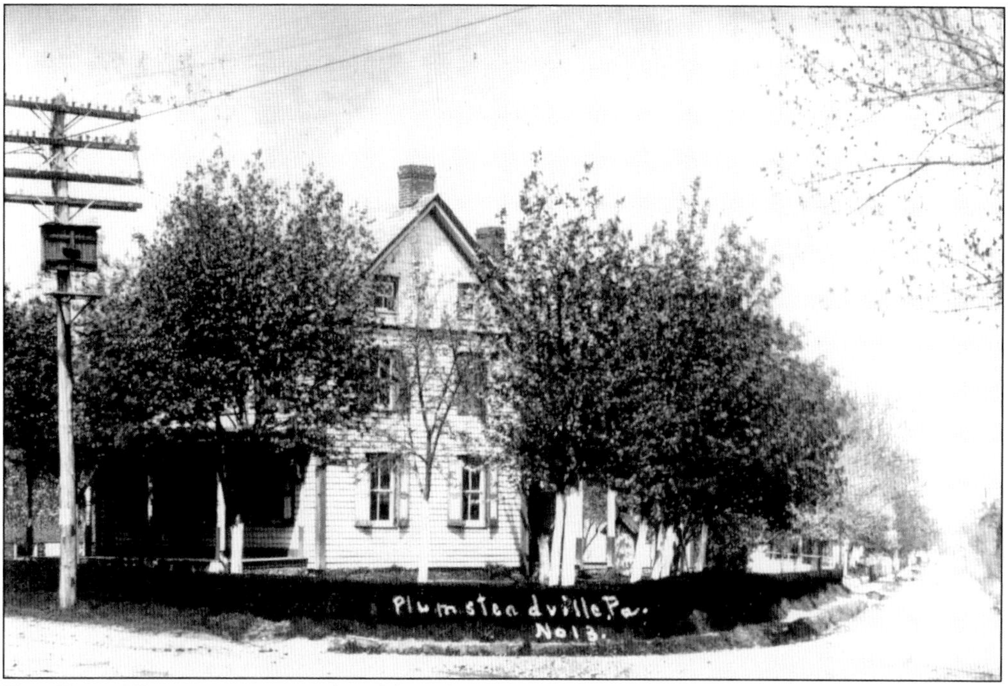

The Rush House, c. 1900. The old Rush House is located at the northeast corner of Stump and Easton Roads. It has undergone many changes since its construction in the mid-1800s. Records indicate that it was the property of J. L. Leatherman in 1876. In the 1920s, it was converted into the Rush Garage, a local landmark for many years.

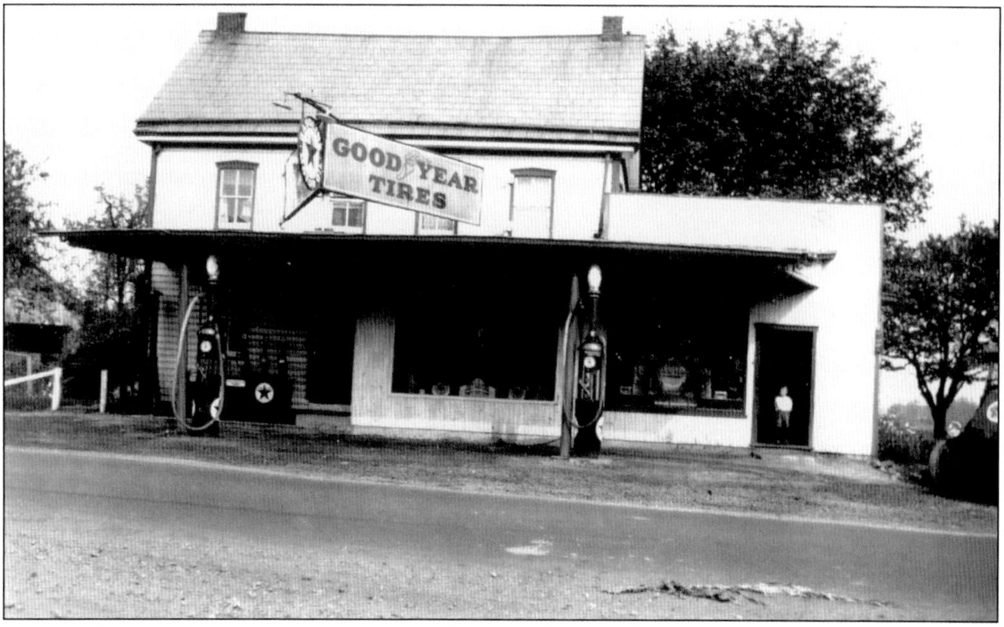

Walter Rush's Garage, c. 1920. Walter Rush opened a Texaco service station in front of his home. The gasoline pumps were moved away from the road, and the shed-roof porch was removed and rebuilt when Easton Road was widened in 1939. Later widening of the road further reduced the frontage.

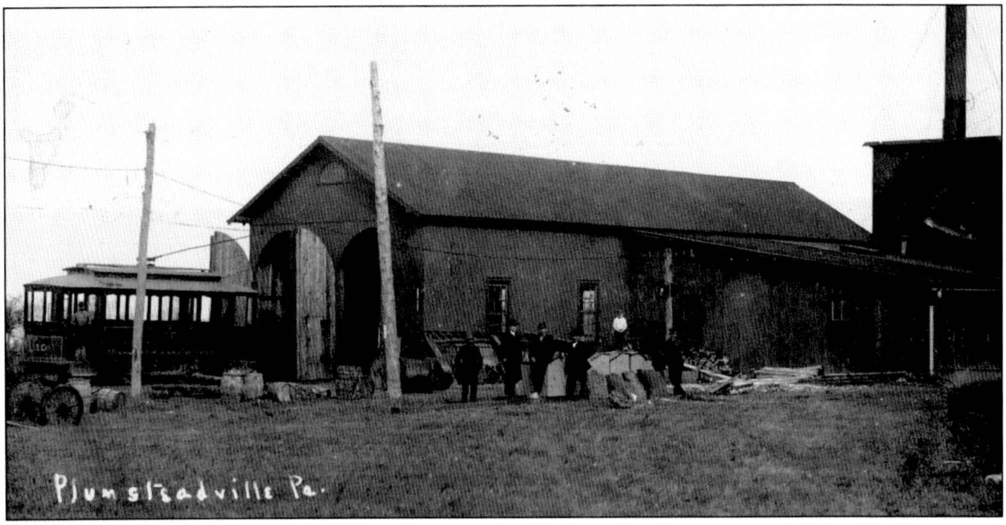

THE PHILADELPHIA AND EASTON CAR SHED, C. 1905. A trolley line was established in Plumstead in 1897, and the first car ran from Pipersville to Doylestown in 1902. The route eventually ran between Doylestown and Easton, along Easton Road, passing the villages of Dyerstown, Danboro, and Plumsteadville. Construction of the line was costly, and the investors, including promoter Aaron Kratz, went bankrupt. Although it was reorganized, the trolley line operated only until the 1920s.

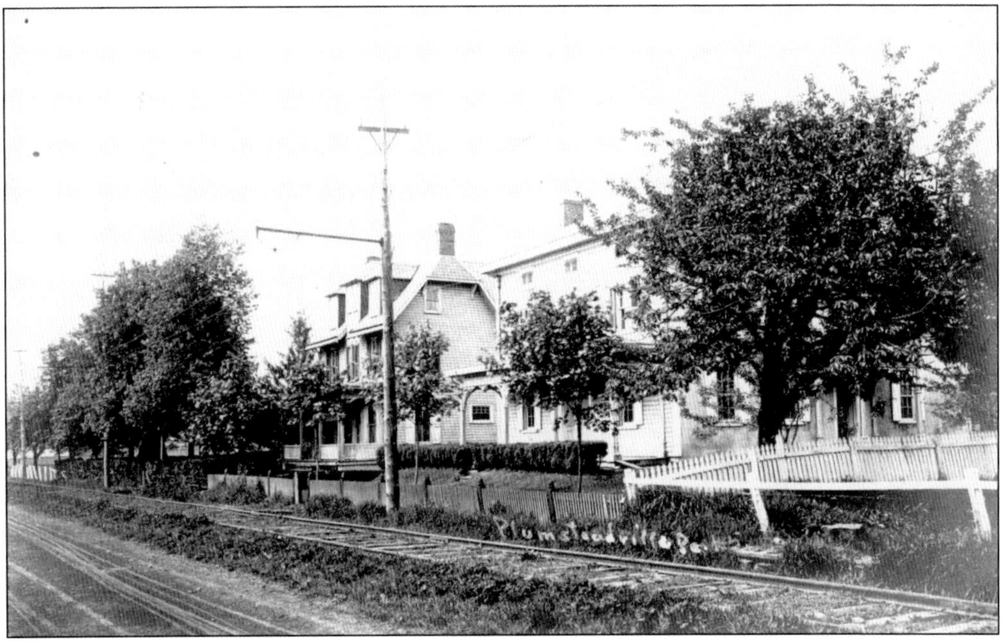

EASTON ROAD LOOKING SOUTH, C. 1910. The trolley tracks are visible along the roadway in the foreground. The trolley provided an important service, making access to nearby Doylestown easy, and providing an economic way for farmers to ship produce to Philadelphia and Easton. The homes pictured here, located just south of the general store, were built by J. B. Snyder between 1850 and 1880.

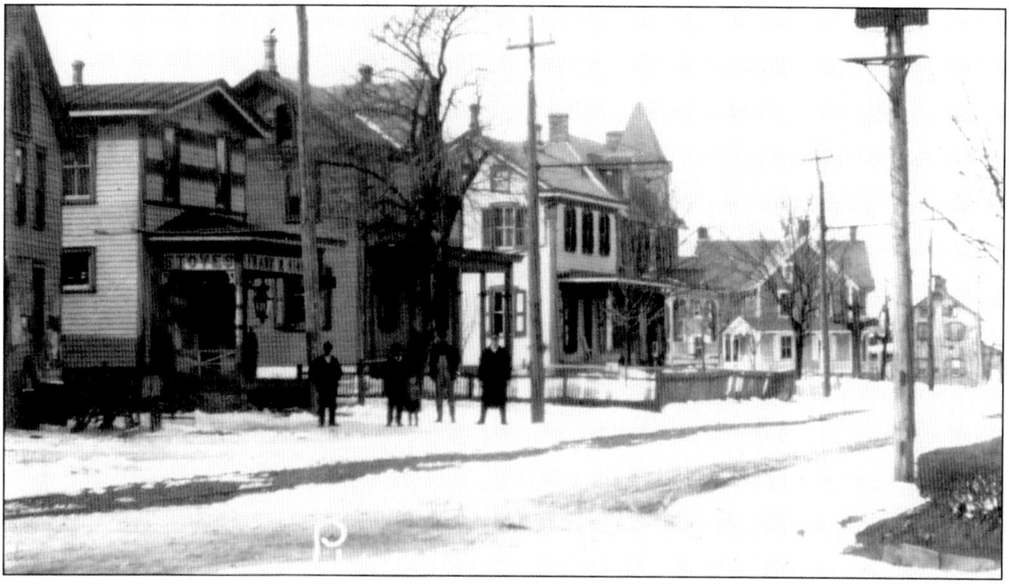

A View up Easton Road, Plumsteadville, c. 1915. Much of the village developed in the second half of the 1800s with the construction of Victorian-style homes. This view shows Easton Road north of the hotel. Seen from left to right are the Hinkle shop and home, the Lloyd Keller homestead, and houses owned by Uriah Schmell and Joseph Myers. The Myers house is now the site of the Shelly Funeral Home.

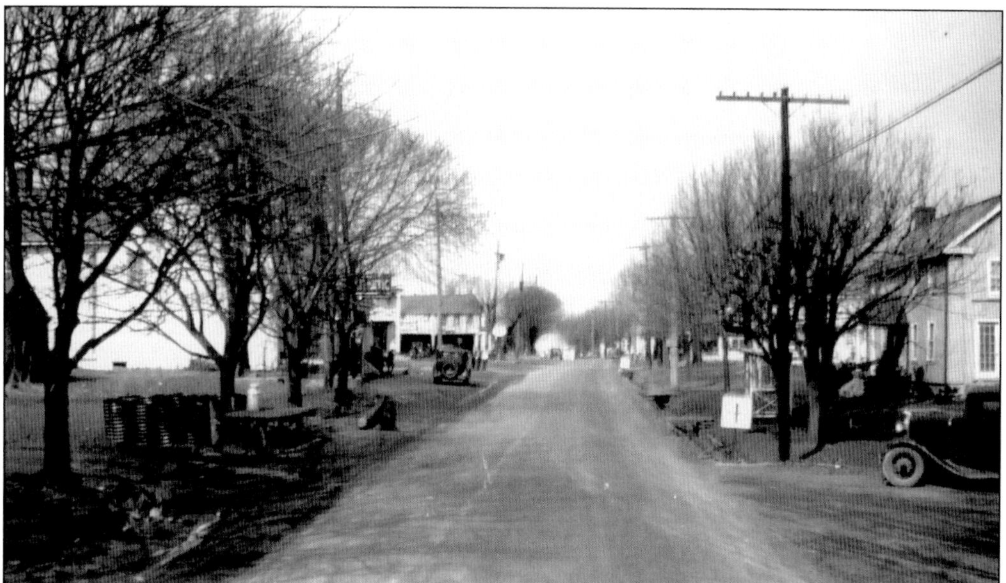

Easton Road Looking North, c. 1910. The old village also extended south of Stump Road. The building on the right was located where Plumstead Square Shopping Center now stands. The milk can on the left is shown in front of the Lady-Lawn Dairy.

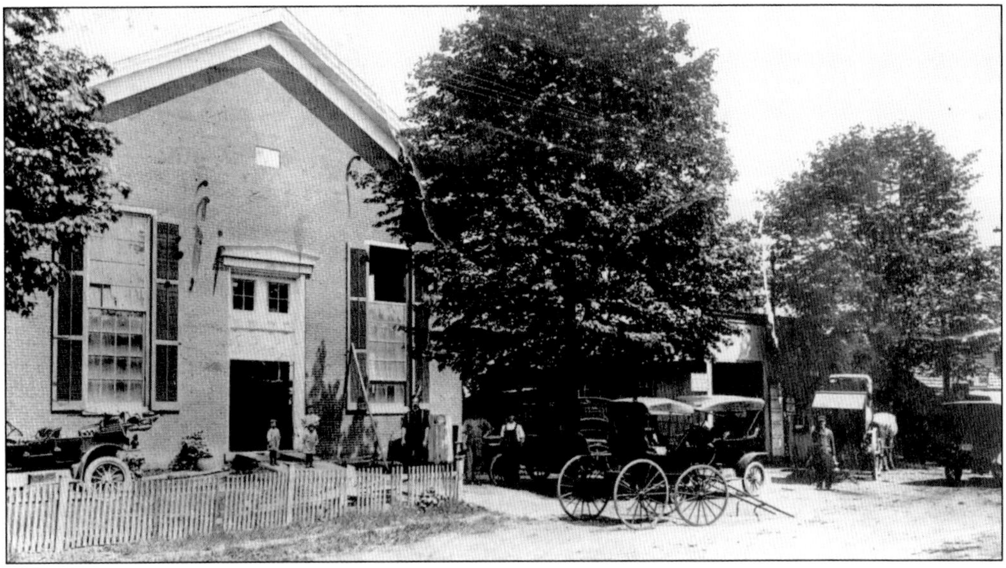

The Presbyterian Church, c. 1900. The Presbyterian Church at Plumsteadville was constructed in the heart of the village in 1861. By the 1880s, the congregation had disbanded and the building was converted for factory use. For many years it housed the Keller Glove Factory. An associated cemetery is still found along Kellers Church Road.

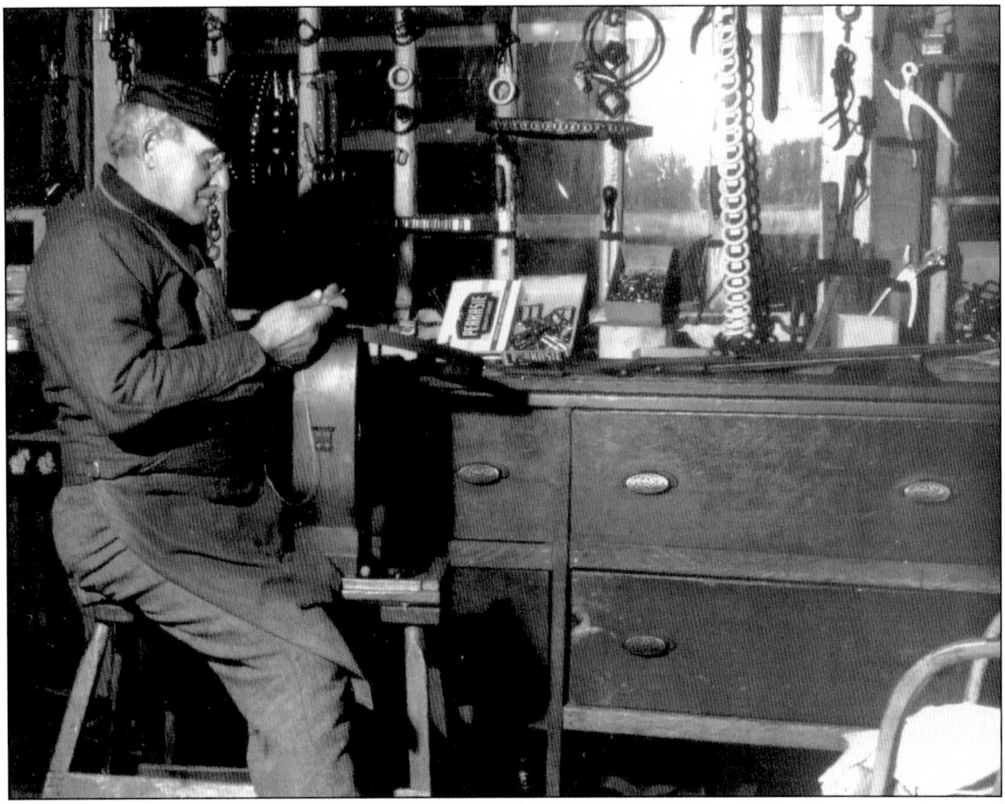

Eli Myers, c. 1940. Eli Myers was the village harness maker. His shop was located on Stump Road.

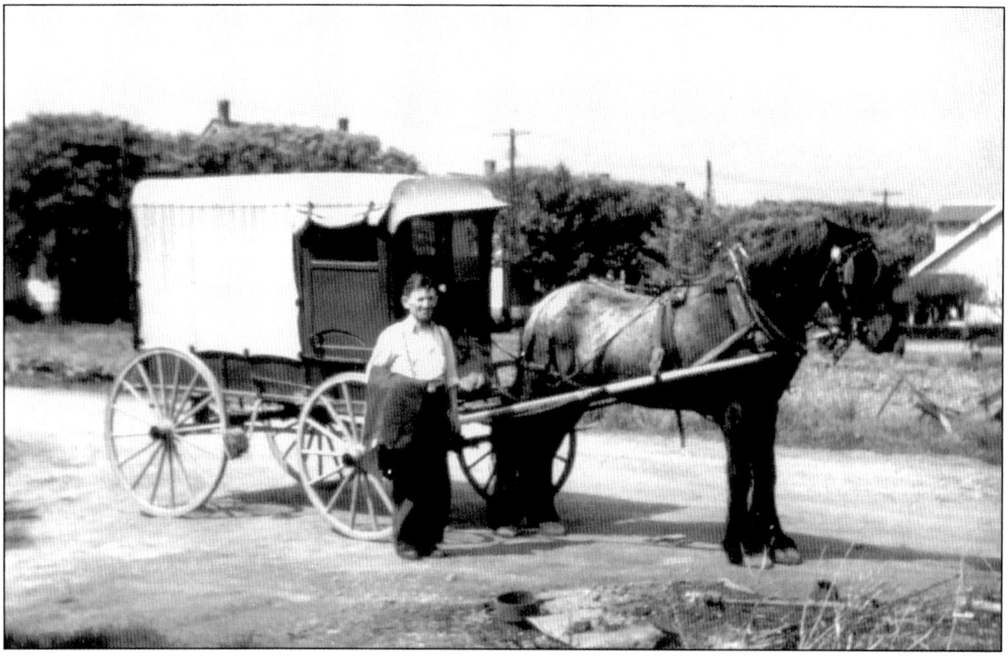

A Peddler in Plumsteadville, c. 1910. Mr. Strickler was one of several salesmen who made his way from farm to farm and house to house selling his wares. He commuted to the area from Philadelphia—keeping his horse and wagon on a farm in the Deep Run area—and traveled to and from work by trolley, and later by bus. He was a common sight at Plumsteadville.

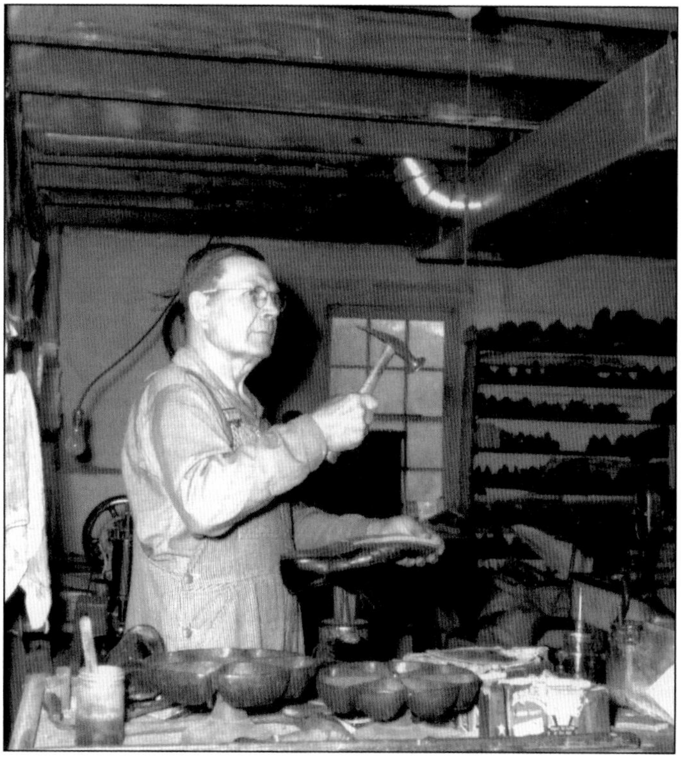

Henry Wagner, c. 1940. The local cobbler in the early 20th century was Henry Wagner.

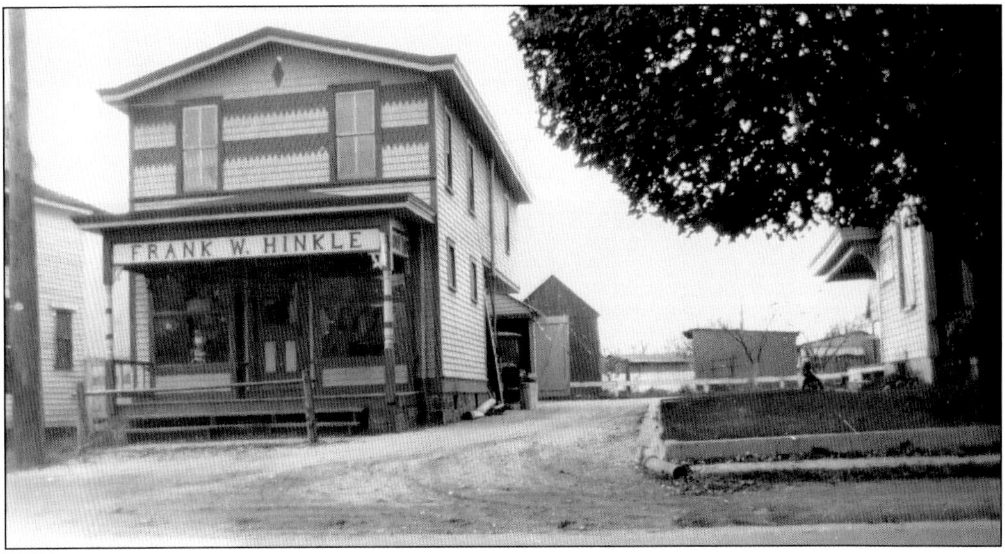

The Hinkle Store, c. 1910. Frank Hinkle, who operated the local tinsmith shop, was a longtime Plumsteadville resident. This building was originally constructed as the Plumstead Rural Telephone Company, but it is locally associated with Hinkle's shop. In the mid-20th century, it housed Farmer John's Food, operated by John and Ruth Bollinger.

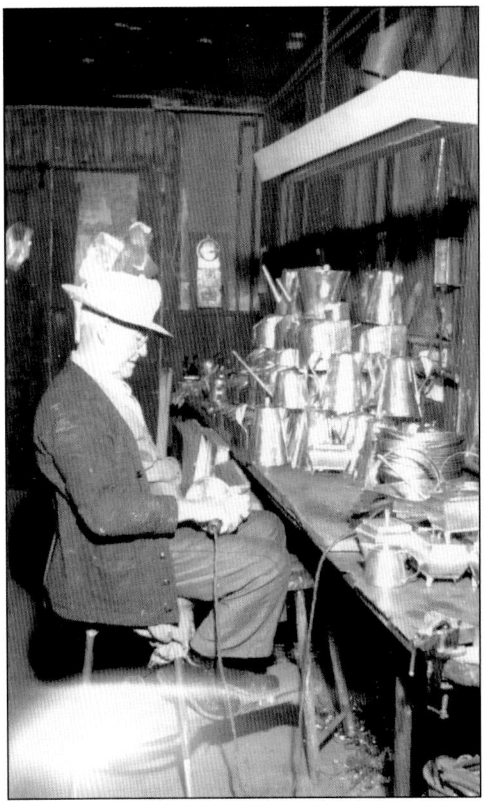

Frank Hinkle, c. 1940. Frank Hinkle continued his work as the local tinsmith for many years. Advertisements indicated he made tin roofing, spouting, plumbing, and stoves.

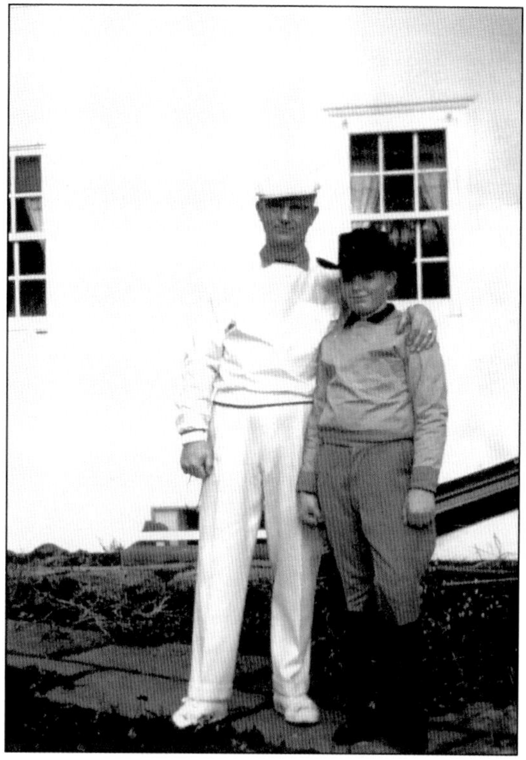

Dr. John W. Ward and Son, c. 1950. Plumsteadville also had other important professionals who served the surrounding community. Dr. Ward was Plumsteadville's family doctor for 23 years. He first came to Plumstead in 1936 as an assistant to Dr. George Brewer, and eventually took his place. Dr. Ward served the community until his death in 1959. He is pictured here with his son Jack.

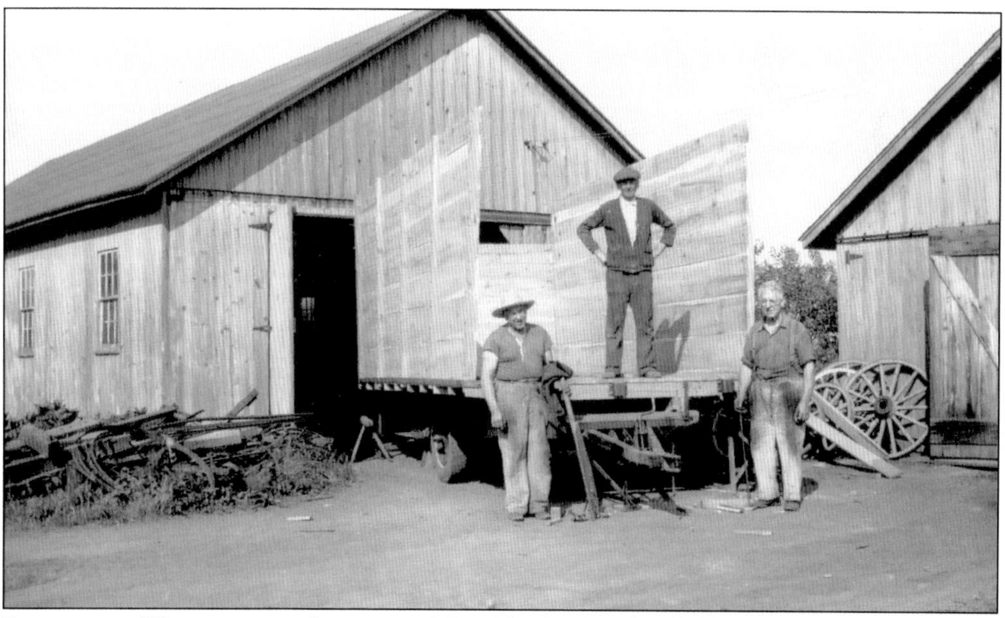

Blacksmith-Wheelwright Shop, c. 1940. Charles Snyder (left), Harry Ott (center), and Howard Kramer pose in front of the shop located on Stump Road.

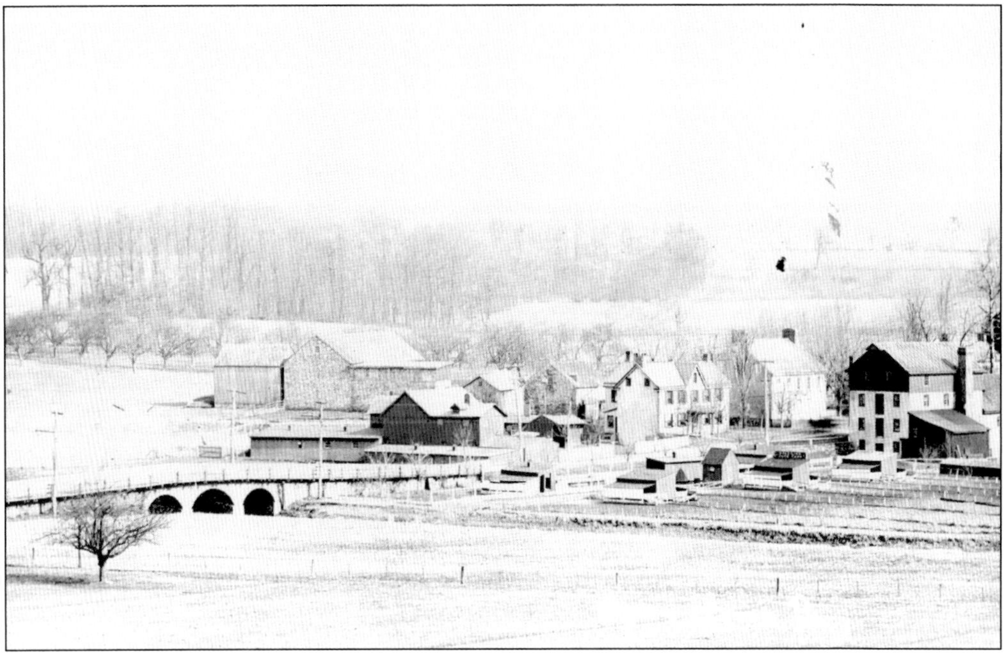

AN EARLY VIEW OF DYERSTOWN, C. 1900. Dyerstown was one of the first villages in Plumstead Township, stretching along the original Easton Road near the Dyer mill. This view, looking southeast from Sawmill Road, shows the gristmill at right, along with the Dyer houses and their associated outbuildings. The bridge, originally constructed in 1798, was replaced in 1928.

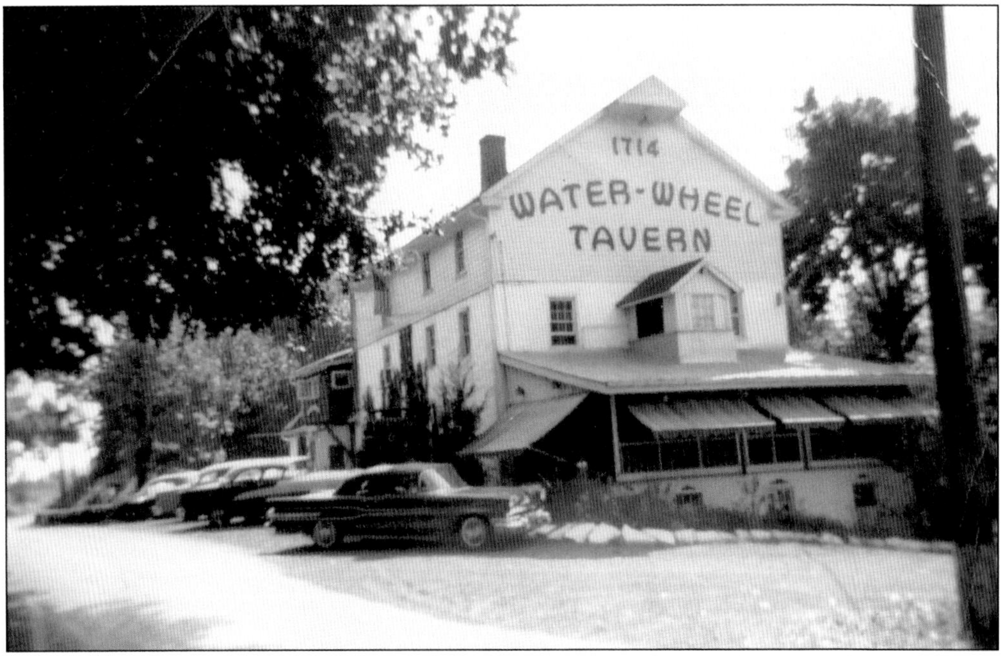

THE DYER MILL, C. 1930. Among the first industries in the township was the gristmill at Dyerstown. The original structure, built in 1722, was destroyed by fire in 1803, rebuilt the following year, and expanded in 1812. By the early 1900s, it was converted into the Water-Wheel Tavern.

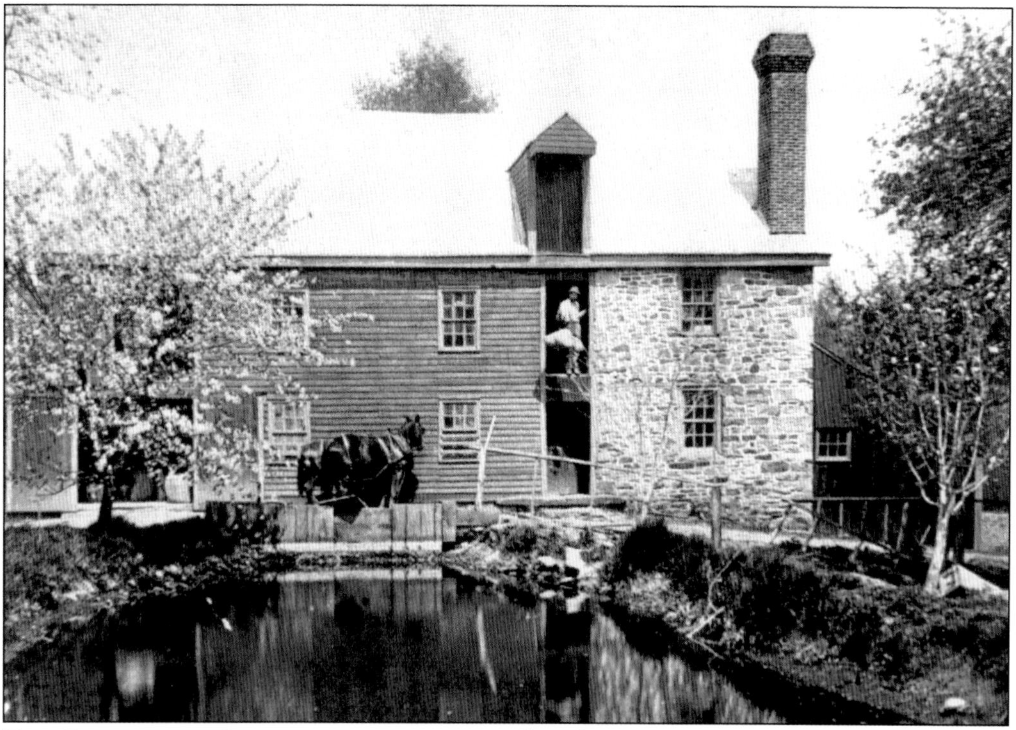

THE LANDISVILLE GRISTMILL, c. 1900. Small villages, such as Landisville, developed around mills. This mill was constructed in the 18th century and was originally operated by Eleazar Fenton. By 1834, it was owned and operated by Abraham Landis. Landis ran the mill for 37 years, and the village and road are named for him. The old mill stood until c. 1930.

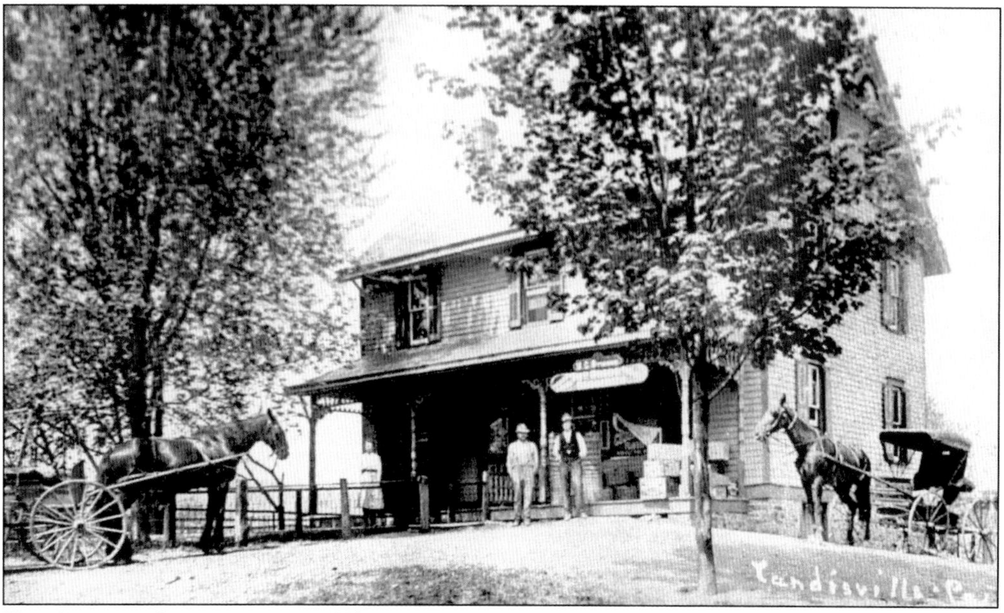

THE STROUSE STORE, c. 1895. Ulysses Grant Strouse, born and raised in Gardenville, acquired the old Fenton Mill in Landisville in 1894. He constructed a house and a store soon after his purchase. The building still stands along the Landisville Road.

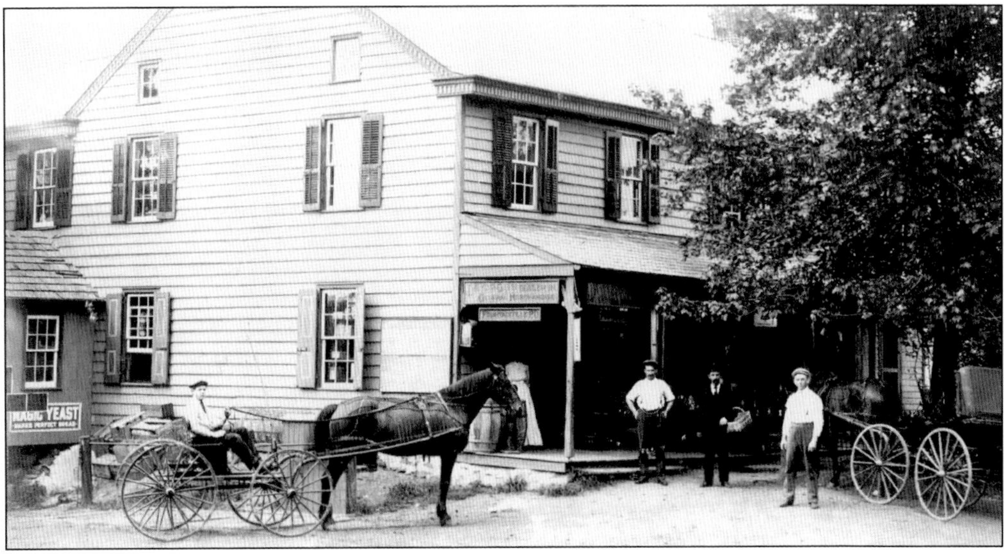

Gross's Store, c. 1870. The village of Fountainville developed in the mid-18th century around a tavern at the southeast corner of Ferry and Swamp Roads. A century later, John L. Gross, along with his brother-in-law Henry Rosenberger, built this structure across the road at the northeast corner of Ferry and Swamp Roads. Gross later bought out Rosenberger and continued the business until his death in 1901. The store also served as the post office and a community gathering place.

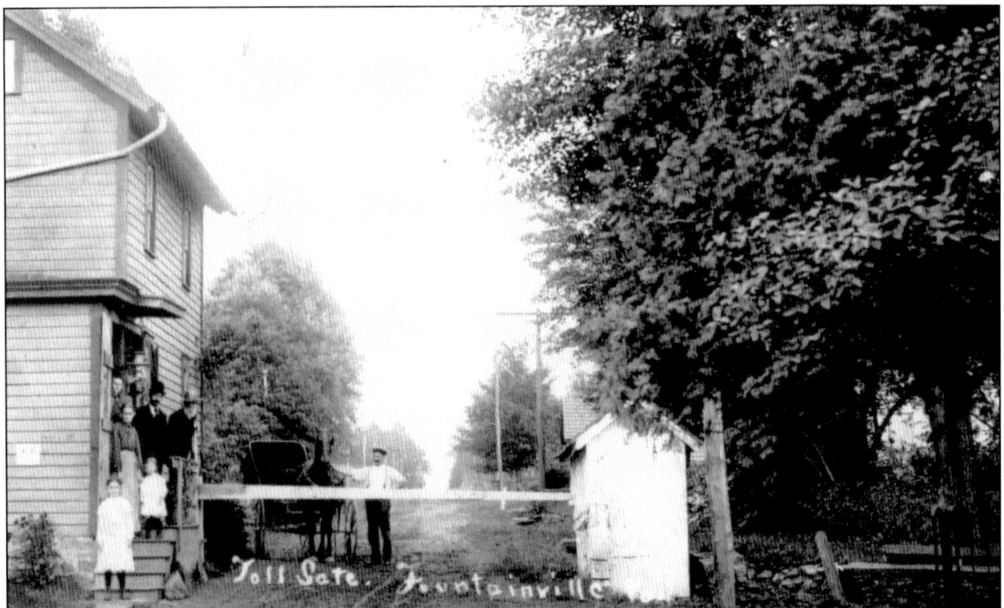

The Tollhouse and Gate at Fountainville, c. 1890. The tollhouse at Fountainville was one of several that served the turnpike roads established in the mid-19th century. This building stood on Swamp Road, just south of Ferry Road.

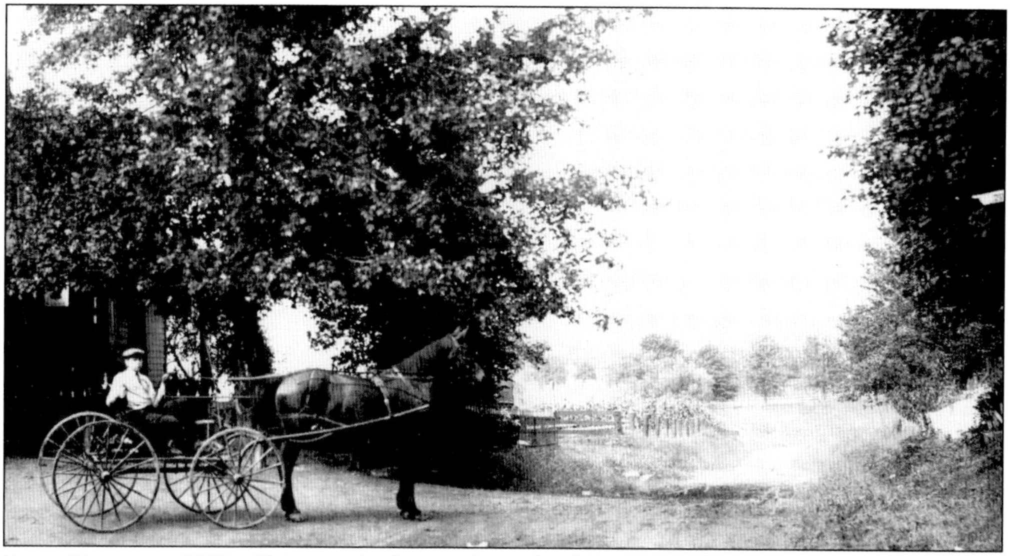

FERRY ROAD, C. 1900. This view looks east from the Gross store along Ferry Road.

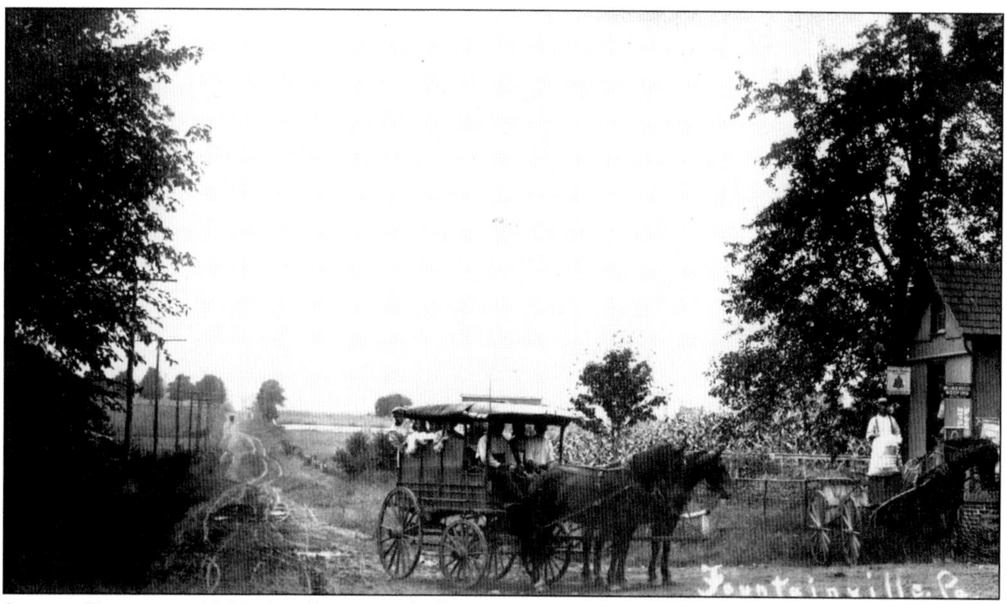

SWAMP ROAD, C. 1900. Looking north from Ferry Road, this view shows Swamp Road, also known as Route 313.

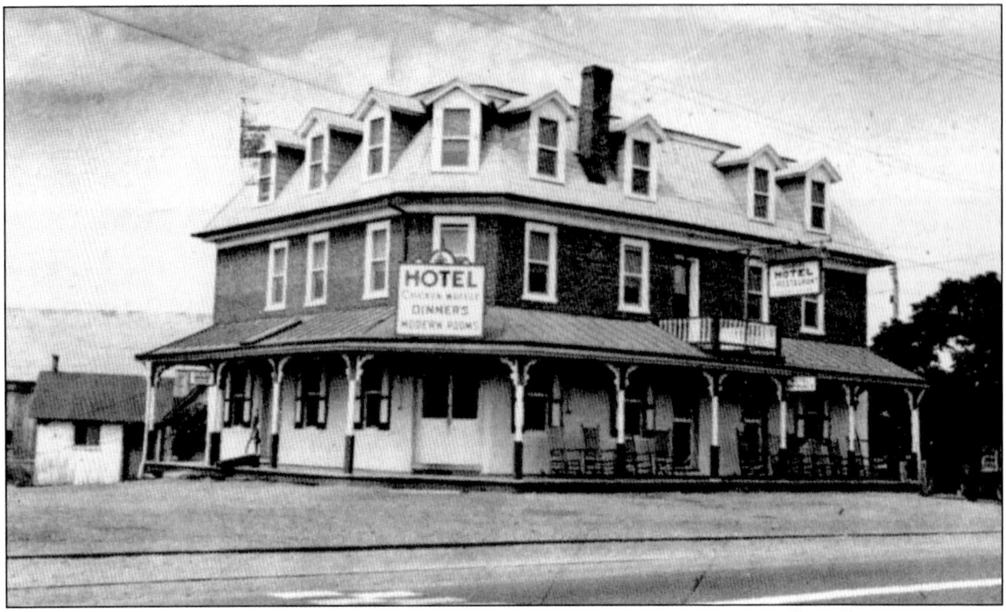

The Danboro Hotel, c. 1910. Records indicate that a tavern was found at the intersection of Easton and Ferry Roads as early as 1810. According to tavern license records, by the 1830s the establishment was known as the Golden Lamb and was operated by Daniel Moore. A fire destroyed the old tavern around 1900, and the present building was constructed soon thereafter.

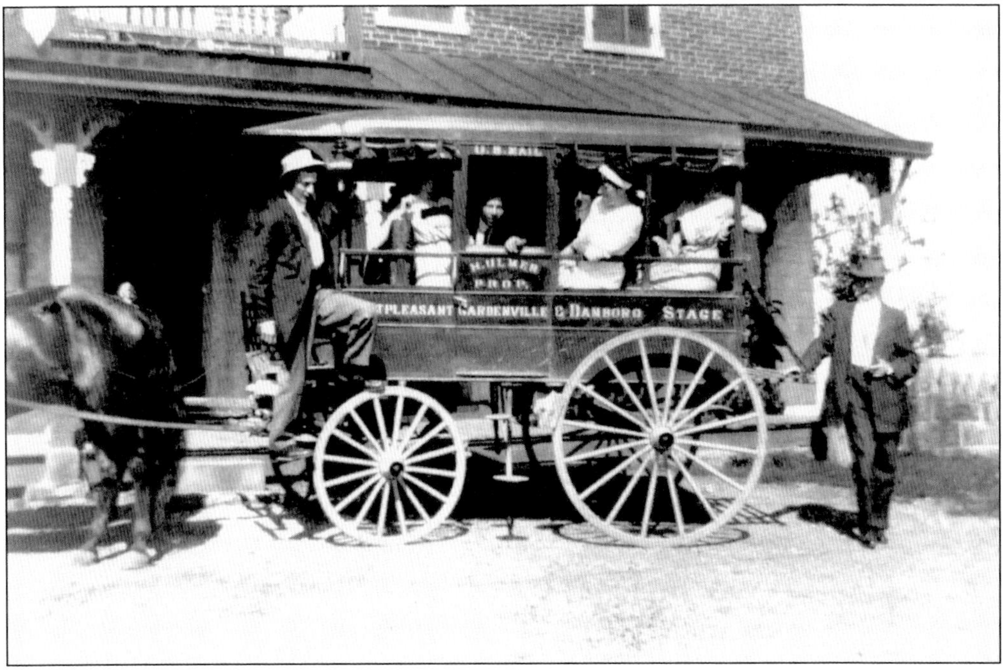

A Stagecoach Stop, c. 1910. The stagecoach was an important means of transportation for township residents, and stagecoach lines ran along the major north–south and east–west routes. Danboro's location at an important crossroads made it a logical stop on the Philadelphia line. The stagecoach pictured here was a local line that ran from the hotel to Point Pleasant by way of Gardenville.

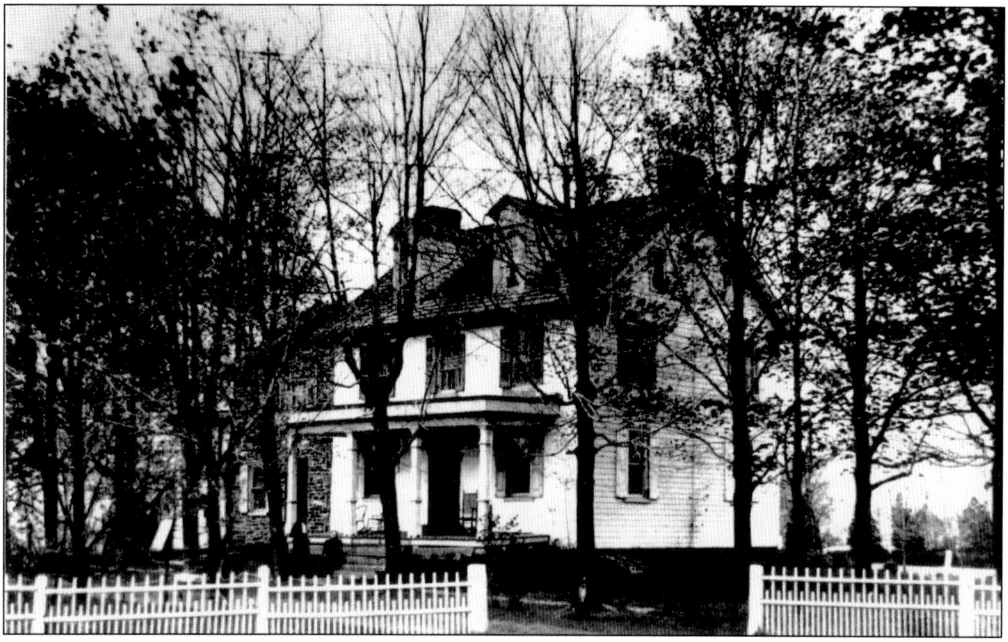

MAPLE KNOLL, C. 1900. Maple Knoll was a summer resort owned and operated by Miss Kate Kratz. Its location on the Philadelphia stagecoach line made it a convenient place for city dwellers and travelers to stop. Deed records indicate that the Kratz family purchased this property in 1858. The house appears to have been constructed prior to the Kratz ownership, most likely by Daniel Moore, for whom the village of Danboro is named. (Collection of the Spruance Library of the Bucks County Historical Society.)

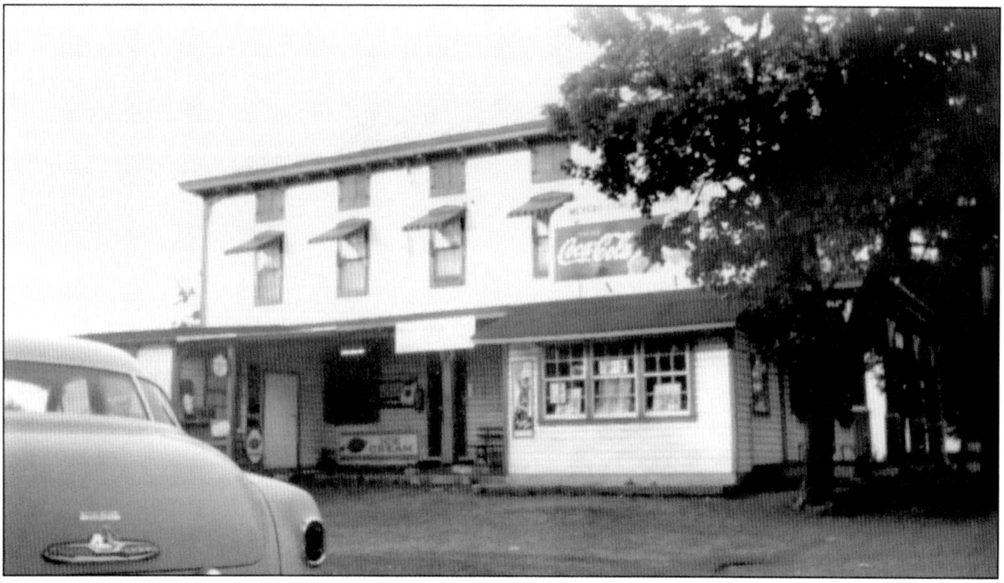

THE MYERS GROCERY STORE, C. 1940. This building was constructed in the mid-19th century as the store and post office. Old advertisements indicate that it was known as Wolf's store as early as 1856. By the 1870s, it was called Keller's store and was operated by Samuel Keller. In the mid-1800s, Danboro was described in reports as containing more than a dozen homes, a school, and several businesses, including a seed store and a carriage and wagon factory.

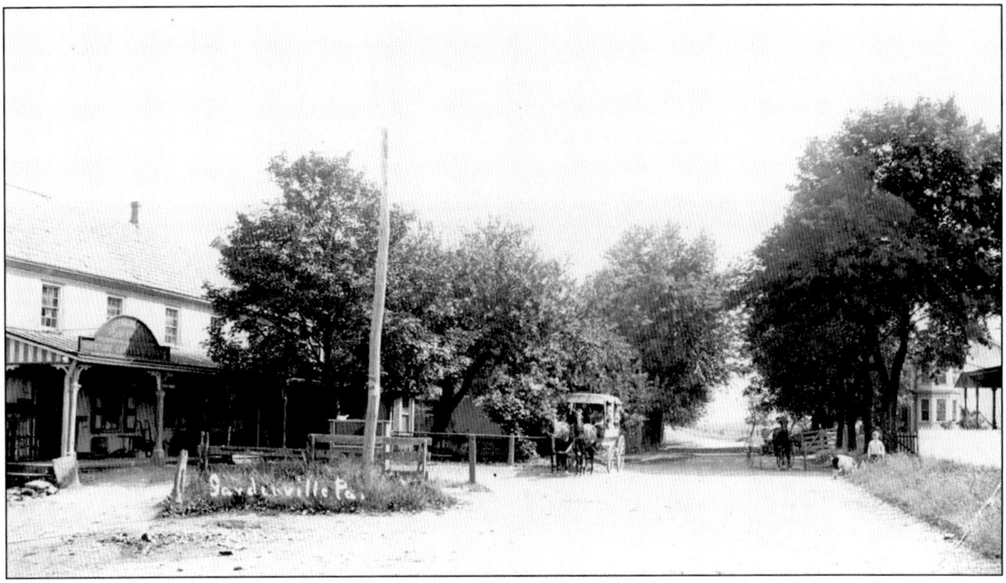

GOTWALS STORE, c. 1900. This store at Gardenville was built *c.* 1845 at the northeast corner of Ferry and Durham Roads. Like most village stores, it was the center of activity for the surrounding farm community. Local historian Edward Matthews described the village at the turn of the 20th century as "a store, hotel, chapel, and creamery, the usual assortment of mechanic shops and ten or eleven dwellings."

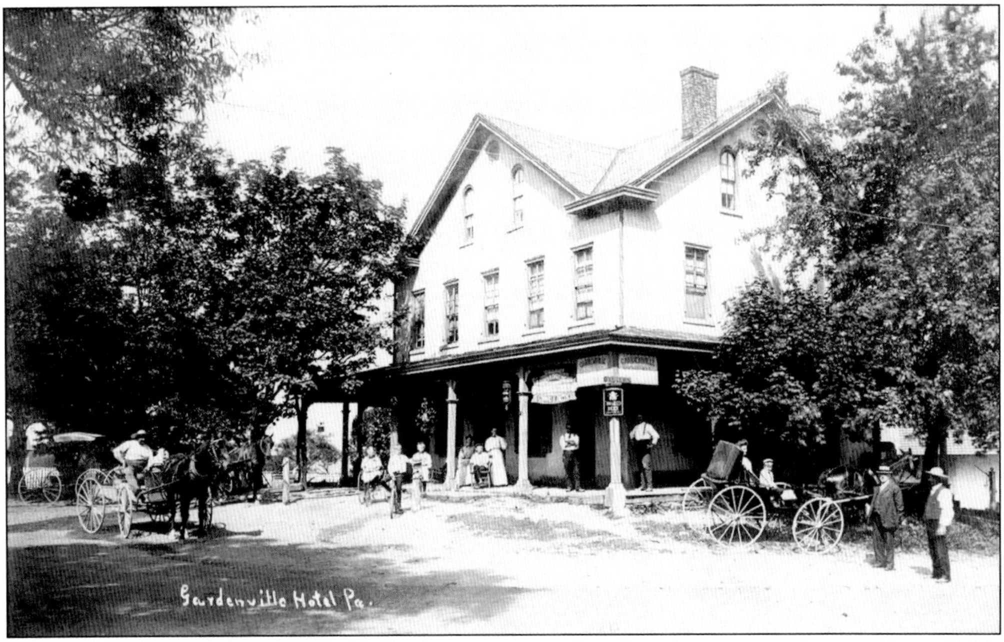

THE GARDENVILLE TAVERN, c. 1906. A tavern was found at the crossroads as early as 1741. The original inn, known as the Sign of the Plough, was destroyed by fire in 1871 and later replaced by this structure. A second tavern was constructed across the road by the mid-1700s and served as a forage station during the Revolutionary War. An 1866 advertisement claimed that "the Gardenville tavern is the site of township elections, and nearly all the township business is done here."

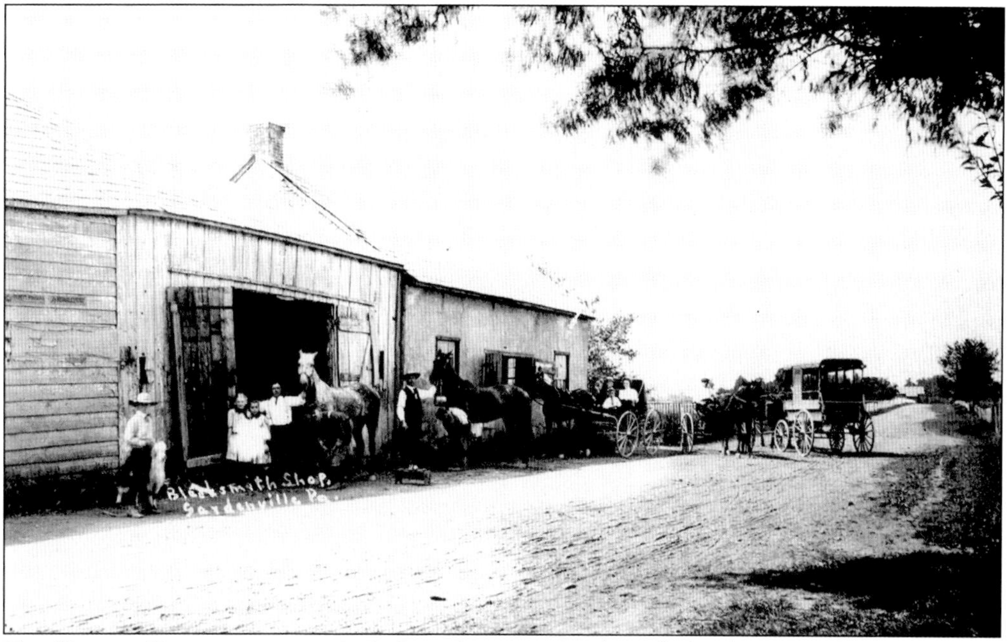

THE VILLAGE BLACKSMITH, C. 1915. Over the years, Gardenville has had several name changes. It was called the Sign of the Plough for the old tavern, Brownsville for the Brown family that held large tracts of land, and by 1857, Gardenville, for its outstanding flower and vegetable gardens. Among the early buildings still standing is the old blacksmith shop pictured here. It is found just west of the Lear garden on Ferry Road.

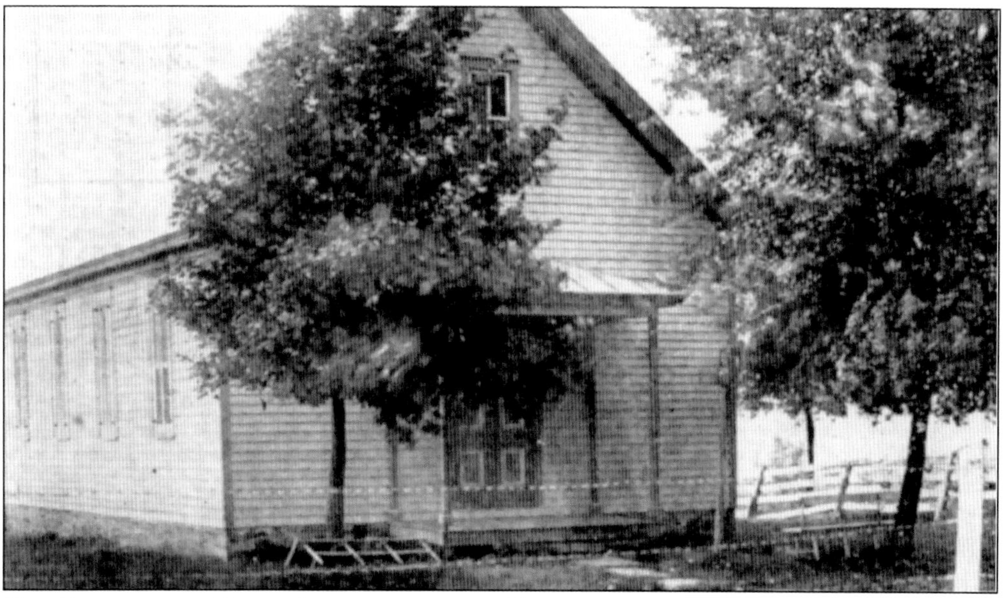

THE GARDENVILLE UNION CHAPEL, C. 1890. The union chapel was constructed in the late 19th century as a nondenominational house of worship. Sunday school and ceremonies, such as eighth-grade graduation, were held here. It is found on the Pike, just west of the crossroads. The Gardenville chapel was one of two union chapels in the township; the other was the community hall in Danboro.

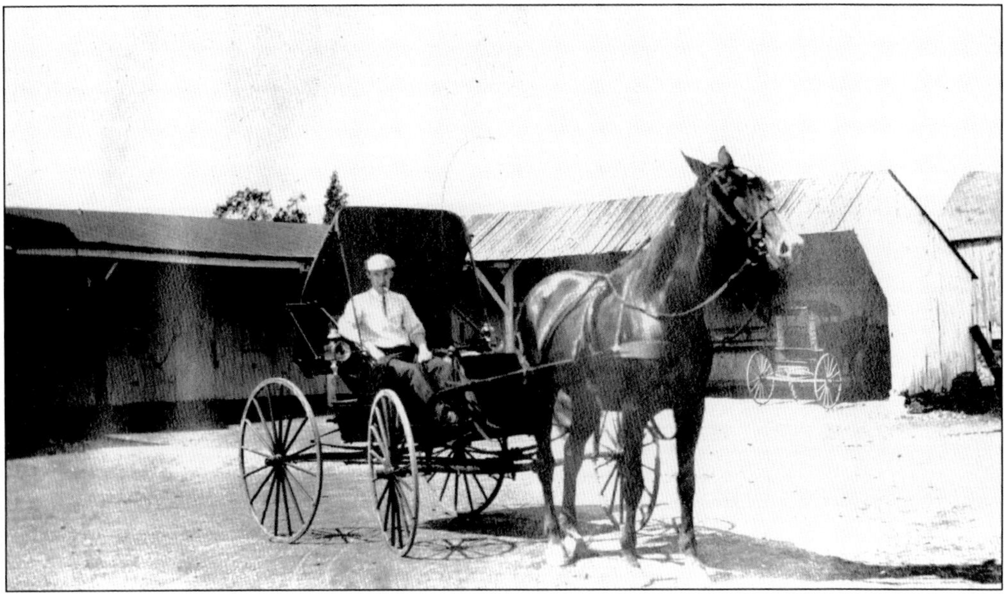

Carriage Sheds, c. 1890. Carriage sheds like those pictured here at the meetinghouse near Gardenville were found in villages and at community meeting places throughout the township.

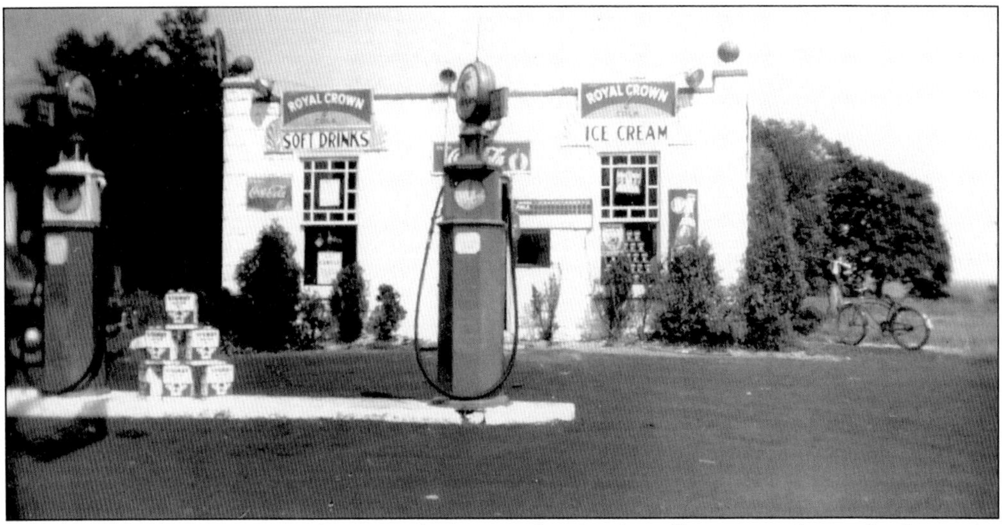

The Old Dairy, c. 1915. The second store at the Gardenville crossroads was built on the southeast corner. This *c.* 1900 building was replaced by the present store around 1950.

MELCHER'S CORNER, THE WISMER POST OFFICE, C. 1953. The Wismer post office began in the village of Wismer, located at the crossroads of Stump and Wismer-Carversville Roads. The post office was moved to Smith's Corner when the Wismer store closed, and in 1938 was relocated to Melcher's Corner, pictured here. This structure still stands at the corner of Groveland and Wismer Roads.

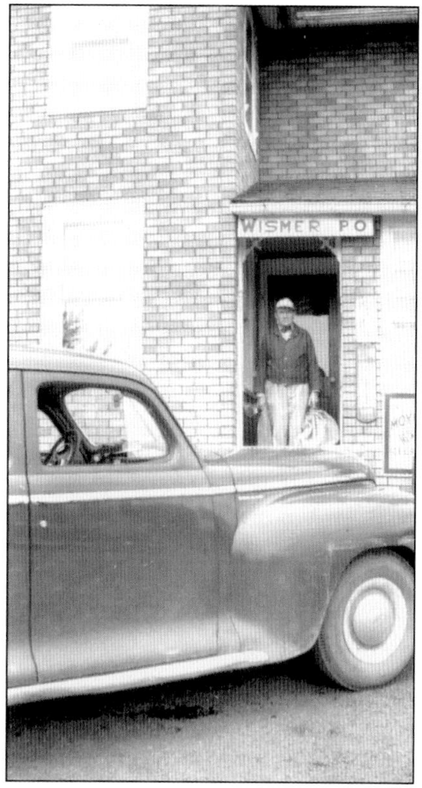

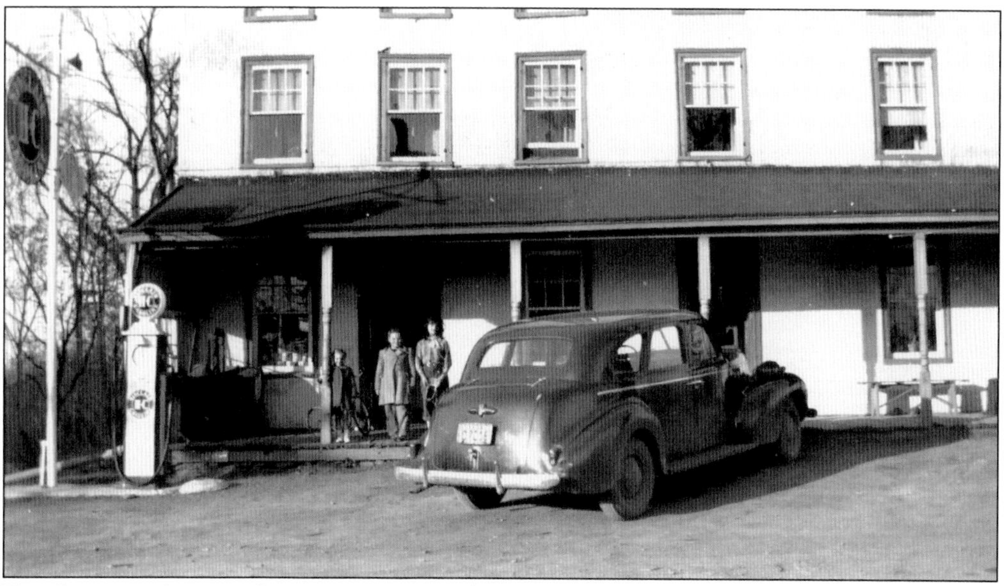

THE STORE AT SMITH'S CORNER, C. 1940. The store at the corner of Stump and Tohickon Hill Roads was established prior to 1867 by Benjamin Hall of Danboro. Local histories indicate that Hall was among the first to ship milk to Philadelphia, and he operated several stores throughout the area. In the 1930s, the Wismer post office was moved here and operated by Arthur Morris. John and Helen Holms operated the store without the post office in the 1940s. David and Jane Burd were the last proprietors of the store when it closed in 1968.

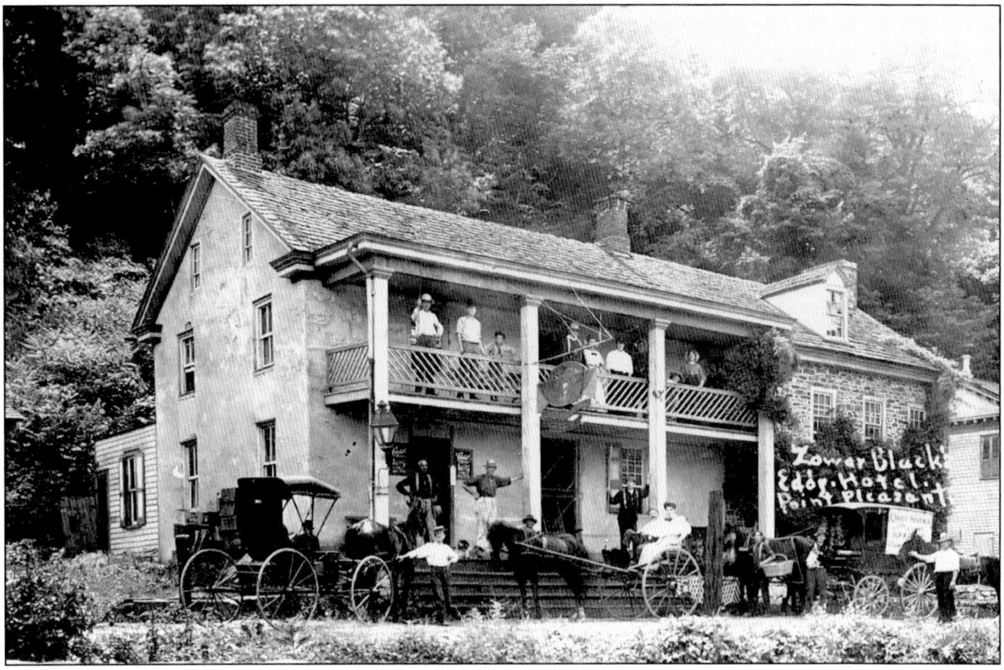

LOWER BLACK'S EDDY HOTEL, C. 1890. Settlement along the Delaware River developed in the early 18th century due to the establishment of a ferry landing. This building was constructed c. 1770, when records show that Jane Hart built a house here and petitioned the court for a tavern license. Michael Black operated the tavern from the 1780s until 1808. By 1848, George Closson owned the inn and held it for the next 48 years. A large portion of the structure appears to date to the Closson ownership. In the 20th century, the building was operated as the Mountainside Inn.

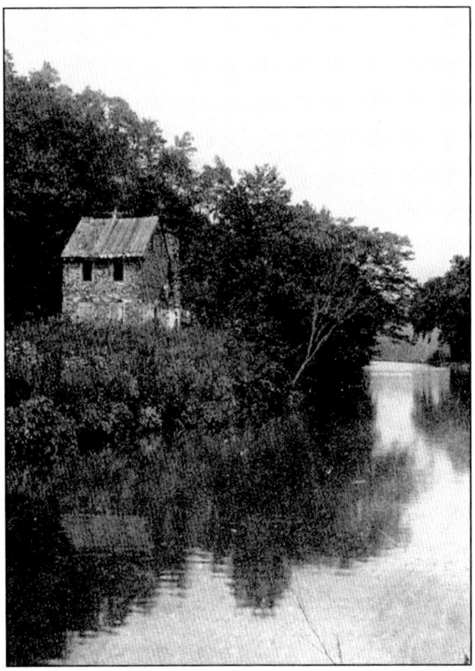

DEVIL'S HALF ACRE, C. 1900. The narrow piece of land along River Road just south of the Mountainside has been known as Devil's Half Acre since the early 19th century. Early records show that the site held a stone house and blacksmith shop by the 1790s. Local tradition suggests the site got its name in the 1830s when it was reportedly a place where boatmen could buy whiskey and drunken revelry prevailed.

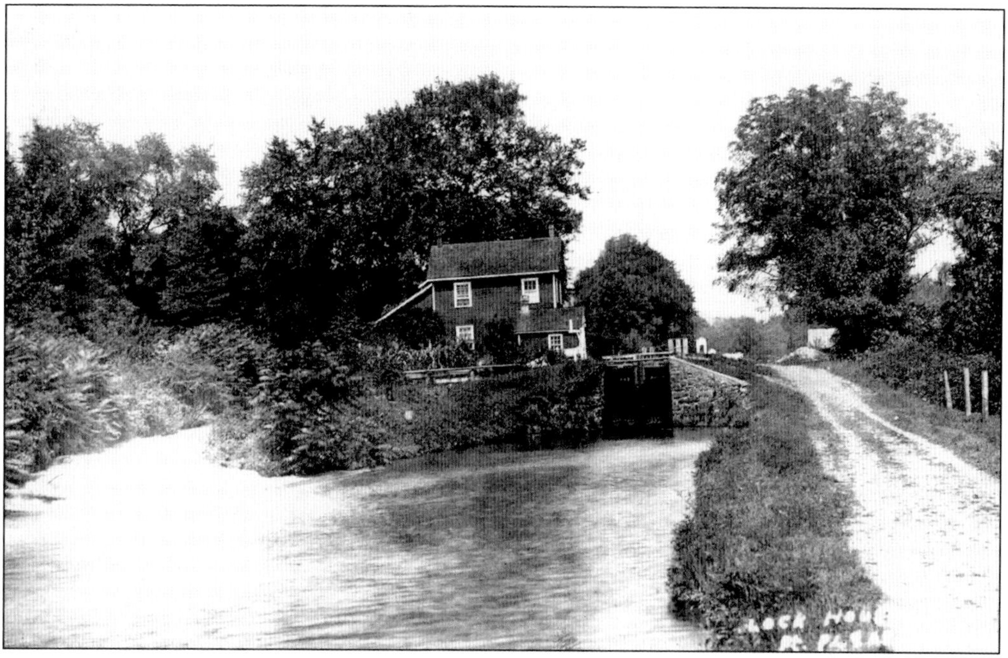

The Canal Locks, Point Pleasant, c. 1900. With the construction of the Delaware division of the Pennsylvania Canal in 1831, the area now known as Point Pleasant grew into a prosperous village. Coal mined in northeast Pennsylvania was the main commodity transported by barge and mule along the canal. The locks, a canal basin, and an aqueduct forced canal traffic to slow and stop here, fueling the village's role as a service area.

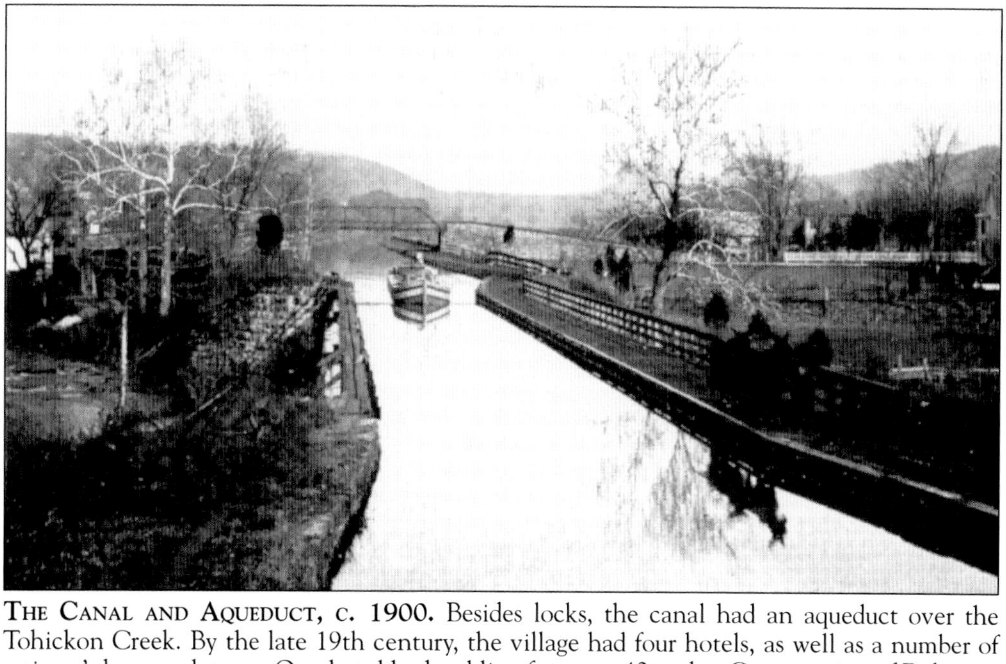

The Canal and Aqueduct, c. 1900. Besides locks, the canal had an aqueduct over the Tohickon Creek. By the late 19th century, the village had four hotels, as well as a number of artisans' shops and stores. One hotel had stabling for up to 40 mules. Construction of Delaware River bridges, improved highways, and the increased use of rail lines caused canal traffic to diminish. The last barge made its way down the canal in 1931.

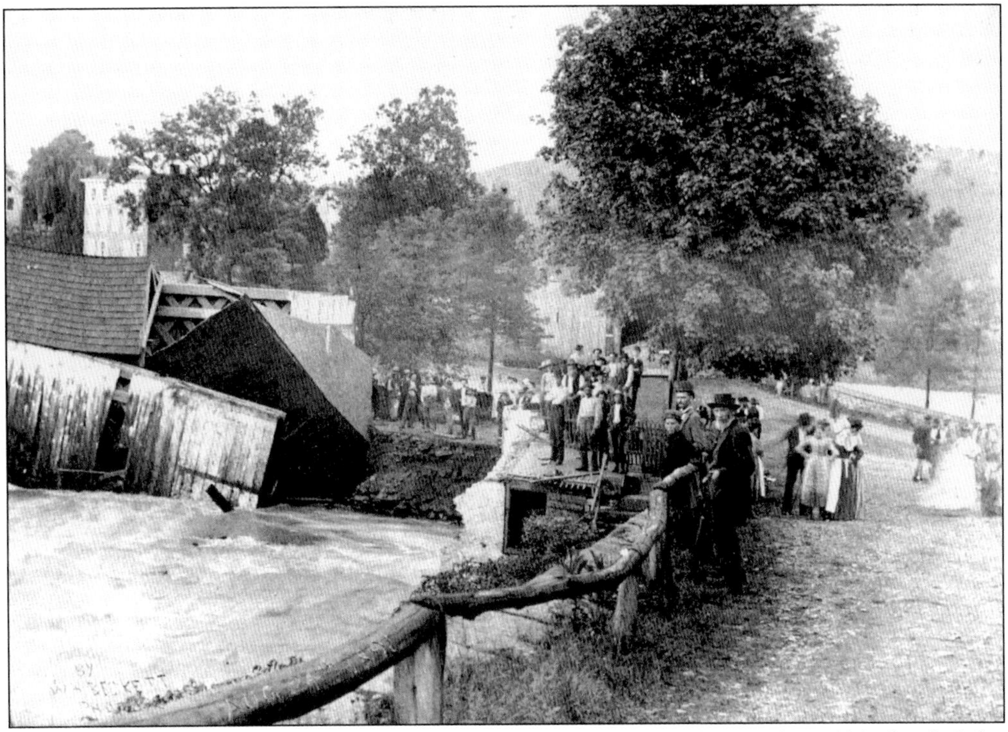

A Freshet at Point Pleasant, c. 1891. A summer storm on August 24, 1891, flooded the Geddes Run and destroyed the Solomon Fulmer general store and the adjacent covered bridge. The location of the village along the river and adjoining hillside has made flooding a danger over the years.

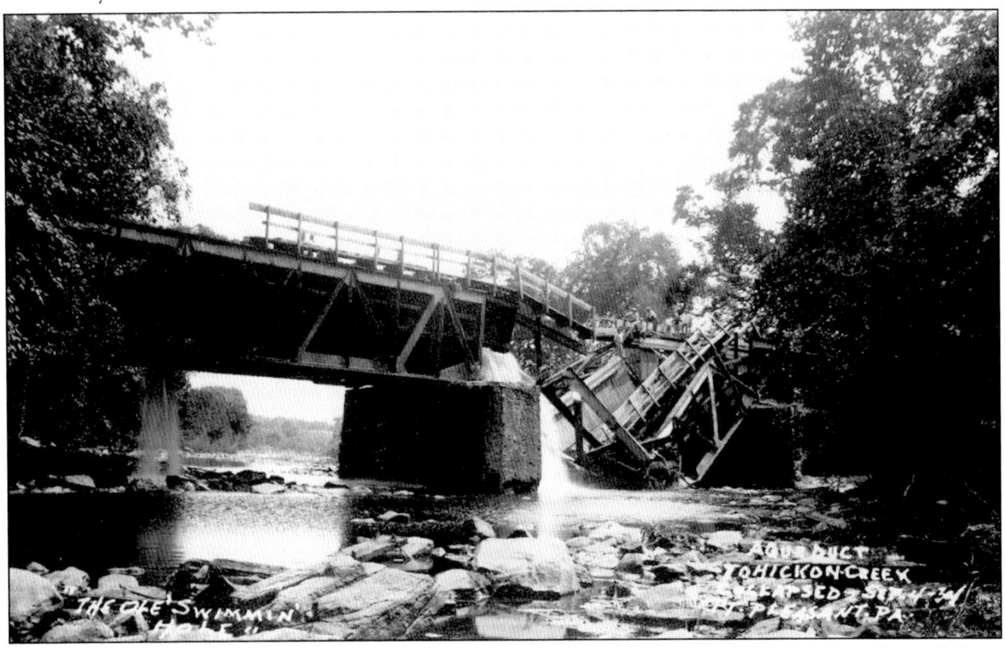

Destruction of the Aqueduct, c. 1920. The aqueduct over Tohickon Creek collapsed from old age. Recently, a new aqueduct was erected of timber-frame construction.

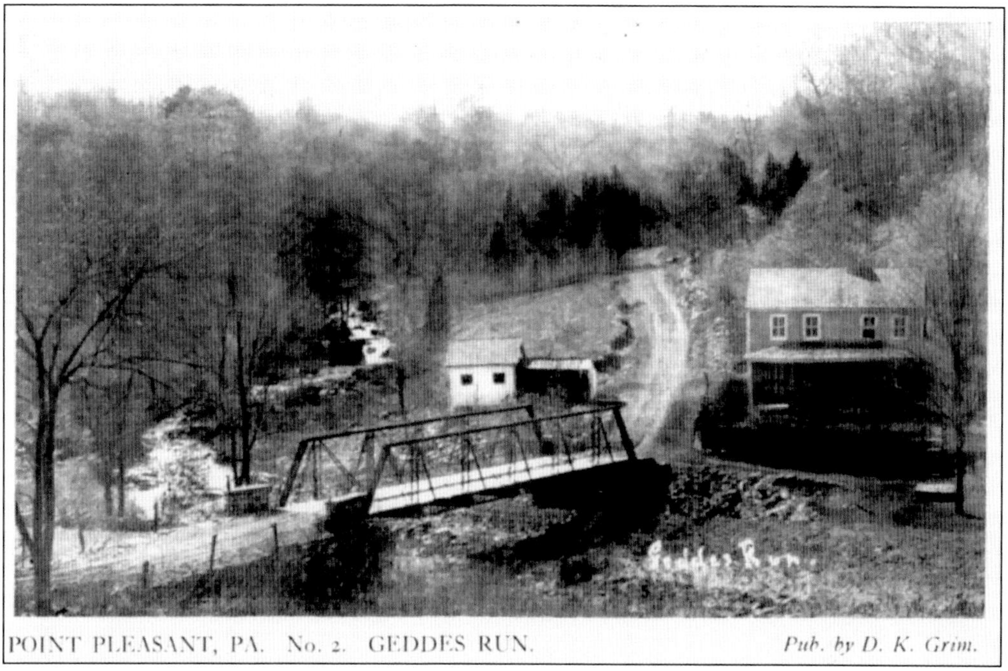

THE GEDDES BRIDGE, C. 1900. Outside Point Pleasant, a new iron bridge was constructed at Tollgate Road. This bridge still stands but no longer is used for vehicular traffic.

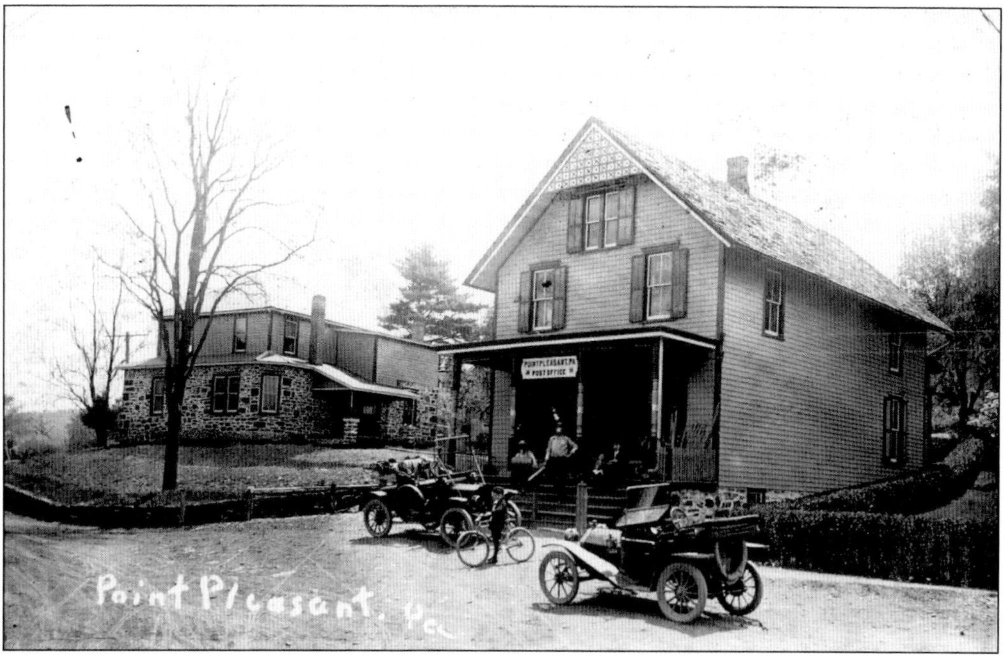

THE GENERAL STORE, C. 1915. The new Solomon Fulmer store and home at left were constructed after the 1891 Geddes Run flood. The new buildings were sited across the road from the original structure. After Fulmer's tenure, the store was operated for many years by Frank P. Kolbe. It later became M. Dobron and Sons, manufacturers of floral supplies.

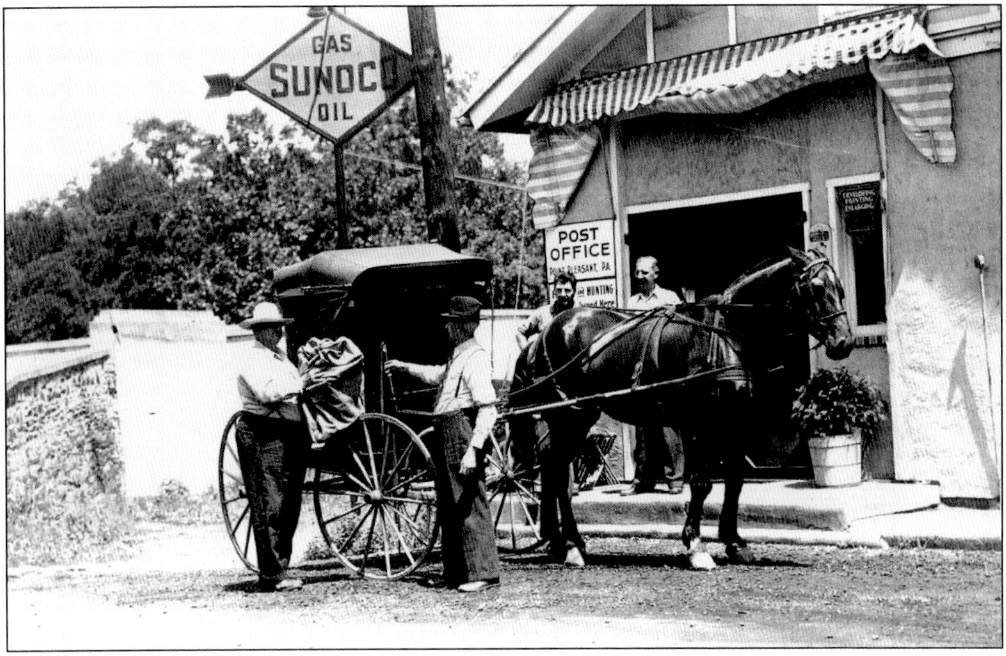

The Point Pleasant Post Office, c. 1930. The post office was located on the site of the old general store. This photograph shows Howard Geddes, postman (on left), delivering the mail to Oliver Yost, postmaster. (The men in the background are unidentified.)

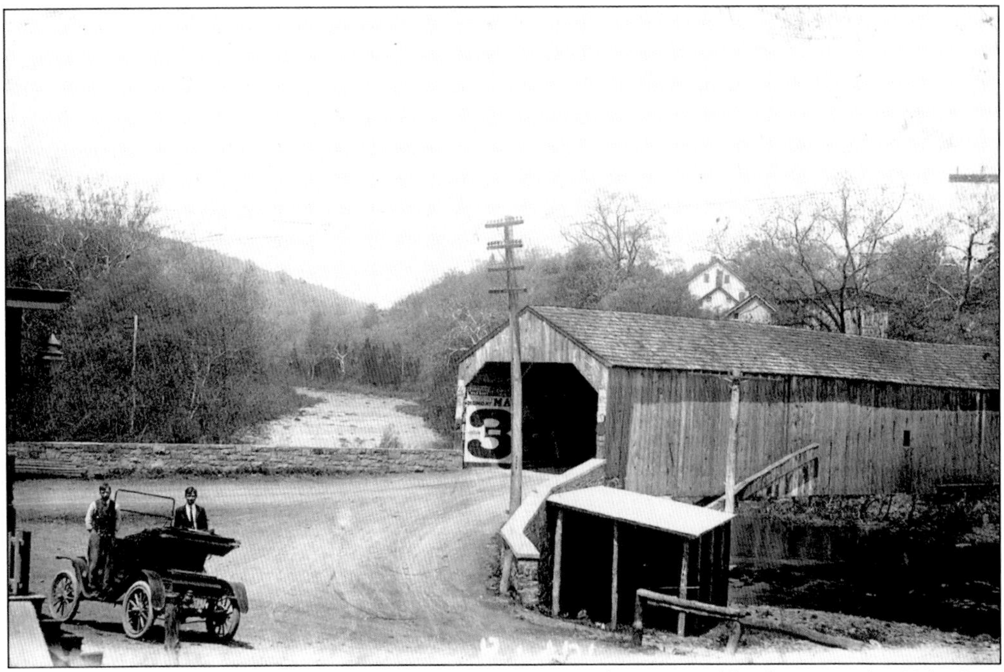

The Covered Bridge over the Tohickon, c. 1920. The covered bridge over the Tohickon Creek in Point Pleasant was torn down in 1922, when the county decreed it unsafe. A new state-of-the-art concrete bridge was completed in 1928.

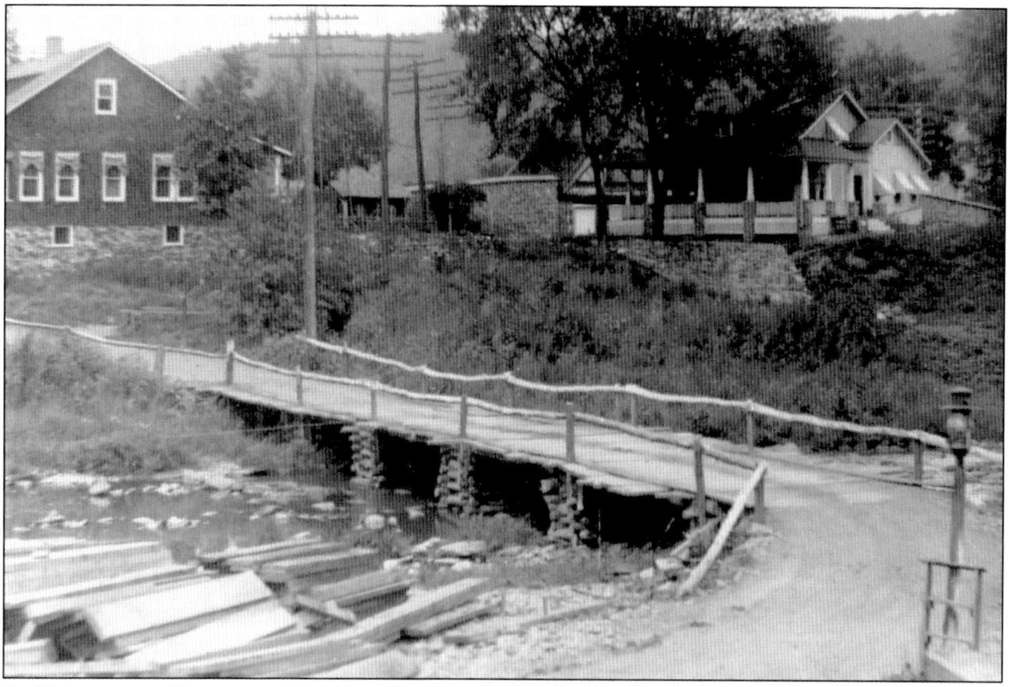

A Temporary Bridge, c. 1922. This temporary bridge was constructed over the creek to connect the two sections of the village prior to the completion of the concrete bridge in 1928.

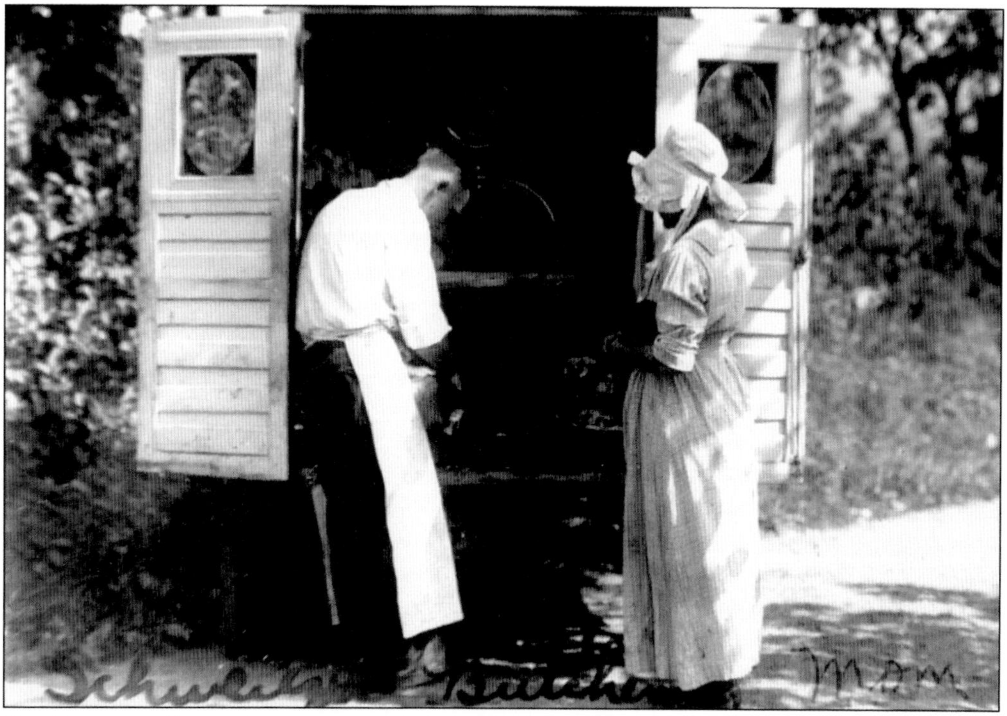

The Butcher, Point Pleasant, c. 1922. In the first half of the 20th century, before there were supermarkets and before most women drove cars, food products were delivered to the home. Here, Marie Stahnten of Point Pleasant makes a purchase from Charles Schweitzer Sr., the local butcher.

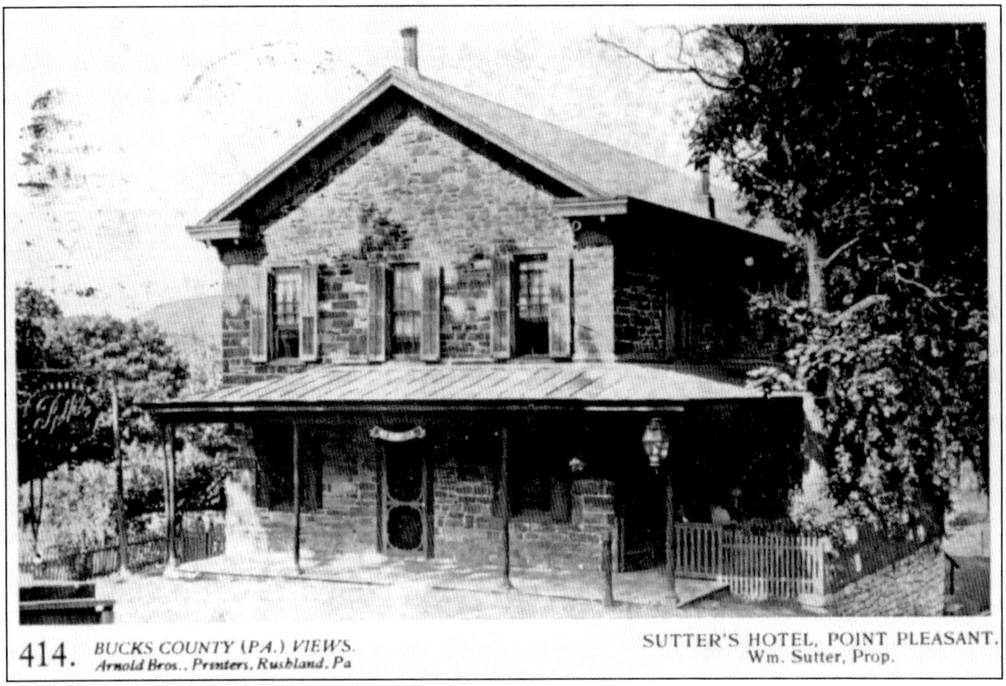

THE SUTTER'S HOTEL, C. 1900. Sutter's was the fourth tavern in the village licensed in 1867. The hotel first catered to the canal traffic but later was a part of a summer resort industry. One of the most popular times to visit Point Pleasant was during shad season, from May to mid-June. Visitors who came to Point Pleasant wishing to fish or dine on a fine shad dinner included Pres. Grover Cleveland.

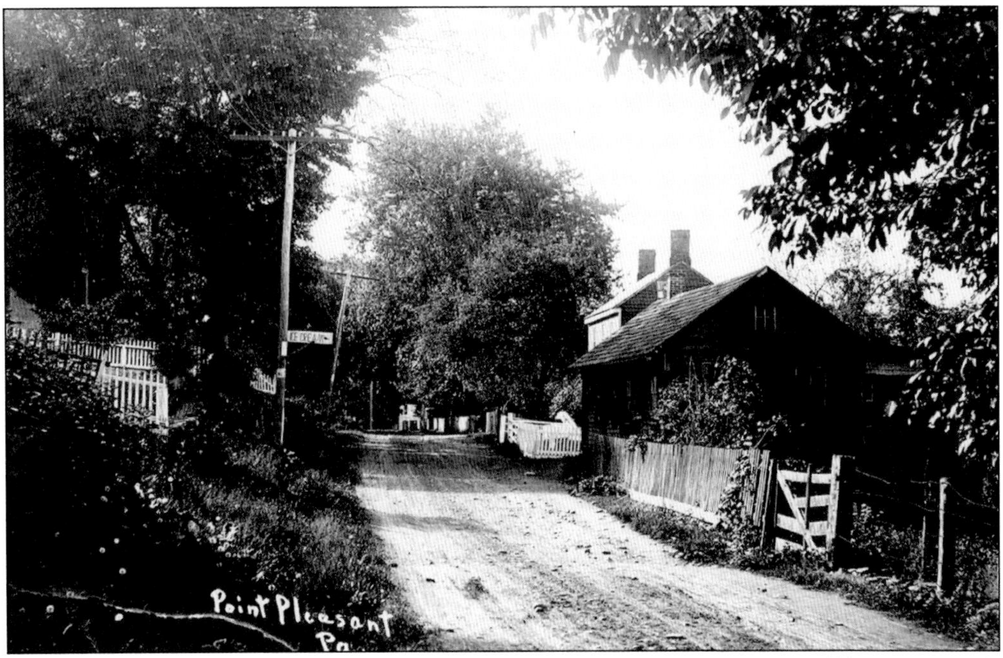

A VIEW OF RIVER ROAD AT POINT PLEASANT WITH PICKET FENCE, C. 1900. Small businesses such as the ice-cream shop and tearoom catered to both residents and travelers along River Road.

Four

SCHOOLS

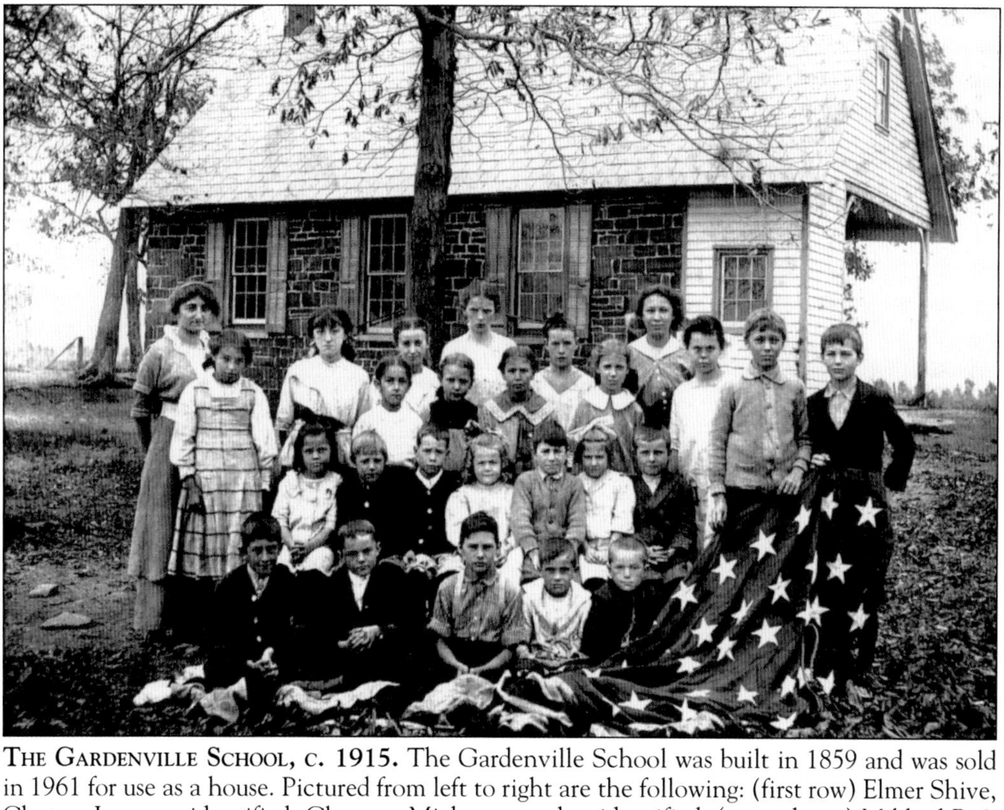

THE GARDENVILLE SCHOOL, C. 1915. The Gardenville School was built in 1859 and was sold in 1961 for use as a house. Pictured from left to right are the following: (first row) Elmer Shive, Clayton Long, unidentified, Clarence Michener, and unidentified; (second row) Mildred B. ?, two unidentified students, Dorothy Walach, unidentified, Ruth Moyer, and Martha Shive; (third row) Helen Lear, unidentified, Dorothy Long, unidentified, Mildred Moyer, Paul Michener, and Lester Michener; (fourth row) teacher Myrtle Archer, Gussie Glantz, Mabel Michener, Edith Long, Helen Michener, Gladys B. ?, and Bertha Long.

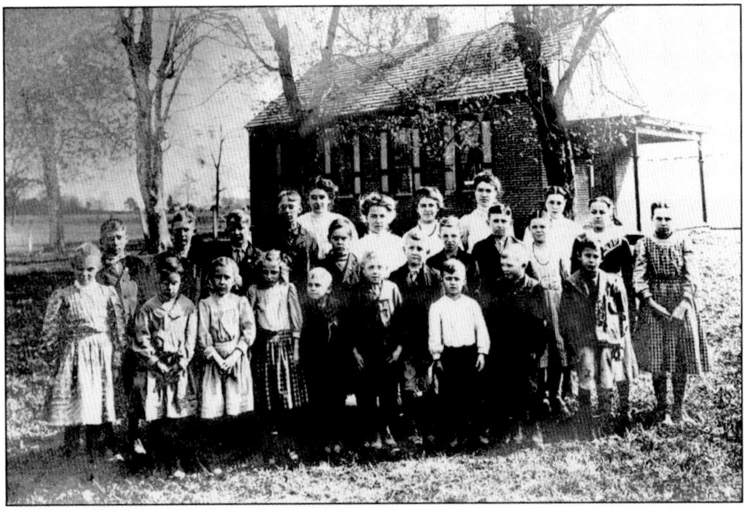

THE WESTERN BRICK SCHOOL, C. 1906. Western Brick, located on Stump Road, was built in 1856 and closed in 1947. Pictured here are unidentified students and their teacher. The building is now faced in stucco and has been converted into a home.

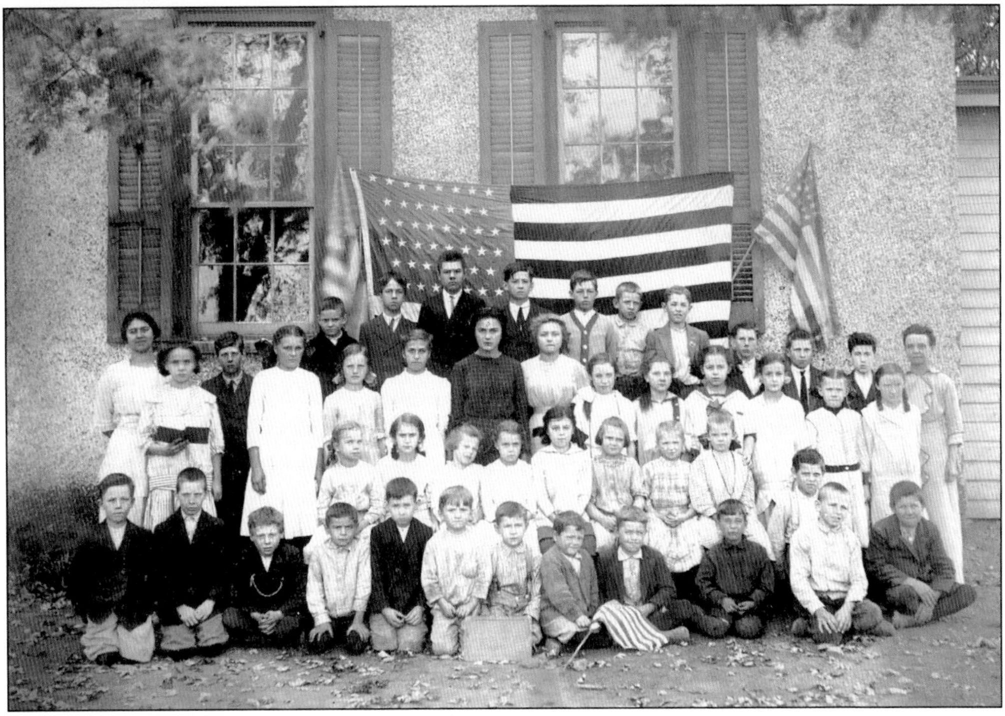

THE PLUMSTEADVILLE SCHOOL, C. 1914. This photograph was taken along the Stump Road side of the 1858 schoolhouse. The Plumsteadville School was one of the largest, containing two classrooms. Shown in this image are, from left to right, the following: (first row) Paul Thomas, Willie Trauger, Marvin Wismer, Willie Gahman, Reuben Keller, Alton Wismer, Williard Hinkle, Reuben Hinkle, unidentified, Joe Smith, Pete Smith, and Alvin Esser; (second row) Adeline Wismer, Anna Fields, Mildred Charles, Katherine Rush, Catherine Kramer, Clara Rush, unidentified, and Rachel Sames; (third row) teacher Mary Buehrle, Margaret Myers, Earl Trauger, Ruth Myers, Ida Labs, Elsie Myers, Ruth Wismer, Viola Myers, Harriet Thomas, Florence Schleicher, Grace Hinkle, Sidney Myers, Florence Sames, and Grace Campbell; (fourth row) Joe Myers, Isaac Rush, Harry Hockman, Irvin Keller, E. Howard Hinkle, Earl Wismer, Orville Frankenfield, Roland Kramer, Ralph Kramer, and an unidentified teacher.

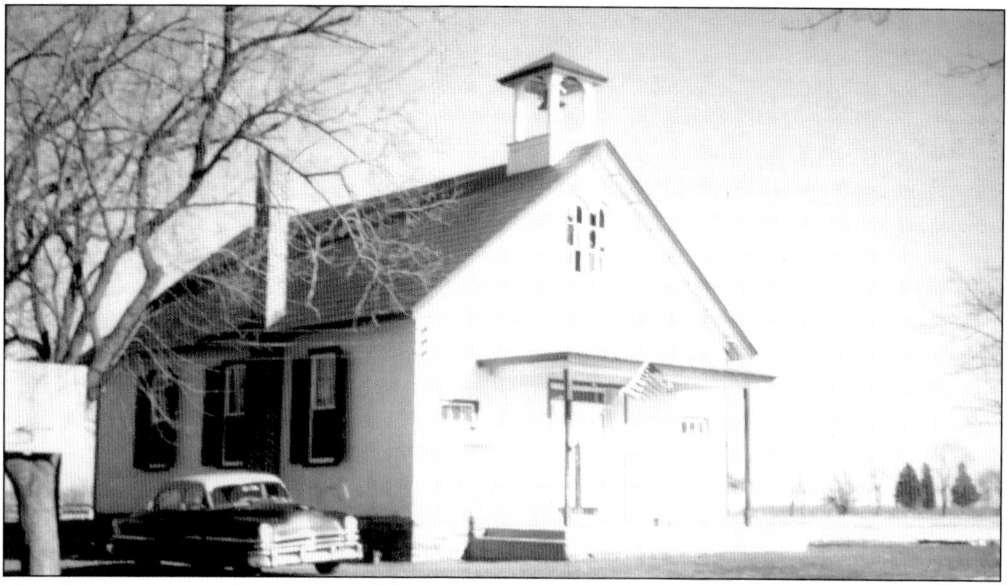

The Southwestern School, c. 1960. The Southwestern School, located on Gayman Road, was built in 1869. It was one of eight schools to be sold at public auction in 1961 upon the completion of the new Gayman Elementary School.

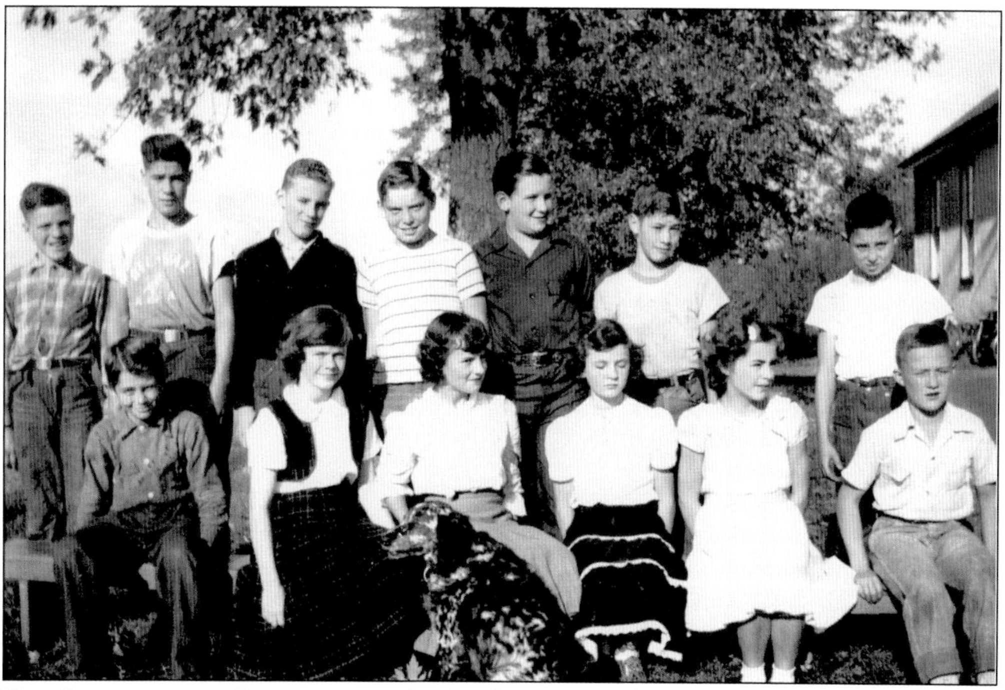

The Southwestern School, c. 1951. Students at Southwestern pose for a class picture. From left to right are the following: (first row) Clarke Hendricks, Joan Hoxworth, Shirley Ament, Margaret Worthington, Margaret Bishop, and Keith Shelly; (second row) Charles Henry, Bill White, Horace Drake, Ronald Sabath, Frank Schwartz, Dale Wolfinger, and Anthony Siron.

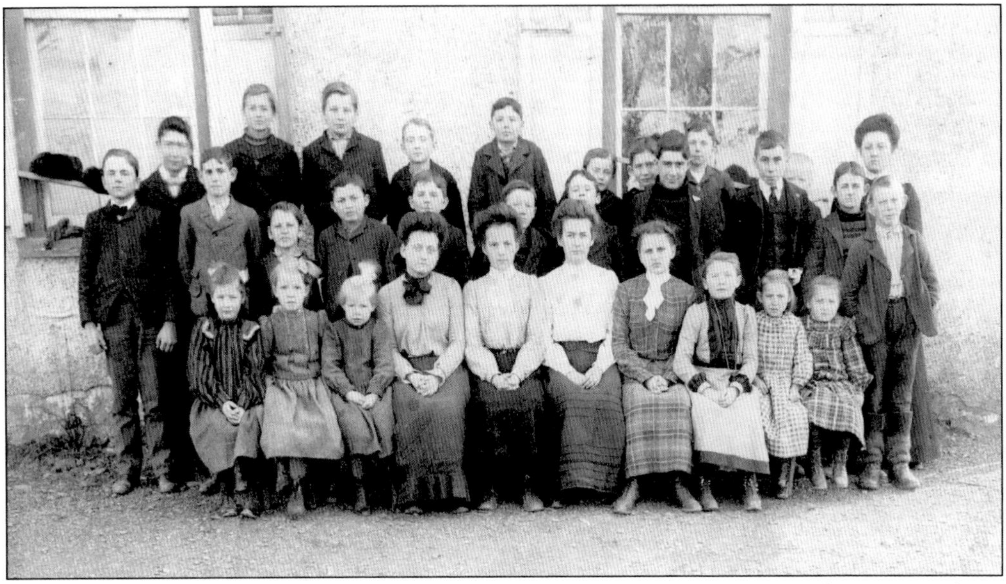

The Smith Corner School, c. 1890. Unidentified students and their teacher pose in front of the school on Stump Road. The Smith Corner School was built in 1863 to replace the old building that was constructed in 1836, found further east on Stump Road. The building was also used as the local Sunday school, which was organized in 1840 by Jonas Bissey and later led to the formation of the Point Pleasant Baptist Church.

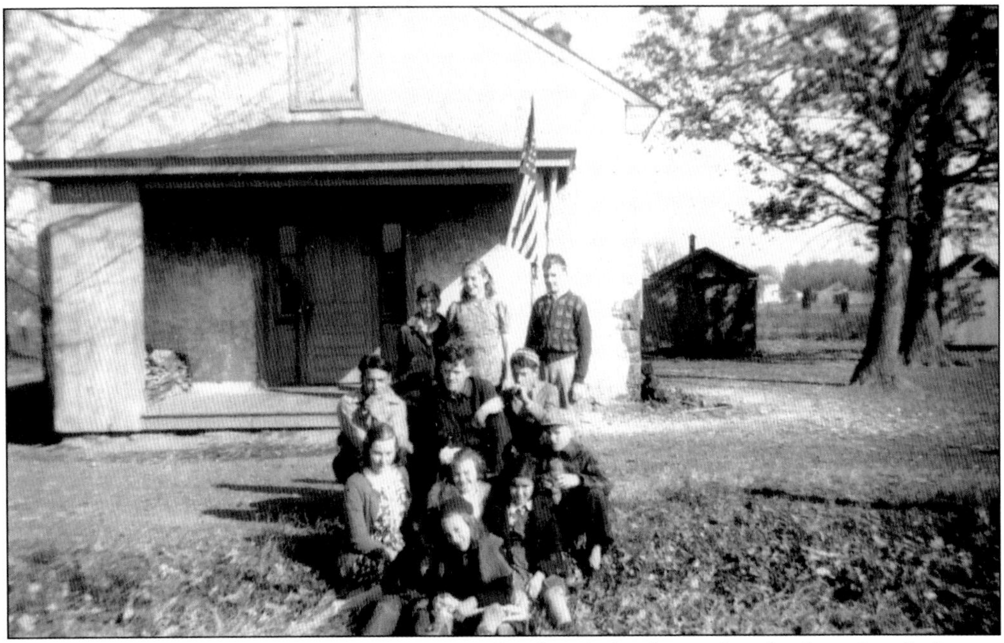

The Smith Corner School, Class of 1940. By the 1940s, the student body at Smith Corner was fairly small. Smith Corner School remained open until 1947 but closed due to dwindling enrollment. The students pictured are, from left to right, as follows: (first row) George Ginn and Doris Kahler; (second row) Esther Mergenthaler, Clare Nash, Dorothy Lear, and John Mergenthaler; (third row) Larry Ginn, Clarence Nash, and William Kahler; (fourth row) James Kahler, Florence Mergenthaler, and Joseph Buehner.

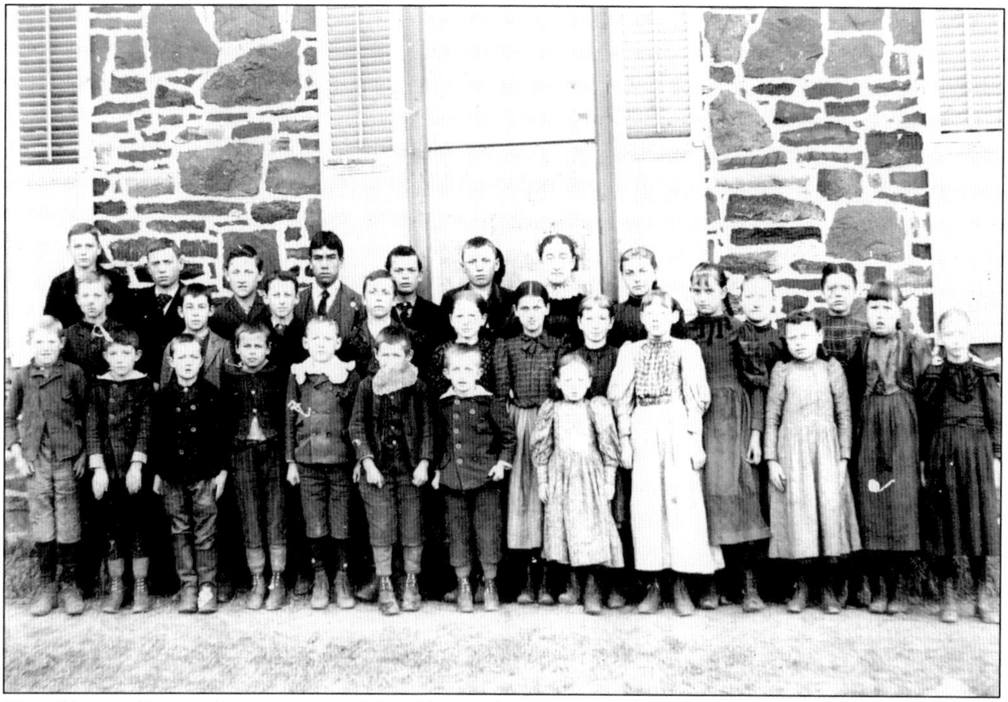

The Rocky Ridge School, c. 1899. Shown here are unidentified students at the old Rocky Ridge School, located on Ferry Road just east of McNeil Road. The structure was built in 1863; however, records indicate the site was used for school purposes as early as 1838. The school's last class was held in 1960.

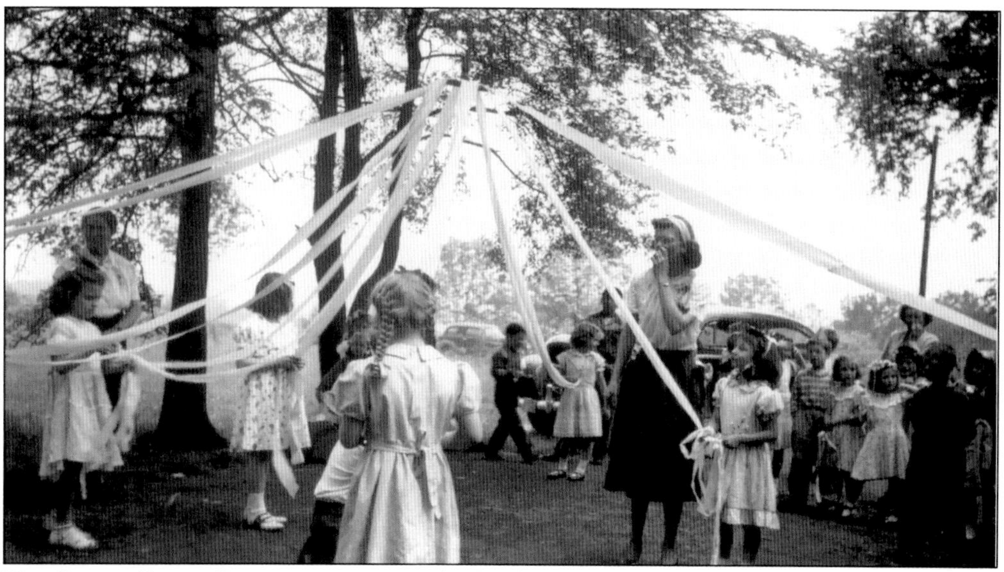

The Rocky Ridge School, c. 1950. The Rocky Ridge School celebrated May Day with a maypole. Participating in this celebration are, from left to right, Janet Free, teacher Agnes Foster, Barbara Althouse, Louise Myers (with her back to the camera), Barbara Beans (holding ribbon in background), an unidentified music teacher, and Carolyn Siron.

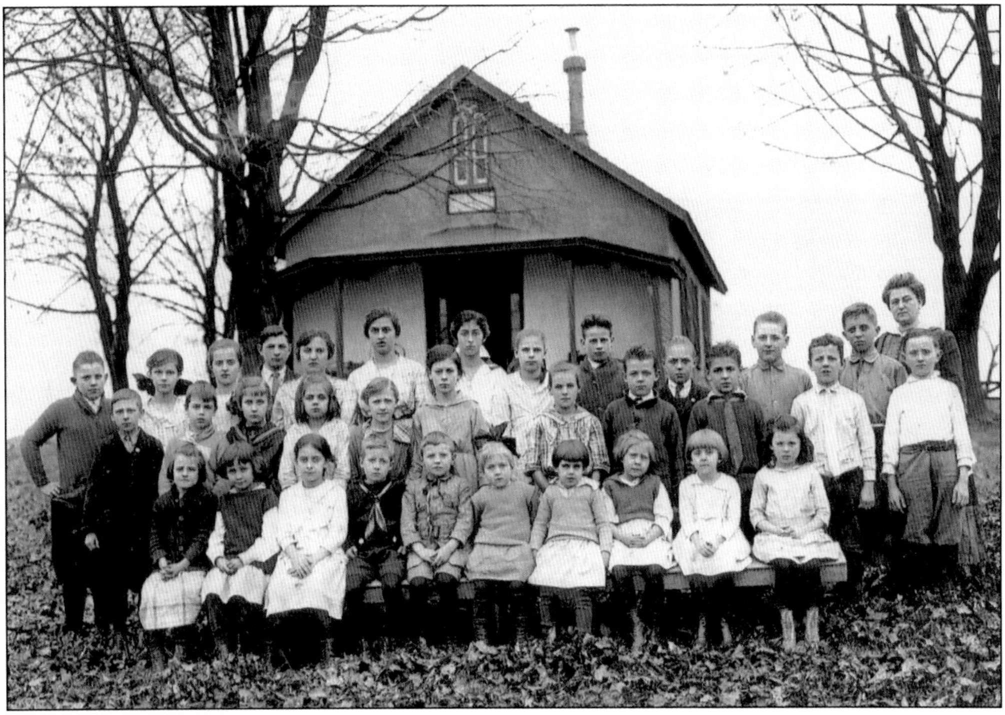

THE DYER'S HILL SCHOOL, C. 1920. Pictured from left to right are the following: (first row) Marion Loux, unidentified, Grace Fluck, Dan Gross, unidentified, Winnie Gross, Martha Wood, Marian Hall, and two unidentified students; (second row) two unidentified students, ? Magee, unidentified, Mert Fellman, unidentified, Grace Loux, and four unidentified students; (third row) Howard Shelly, unidentified, Elma Fluck, unidentified, Margaret Shelly, Clara Wood, six unidentified students, and teacher Amanda Strouse.

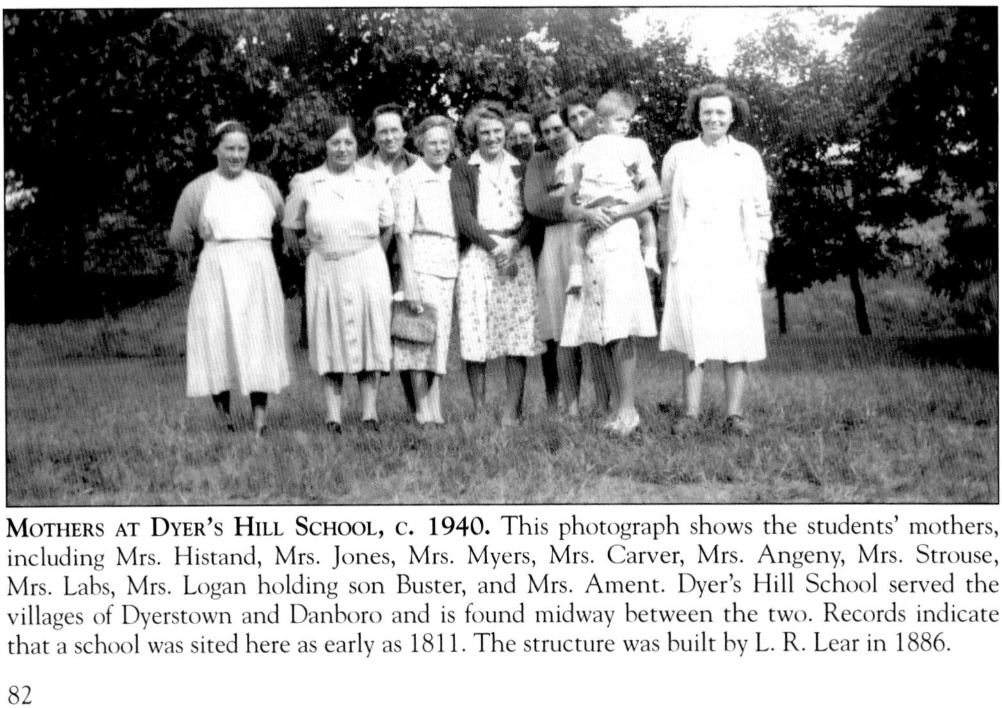

MOTHERS AT DYER'S HILL SCHOOL, C. 1940. This photograph shows the students' mothers, including Mrs. Histand, Mrs. Jones, Mrs. Myers, Mrs. Carver, Mrs. Angeny, Mrs. Strouse, Mrs. Labs, Mrs. Logan holding son Buster, and Mrs. Ament. Dyer's Hill School served the villages of Dyerstown and Danboro and is found midway between the two. Records indicate that a school was sited here as early as 1811. The structure was built by L. R. Lear in 1886.

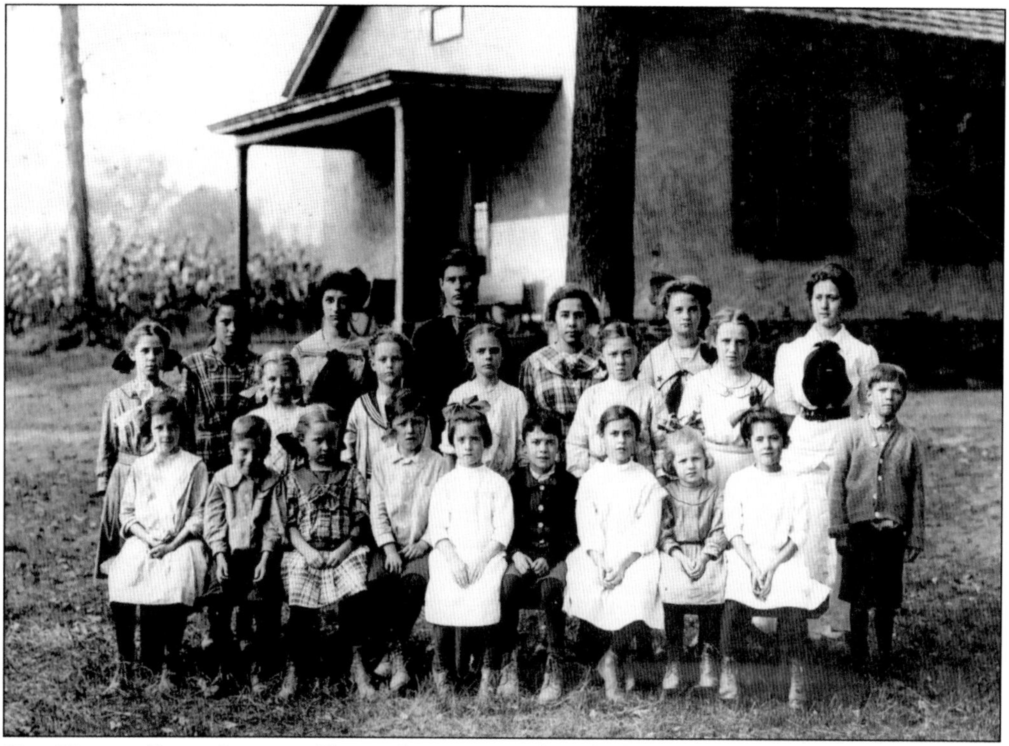

THE VALLEY PARK SCHOOL. Shown here are unidentified students and their teachers at the Valley Park School *c.* 1913 (above) and *c.* 1921 (below). The site, acquired in 1851, appears to have held an earlier building that was replaced by the present structure in 1878. The school was one of eight sold at public auction for residential use in 1961. Today, the old school has been converted into a home and can still be found on Valley Park Road. The bell for the school is now located at Randolph Macon College in Virginia.

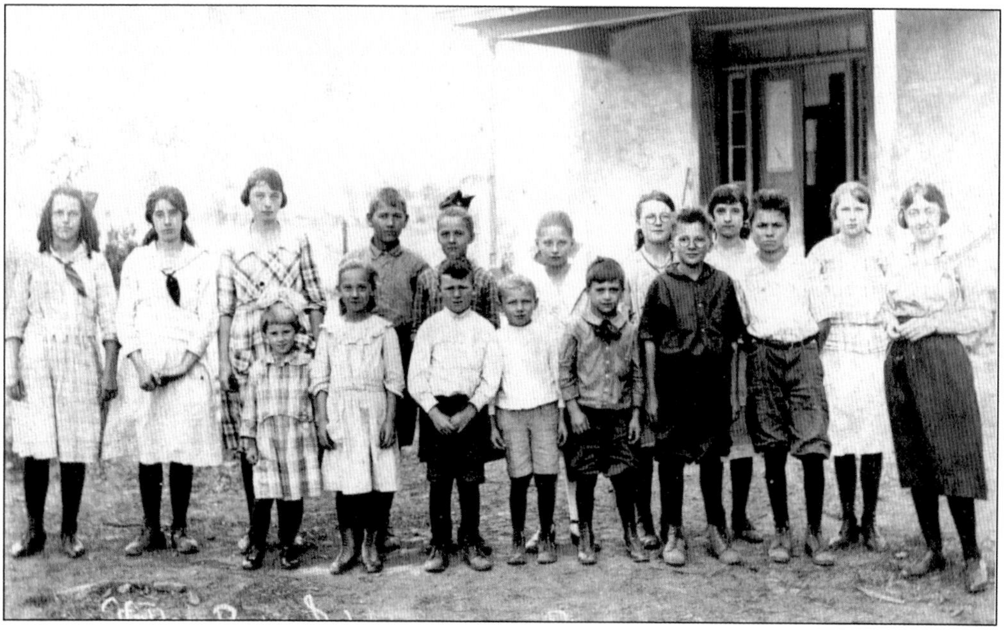

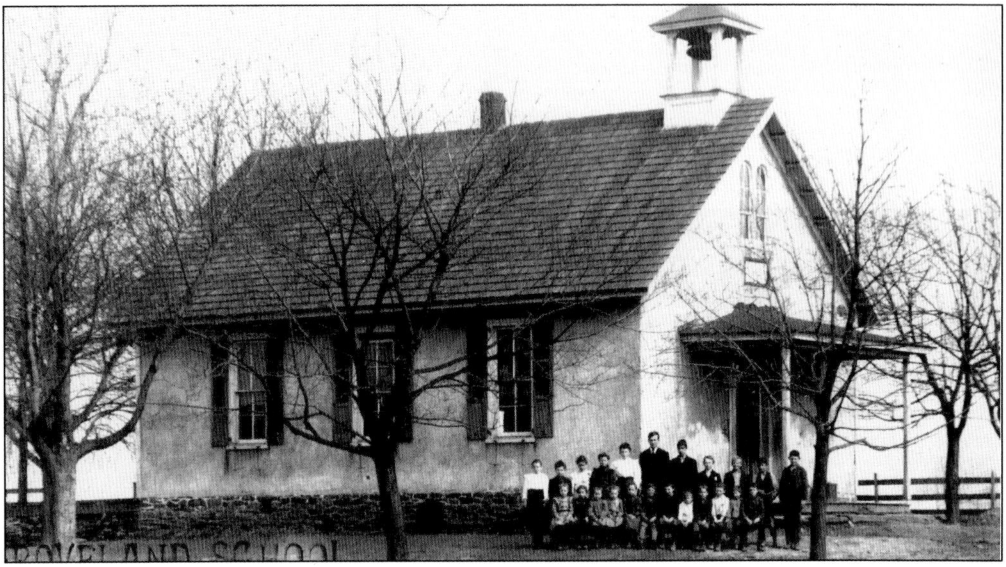

THE GROVELAND SCHOOL, C. 1923. The Groveland School was used for public schooling on weekdays and for Bible classes by the adjacent meetinghouse on Sundays. This is a photograph of a Sunday school class. The Groveland School was built in 1887 to replace the Funk Octagonal Schoolhouse, which had been located on the site as early as the 1830s. The old bell is now at the new Groveland Elementary School on Easton Road.

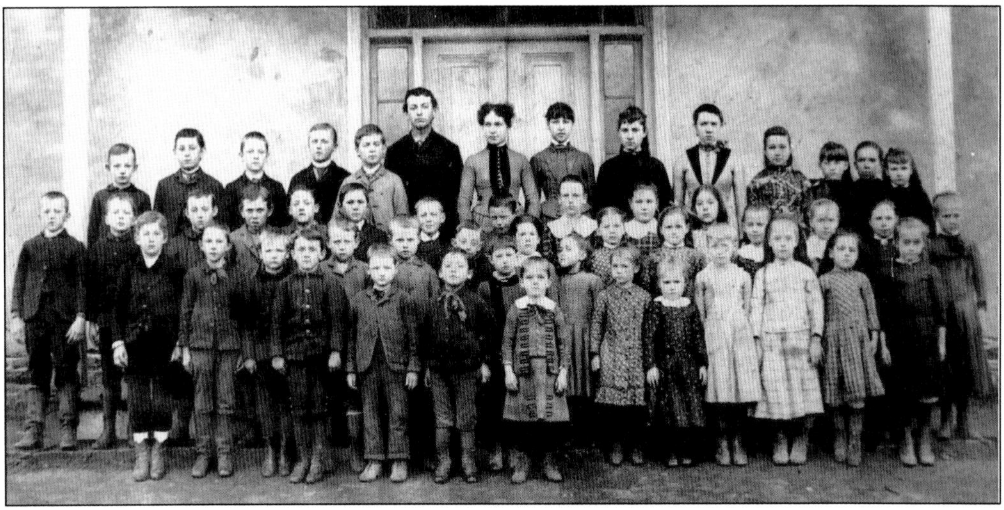

THE GROVELAND SCHOOL, C. 1900. Individuals identified in this school picture include: Theodore Michener, Walter Shaddinger, Elmer Michener, Henry Gaugle, Wilson Wismer, Cooper Swope, Edna Michener (Leatherman), Anna Michener, Harry Rickert, Susie Kriebel (Strawn), Lottie Melcher (Shelley), Susie Roat, Bertha Keller (Haring), Silas Myers, Wilson Fretz, Willie Myers, Albertis Wismer, Levis Swope, Bill Kriebel, Harvey Michener, James Melcher, Frank Benner, Frank Wismer, Rose Ella Wismer (Long), Lizzie Wismer, Mabel Melcher (Kriebel), Flora Michener (Myers), Katie Swartz (Keller), Cassie Sine, Ella Swartz, Mamie Melcher (Shaddinger), Annie Swartz, Ella Wismer, Clara Myers (Moyer), Annie Keller (Shaddinger), Willie Schrauger, Harry Myers, John Rickert, Leidy Landis, Herbert Swope, Newberry Myers, teacher Rebie V. Doan, Anna Swope (Wismer), Rose Emma Wismer (Rufe), Clara Atkinson (Shaddinger), Edith Schrauger, Sara Wismer, and Rose Michener (Shaddinger).

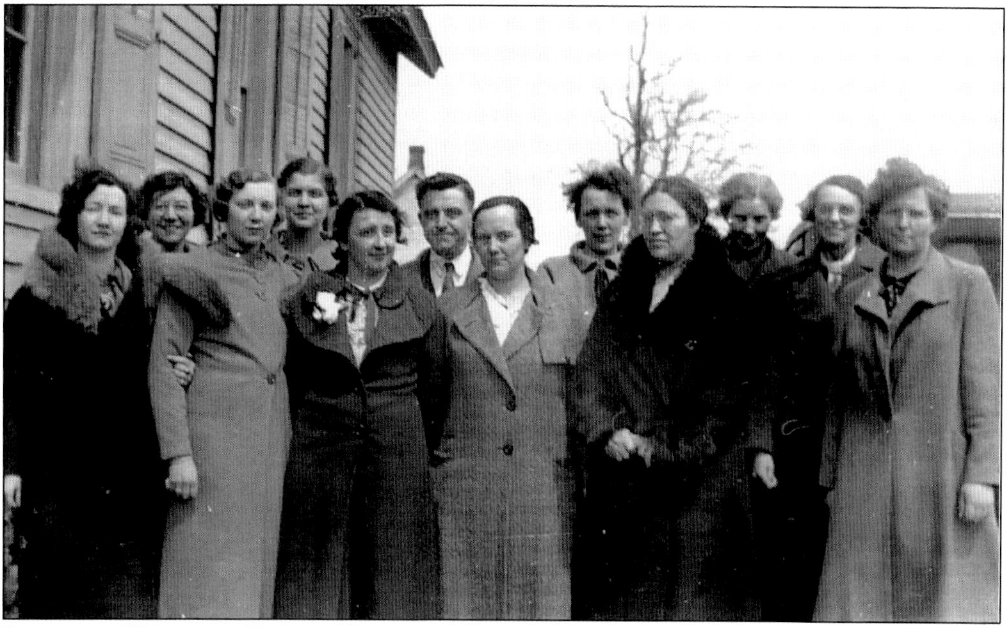

PLUMSTEAD TOWNSHIP TEACHERS, C. 1936. Teachers who taught in all 12 schools in the township are assembled here. Pictured from left to right are Mary Peoples (River Hill), Helen Gayman (Southwestern), Carol Permar (Valley Park), Eleanor Whitman (Rocky Ridge), Ethel Furness (Groveland), Carver Weisel (Plumsteadville), Helen Lord (Tohickon Hill), Dorothy Bergstrom (Dyer's Hill), Agnes Foster (Prospect Corner), Alma Myers (Gardenville), Elsie Gill (Western Brick), and Edith Diarman (Smith Corner). Mary Furness, who taught the first four grades at Plumsteadville, is not pictured.

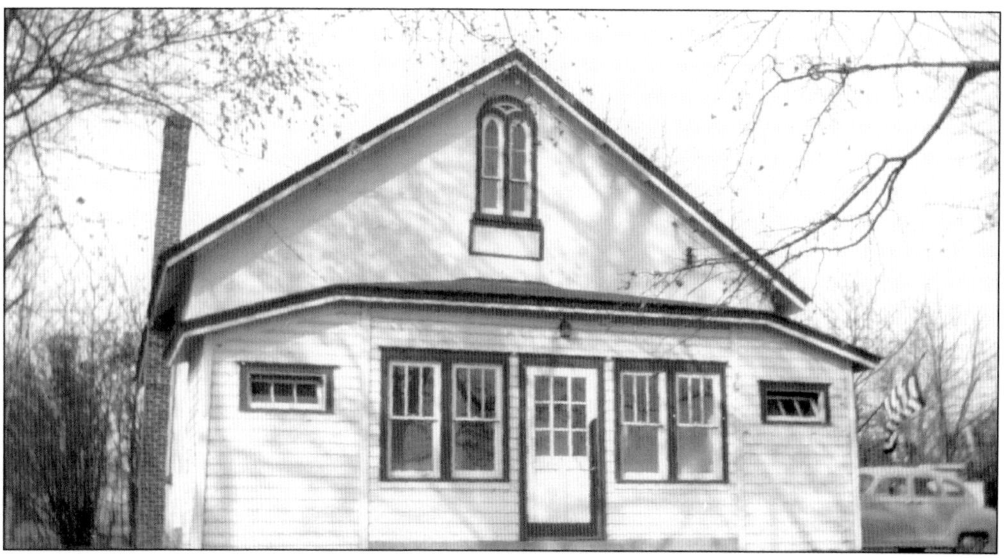

THE DYER'S HILL SCHOOL, C. 1950. The last of the township's small one- and two-room schoolhouses was upgraded in the 1950s. The porches were enclosed with restroom facilities and cloakrooms; the old stoves were removed and central heating was installed.

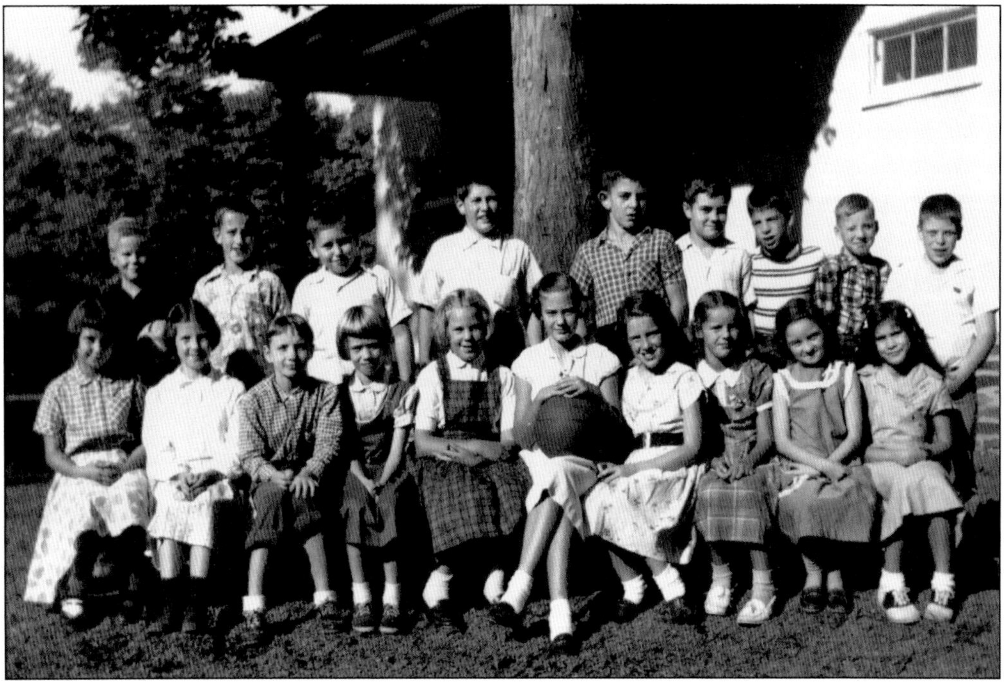

THE TOHICKON HILL SCHOOL, C. 1956. The original school at this site was constructed in 1850 and was replaced by this building in 1880. Pictured from left to right are the following: (first row) Elsie Schwartz, Karen Steinbinder, Edith Roth, Doris Wolford, Alda Scheingold, Beverly Bender, Carol Landis, Ruth ?, Karin Engleke, and Helen Myers; (second row) Peter Frome, Albert Buehler, Chris Sadow, Paul High, Jerry Folke, unidentified, Robin Heller, Dennis Burd, and Eugene Stahlneker.

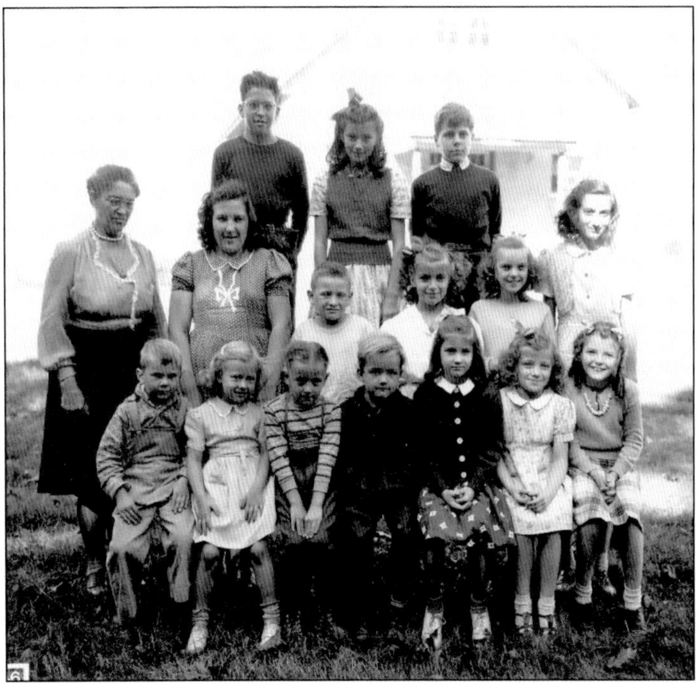

THE PROSPECT CORNER SCHOOL, C. 1946. This schoolhouse on Tollgate Road was built in 1917 and served the township until it was sold in 1947 to become a residence. Pictured from left to right are the following: (first row) Frank Kosloski, Carol Althouse, Robert Wenner, unidentified, Christine Freed, Jeannette Wenner, and Susan Black; (second row) teacher Agnes Foster, Alberta Morris, Frank Pool, Jackie Wenner, Marion Busik, and Gertrude Klenert; (third row) Donald Morris, Doris Wenner, and Gilbert Dixon.

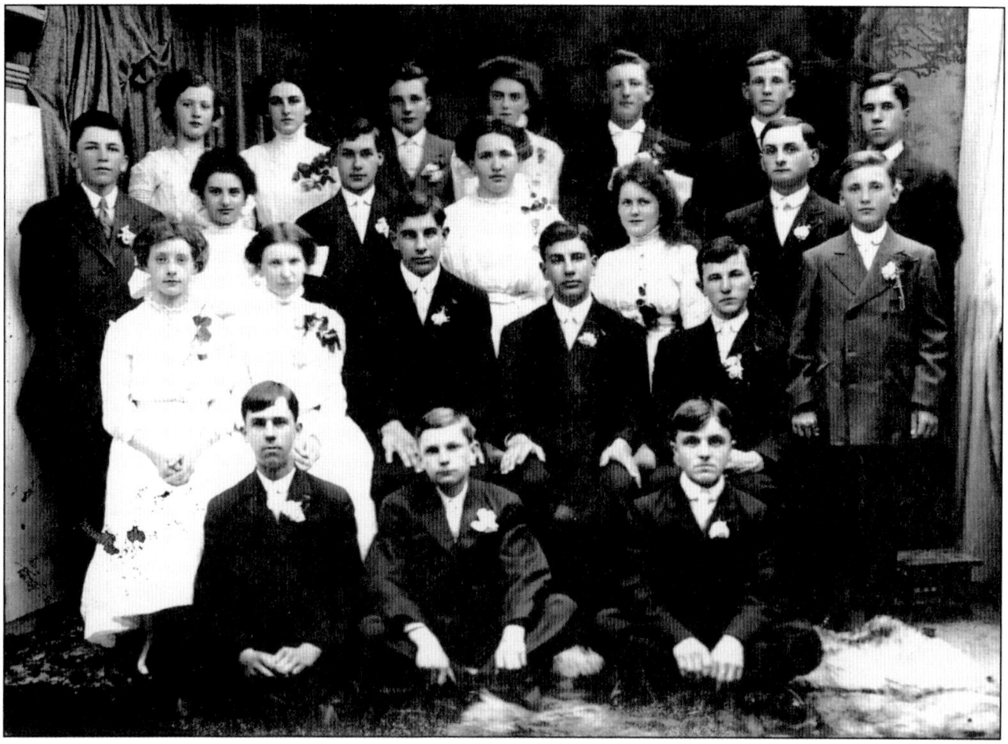

THE GRADUATION CLASS OF 1909. Over the years, eighth-grade graduation ceremonies for each of the 12 township schoolhouses took place together at various locations. The 1909 class commencement was held at Point Pleasant.

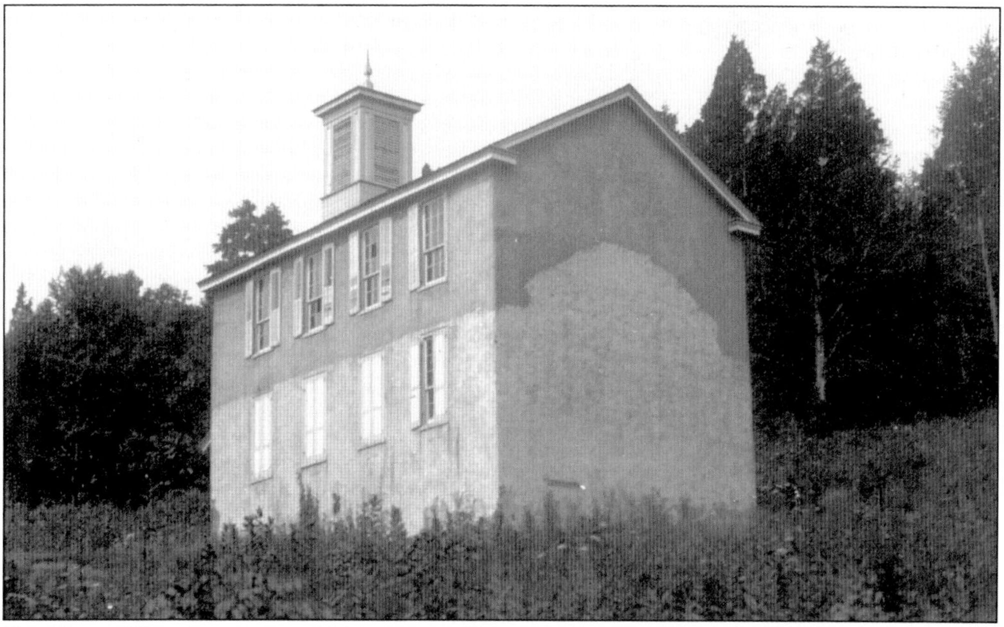

THE RIVER HILL SCHOOL, c. 1922. Originally a one-story structure, the River Hill School was built in 1856 and was enlarged in the late 1800s. It was closed by the school district in 1943 due to dwindling student enrollment.

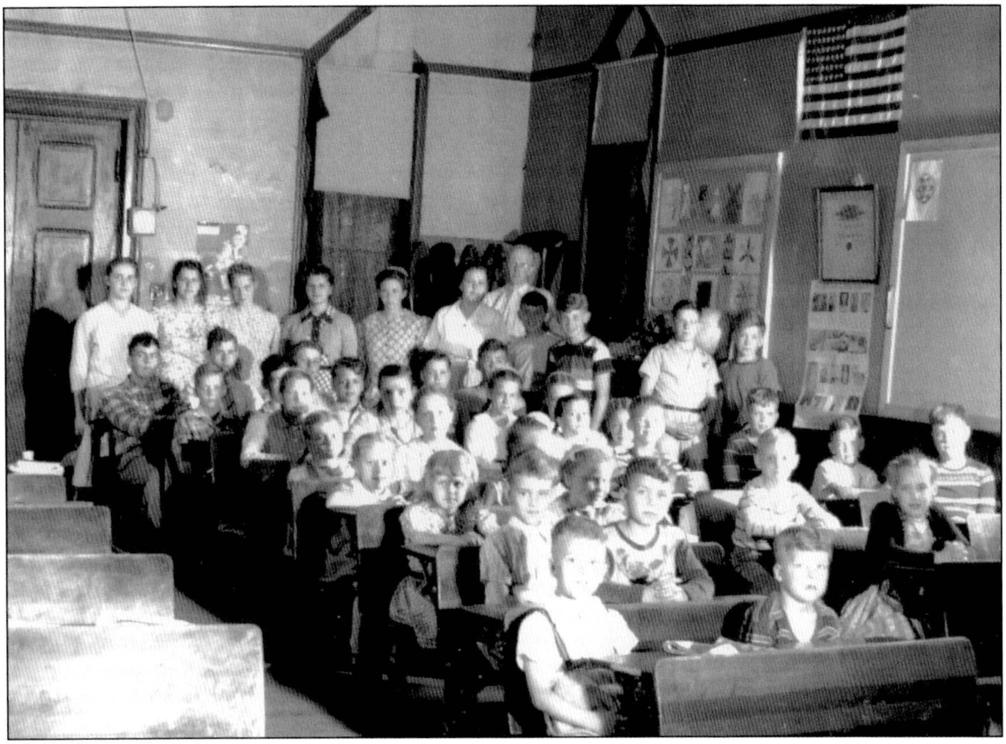

THE PLUMSTEAD CHRISTIAN SCHOOL, C. 1945. The Danboro chapel was used as the Plumstead Christian School in the 1940s, prior to the school's relocation to its new building in Plumsteadville.

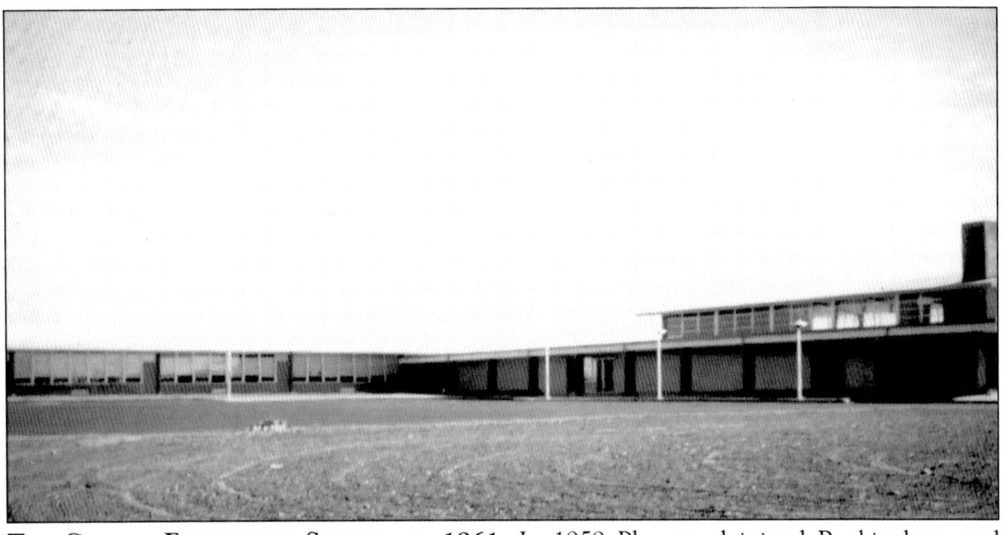

THE GAYMAN ELEMENTARY SCHOOL, C. 1961. In 1959 Plumstead joined Buckingham and Doylestown townships to form the Central Bucks Joint Elementary School Board. A central school was constructed in Plumstead on Point Pleasant Pike. The new school was finished in 1961 and included 14 classrooms, a large multipurpose room for lunch and meetings, offices, and the necessary storage and utility rooms.

Five

LEISURE

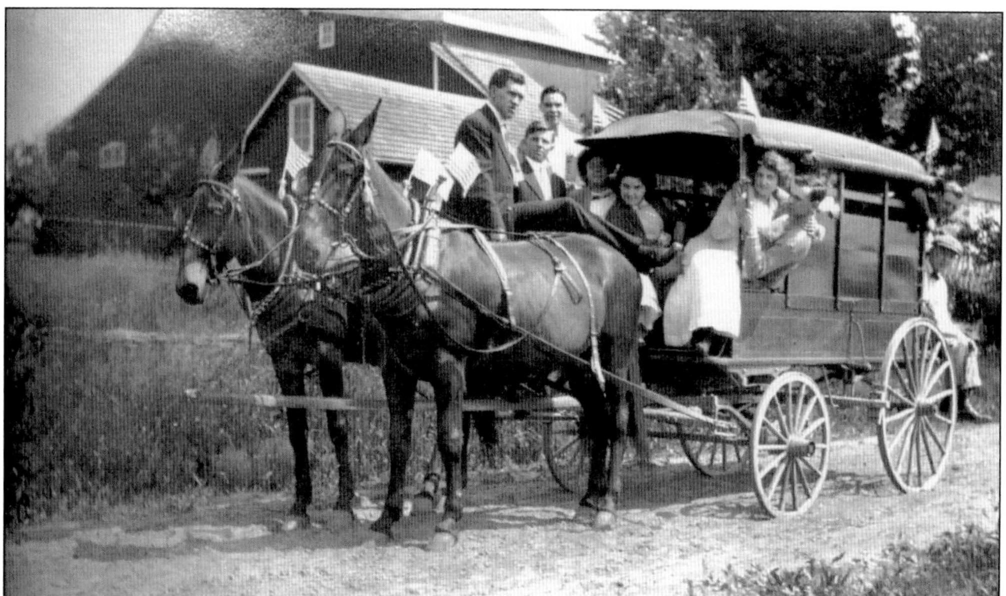

ON THE WAY TO POINT PLEASANT, JULY 4, 1912. Members of the Beidler family and friends head to the Point for an afternoon of recreation. The horse and carriage are pictured in front of the family farm on Curly Hill Road. By the late 19th century, Point Pleasant was a vacation destination, and the canal, river, and cliffs surrounding it made for a great Sunday excursion.

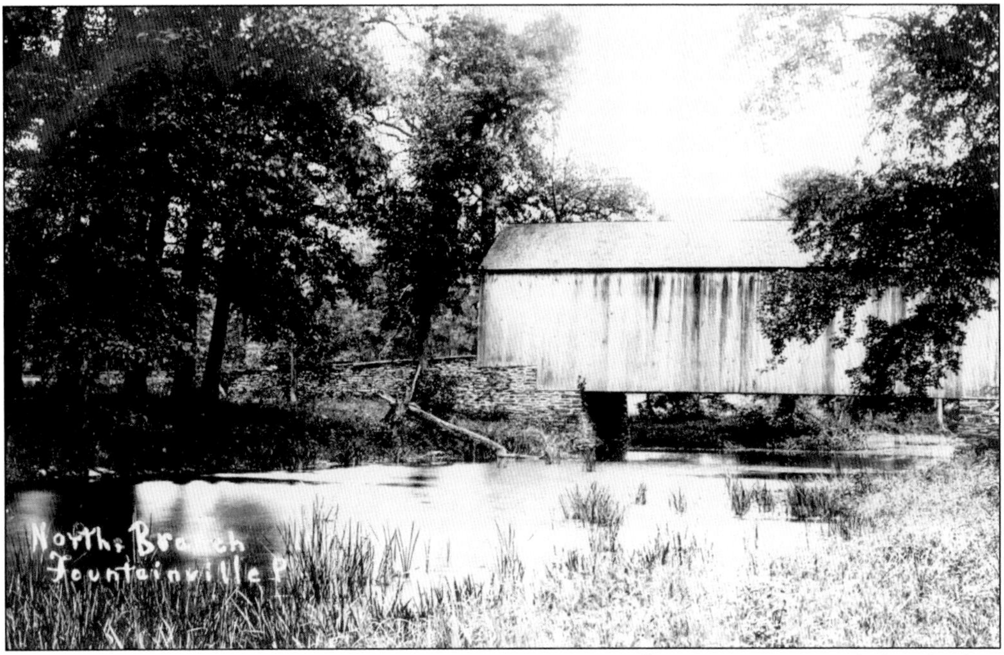

THE NORTH BRANCH COVERED BRIDGE, C. 1900. Major road improvements, including bridges and highways, were made in the region in the 19th century. By the early 20th century, covered bridges were so rare that they became tourist attractions. Pictured here is the North Branch Covered Bridge, which once stood along Swamp Road. Today, only two of the township's original covered bridges remain.

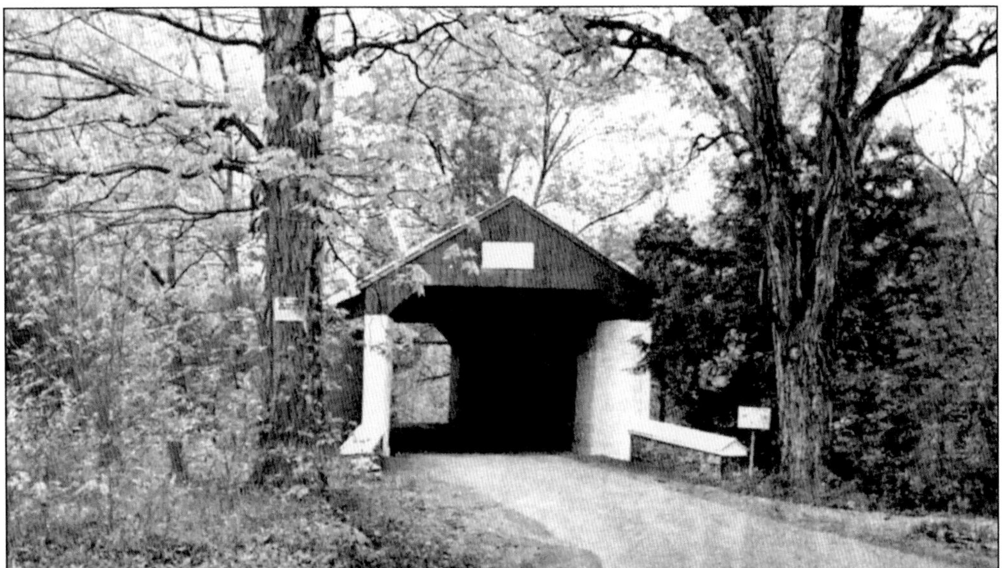

THE LOUX COVERED BRIDGE, C. 1950. The 60-foot-long Loux Covered Bridge is a popular landmark and tourist destination. The bridge is named for the Loux Mill, which once stood nearby. It was built following the drowning of Reed Myers on July 16, 1865. Myers attempted to ford the swollen Cabin Run Creek after a heavy rainfall. His buggy and drowned horse were found a half-mile downstream, and his body was eventually recovered in Tohickon Creek.

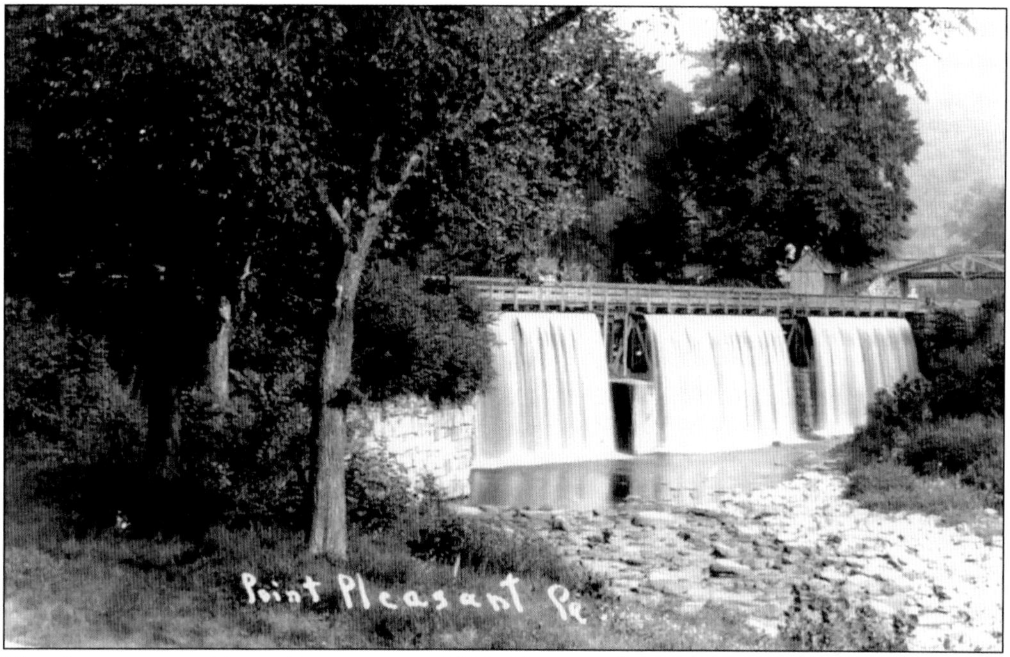

The Aqueduct at Point Pleasant, c. 1900. The aqueduct at Point Pleasant was not only a picturesque sight, but also a popular swimming spot for many years. A reconstructed aqueduct is now located on this site.

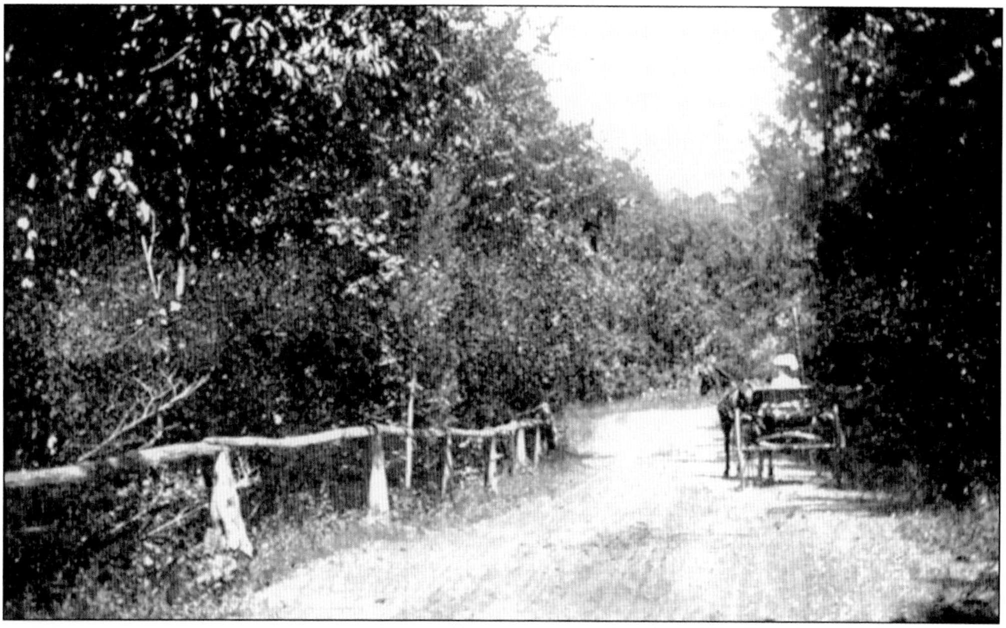

A Delightful Drive on River Road, c. 1915. Driving along the river by horse and buggy, and later by car, provided the rider marvelous scenic views. River Road remains a popular destination for residents and visitors alike. It has changed little since the early 1900s.

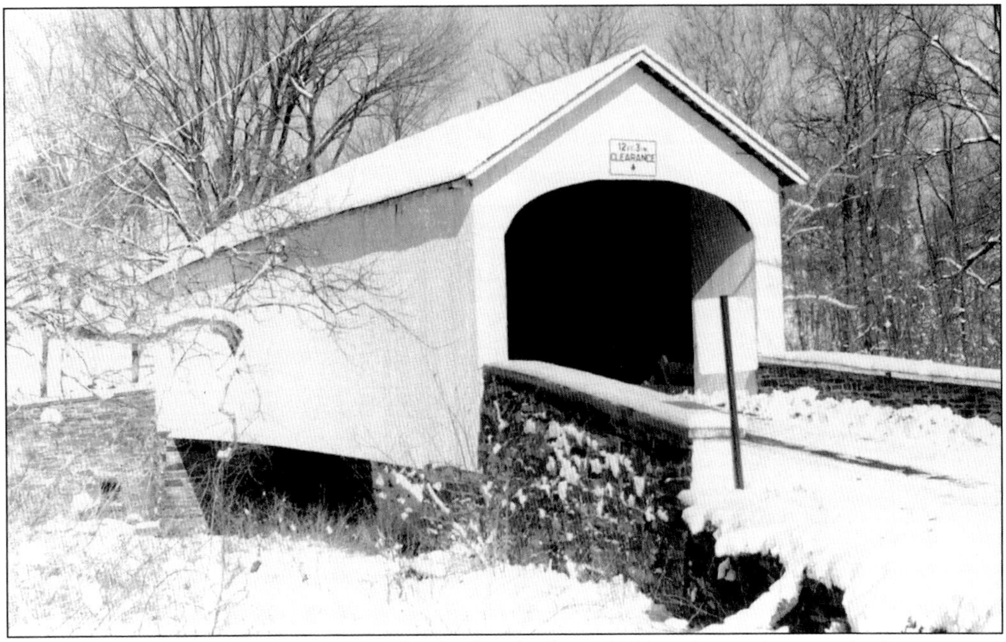

The Cabin Run Bridge, c. 1960. This bridge, built in 1871, is located one mile downstream from the Loux Covered Bridge, where the Cabin Run Creek meets Tohickon Creek. It measures 82 feet in length and is larger than the Loux Bridge.

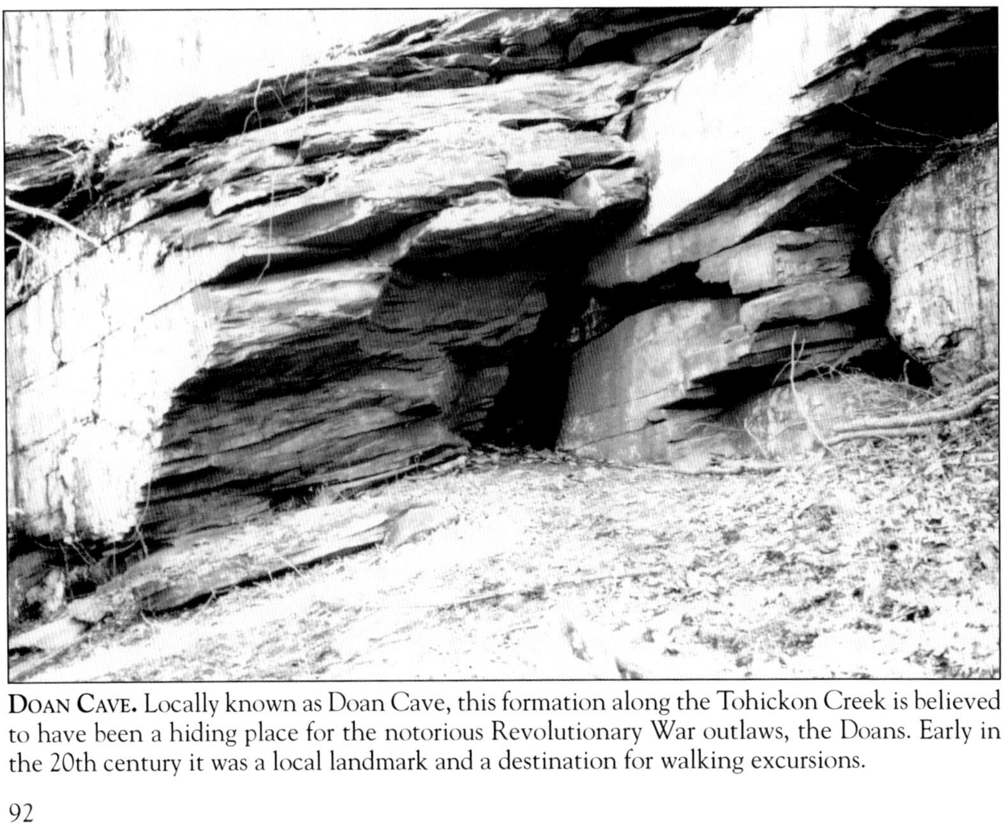

Doan Cave. Locally known as Doan Cave, this formation along the Tohickon Creek is believed to have been a hiding place for the notorious Revolutionary War outlaws, the Doans. Early in the 20th century it was a local landmark and a destination for walking excursions.

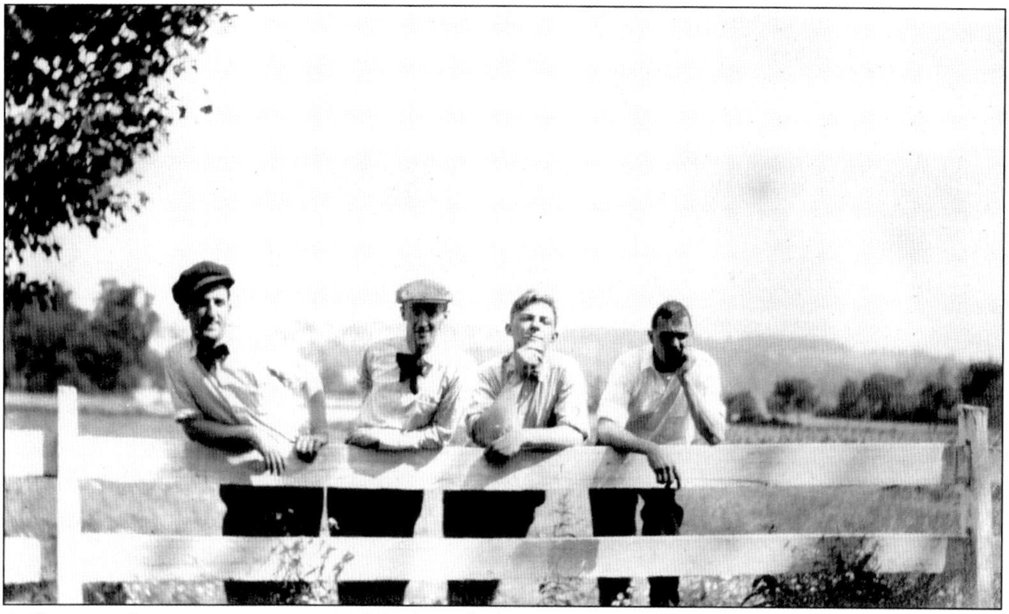

A Sunday Afternoon, c. 1915. Unidentified young men, dressed in their Sunday best, relax along a fence on Curly Hill Road.

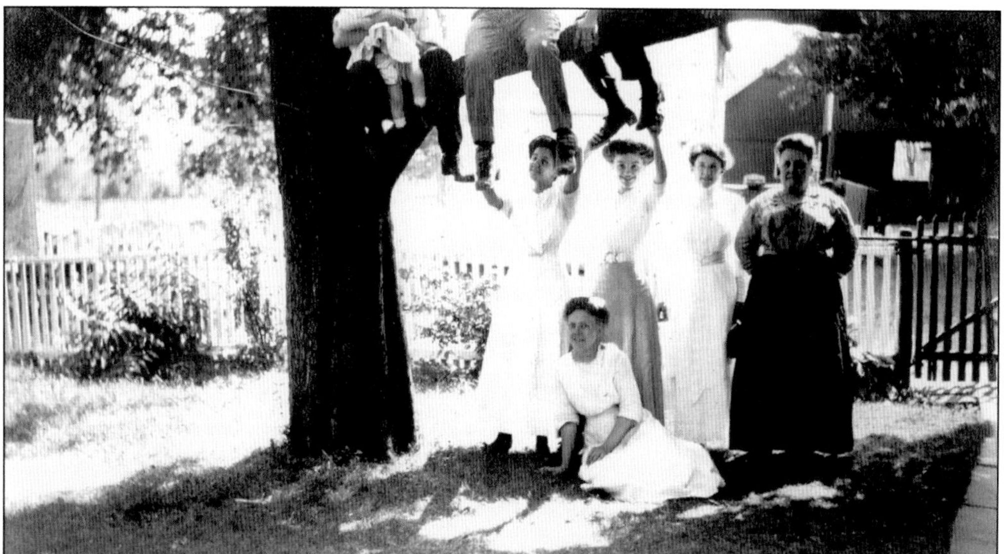

Horsing Around, c. 1915. Holidays and family gatherings often called for some good, old-fashioned horsing around. This group is pictured in front of the Beidler home on Curly Hill Road.

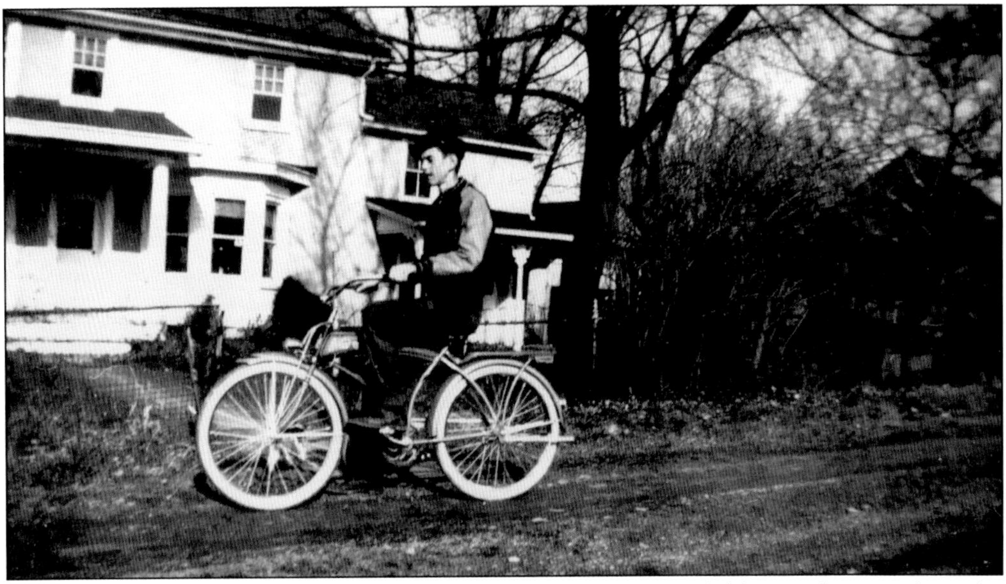

The New Bike, c. 1939. Bicycling was a popular pastime for most children in the township. The major and minor country roads at that time were ideal for biking. Here, William John Jacobs Jr. tries out his new bike in front of the old Loux farmhouse.

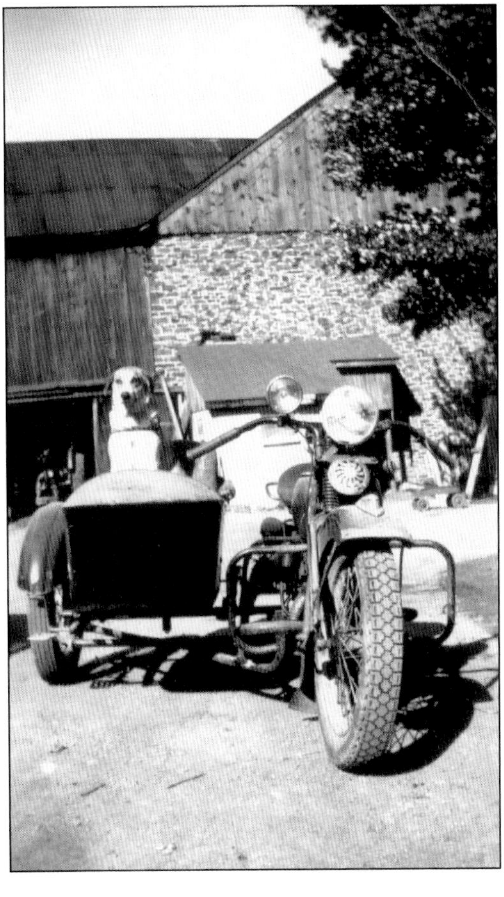

Shep the Dog, c. 1940. Most farms had a dog; usually it was a watchdog, a companion, or a herder. Here, the Myers family's dog, Shep, decides to take some leisure time.

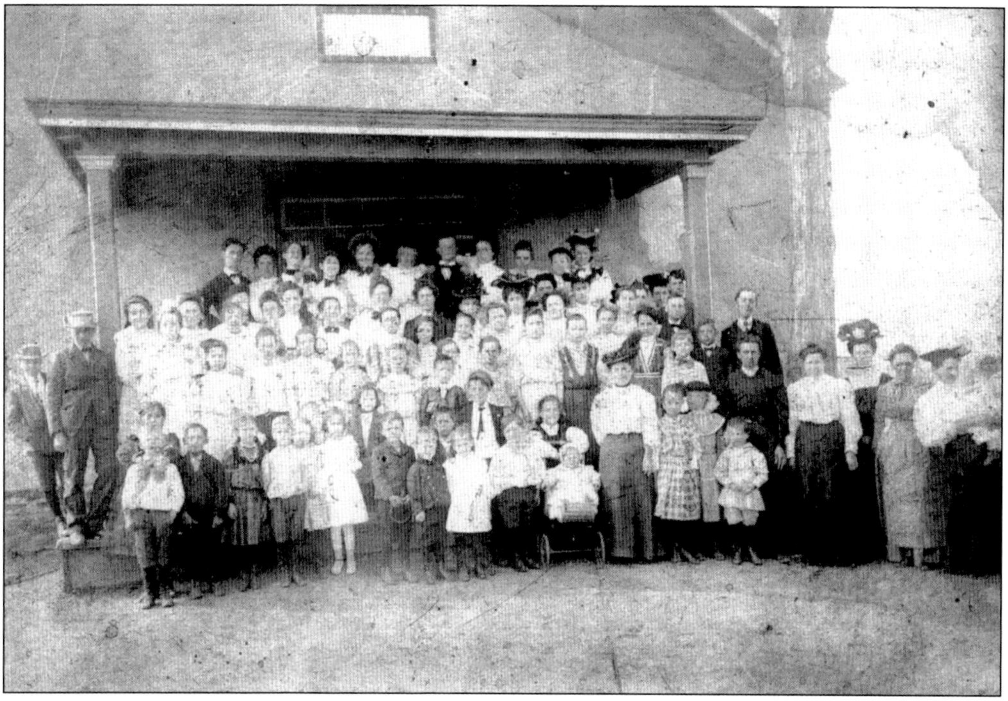

The Point Pleasant Literary Club, c. 1890. Among the area's early clubs was the Literary Club that met in the River Hill School. Other early clubs established in the first decade of the 1800s, including Plumstead's lending library, are largely forgotten.

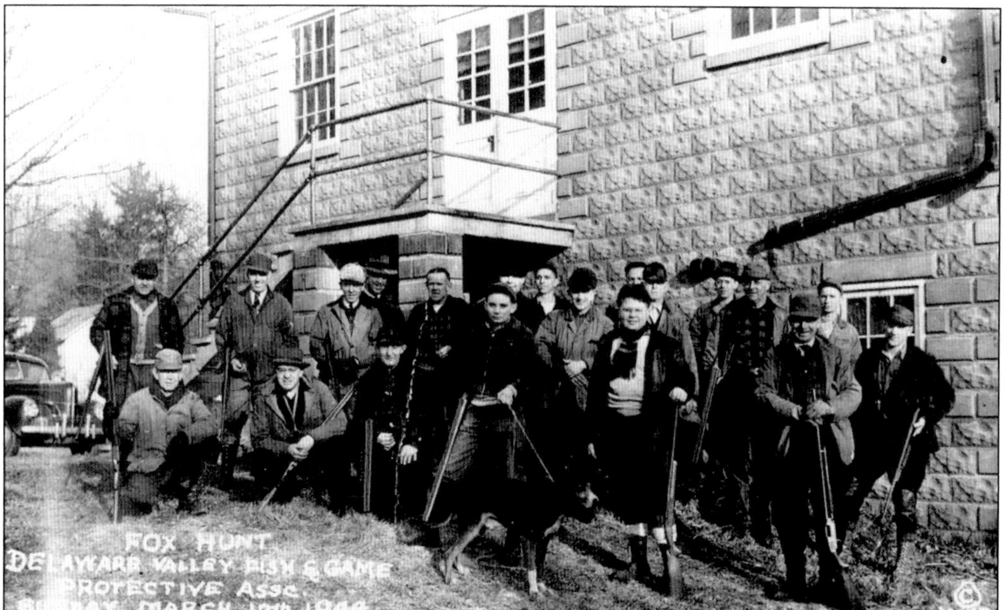

A Fox Hunt, c. 1944. Members of the Delaware Valley Fish and Game Protective Association gather at the Point Pleasant Firehouse prior to their fox hunt. The association met at the firehouse before the group purchased land on Ferry Road.

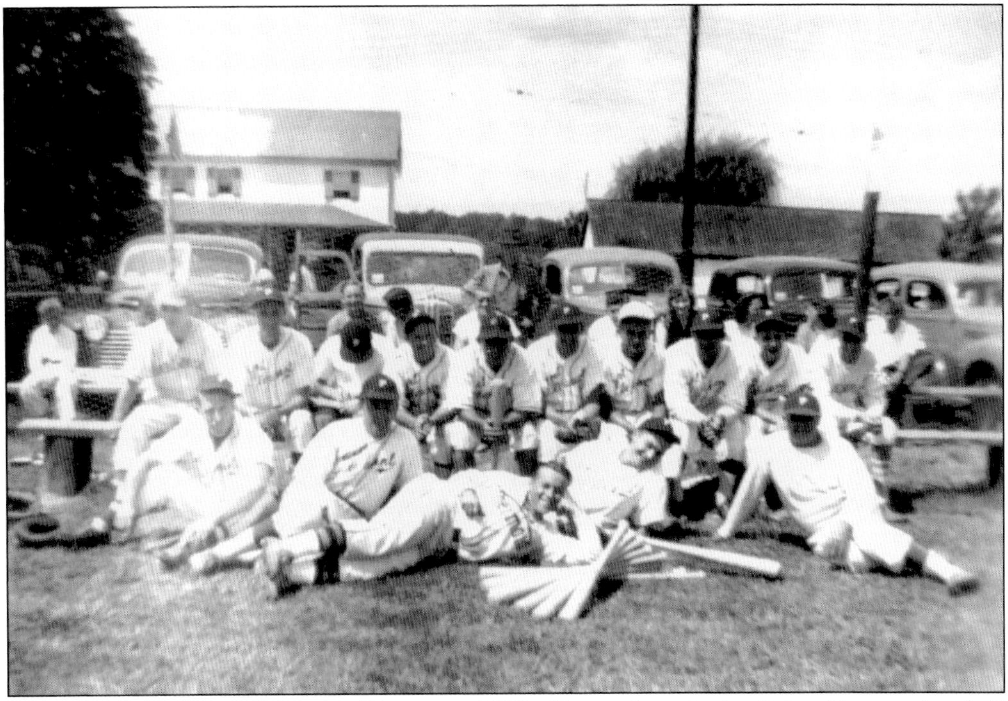

The Point Pleasant Baseball Team, c. 1958. Shown here is the Point Pleasant baseball team. Their field was located at Mary Max's corner, at the intersection of Wismer Road and Point Pleasant Pike. Mary Max operated a roadside refreshment stand across the road for many years. Also adjoining the field was the home of Harry Fulmer, the local beekeeper and broom maker.

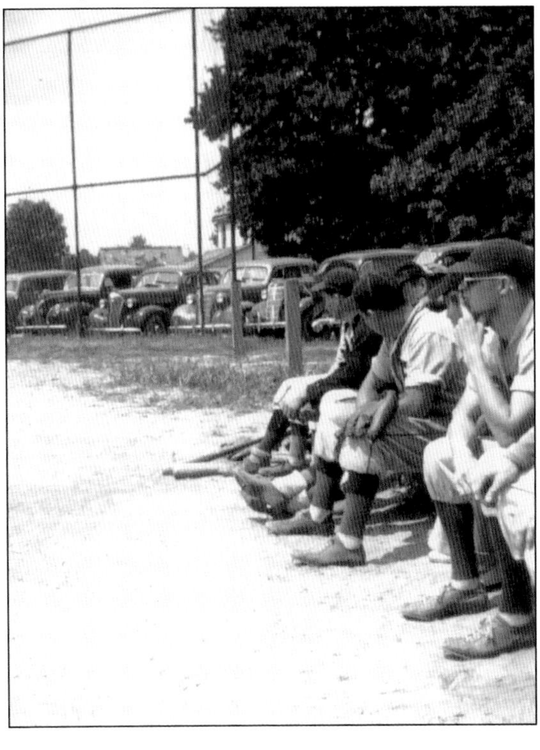

Baseball Players, c. 1945. Plumsteadville also had a baseball team. Their playing field was located on the site of the current firehouse.

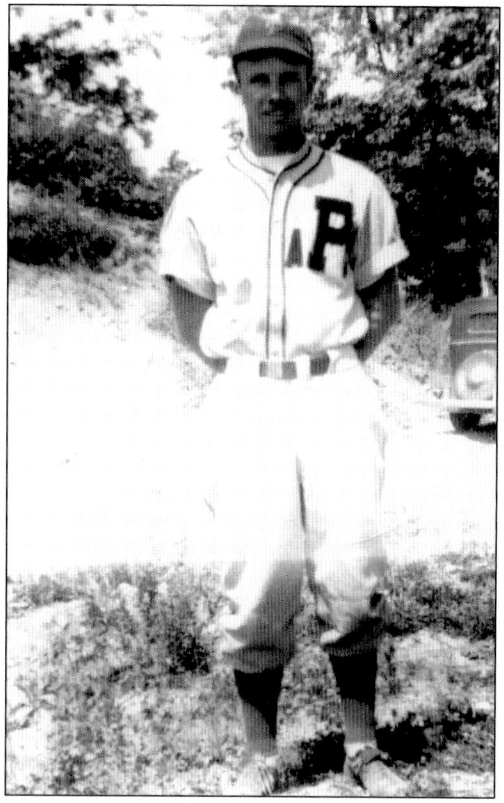

A Ballplayer, c. 1945. Joseph Roman, a member of the Plumsteadville team, poses in his uniform.

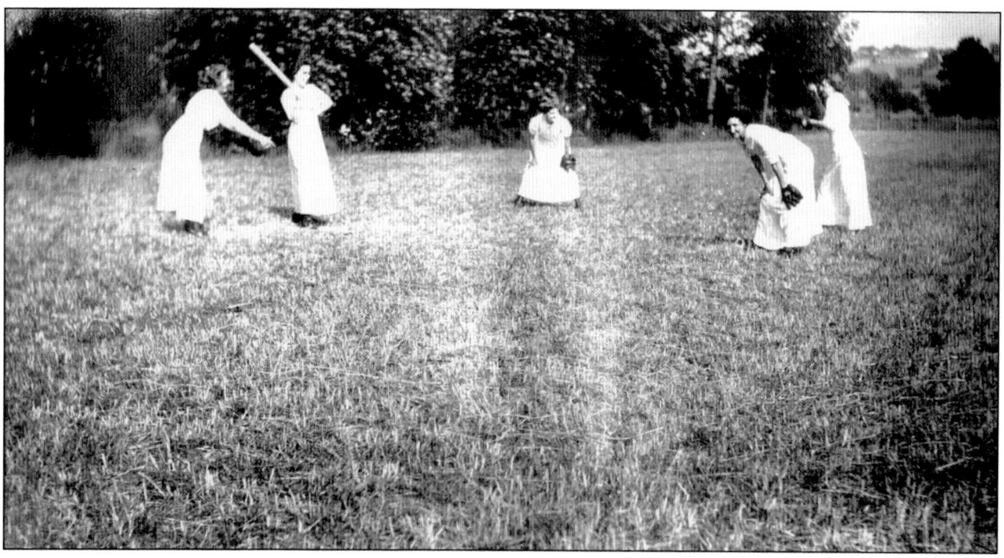

Girls in the Field, c. 1915. Baseball or softball was also played by local girls.

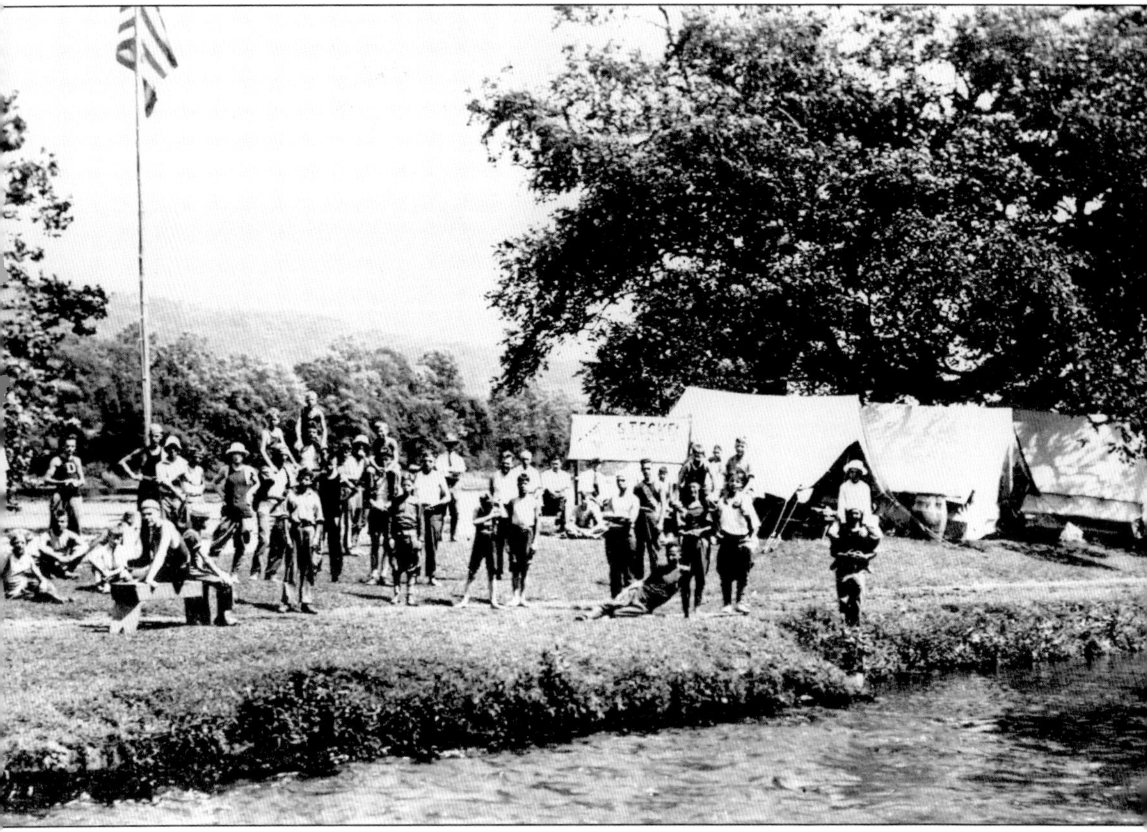

CAMPING ALONG THE CANAL, C. 1920. The Boy's Brigade was founded in 1906 by George C. Murray of Doylestown in association with the Presbyterian church. Brigade members camped along the canal towpath at Point Pleasant, along with other groups shown here.

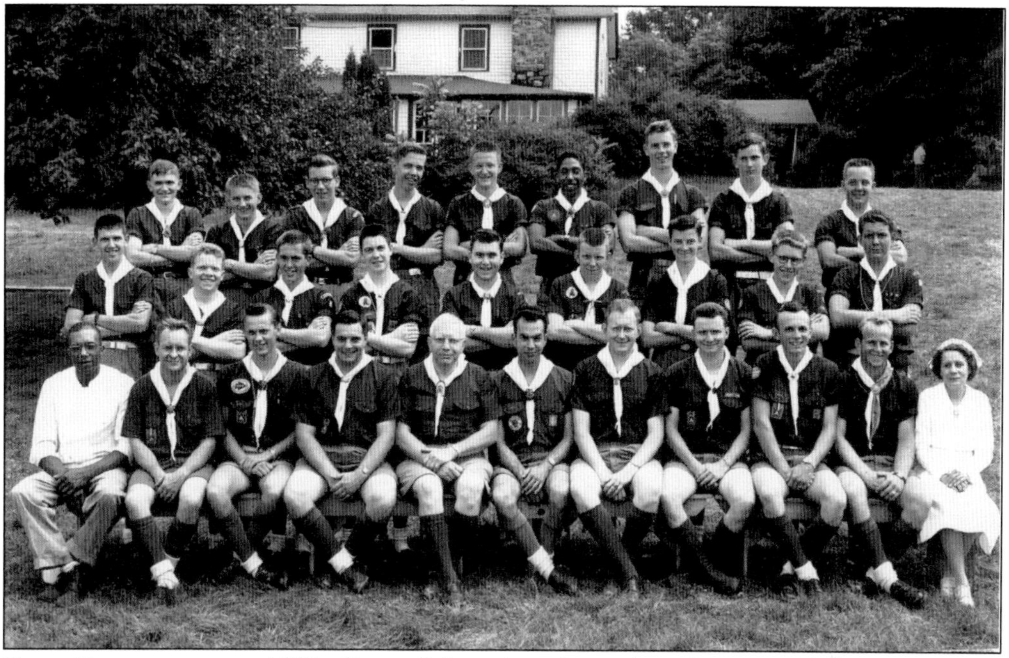

CAMP OCKANICKON, C. 1953. Camp Ockanickon, located in the east end of the township, along State Park Road, was established in Plumstead in 1940. Pictured here are senior staff members and other camp employees (names unknown).

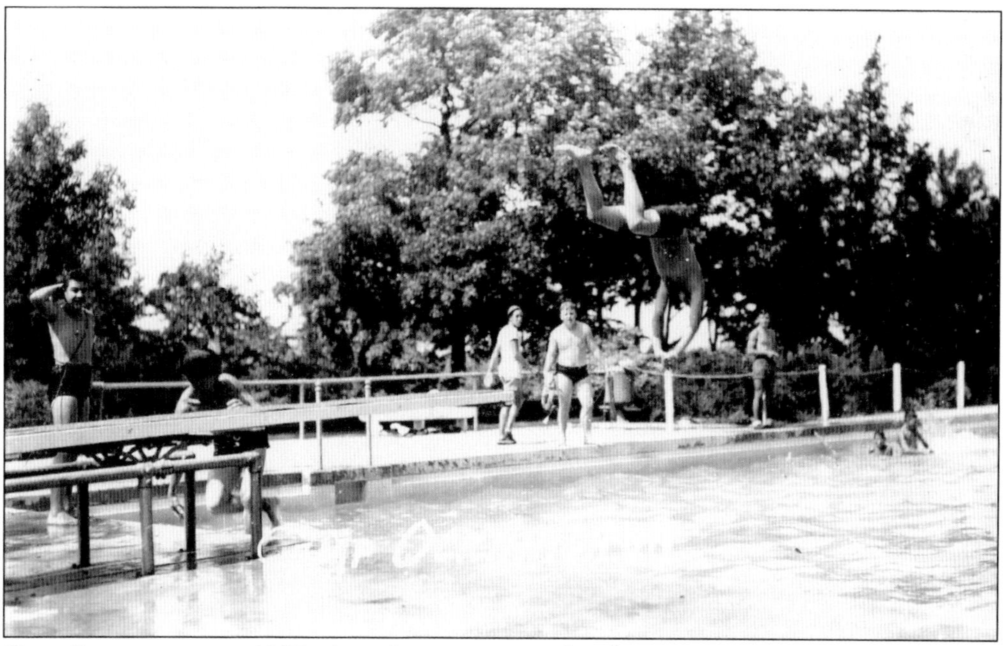

CAMP OCKANICKON, C. 1950. A pool was constructed at the camp in 1941.

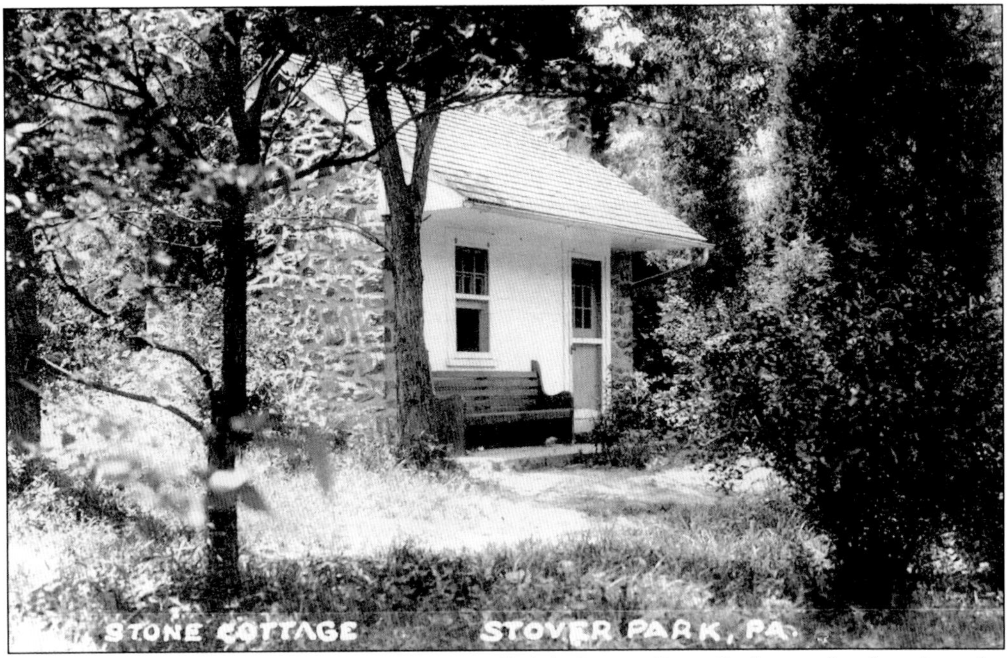

A STONE COTTAGE, STOVER PARK, c. 1940. Ralph Stover State Park was developed in the 1930s by the federal Works Progress Administration (WPA). The cabins at Stover Park were constructed of native stone to reflect the local architecture. Today, only one cottage remains.

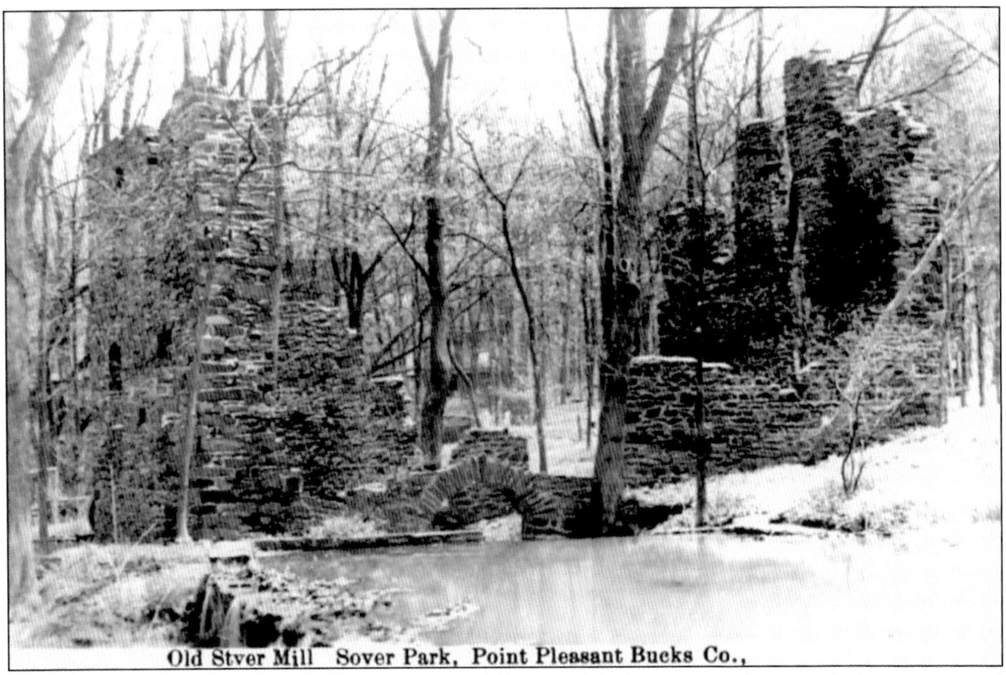

THE MILL, STOVER PARK, c. 1930. The old Long Mill, located in Stover Park, was one of many found along the Tohickon Creek. It was destroyed by fire around 1890, but the stone ruins became a destination for many area residents and visitors lured by history and the natural beauty of the area.

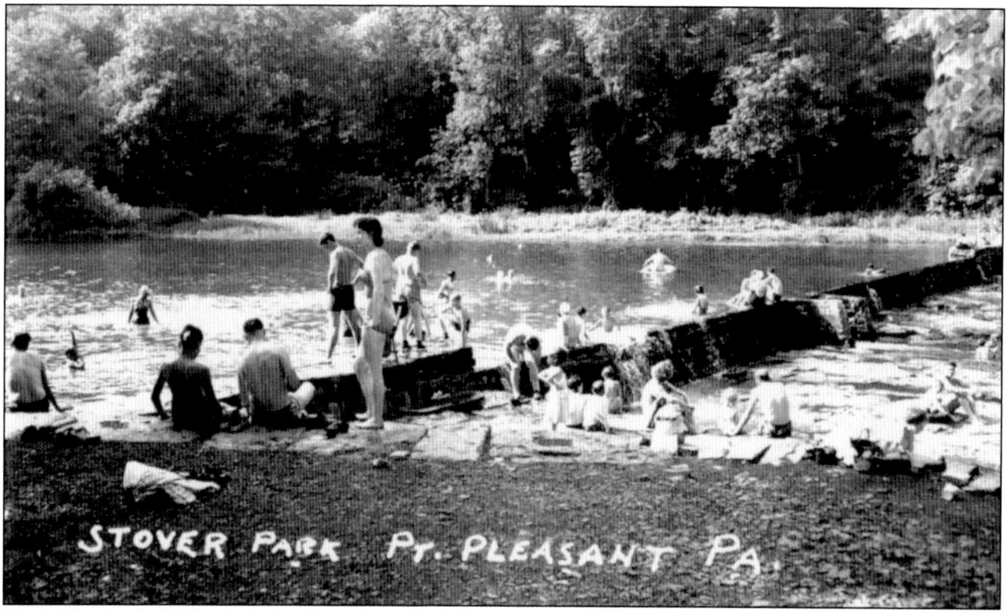

THE SWIMMING HOLE, STOVER PARK, c. 1930. The area near the old dam across the Tohickon Creek at Stover Park was a popular swimming hole for much of the 20th century. The dam had been built to supply water to the mill.

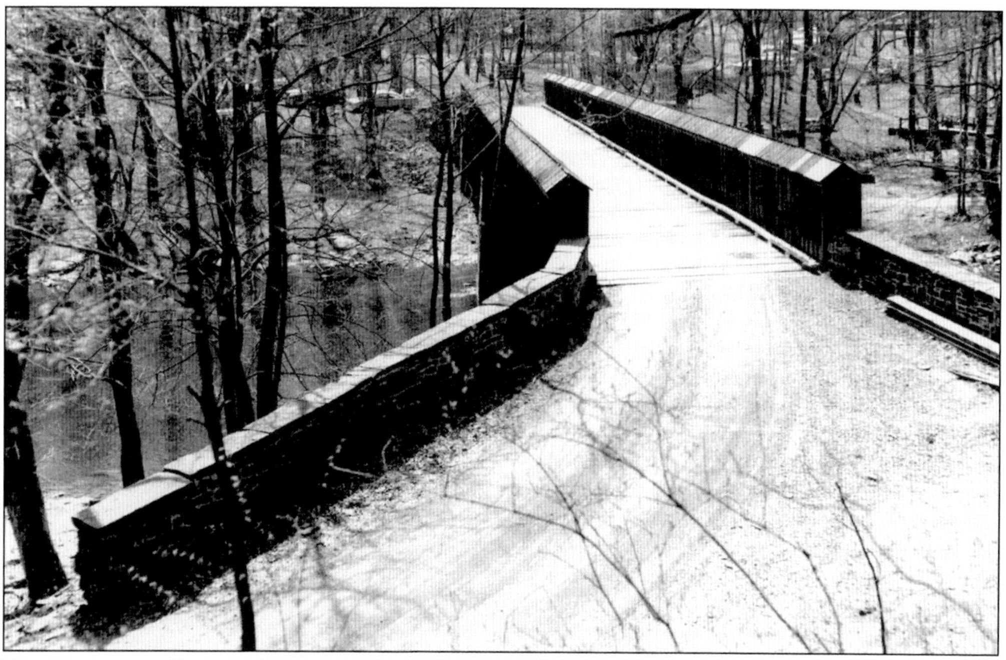

THE BRIDGE AT STOVER PARK, c. 1960. The covered truss bridge over the Tohickon Creek was constructed c. 1900. It still stands but is not open to vehicular traffic.

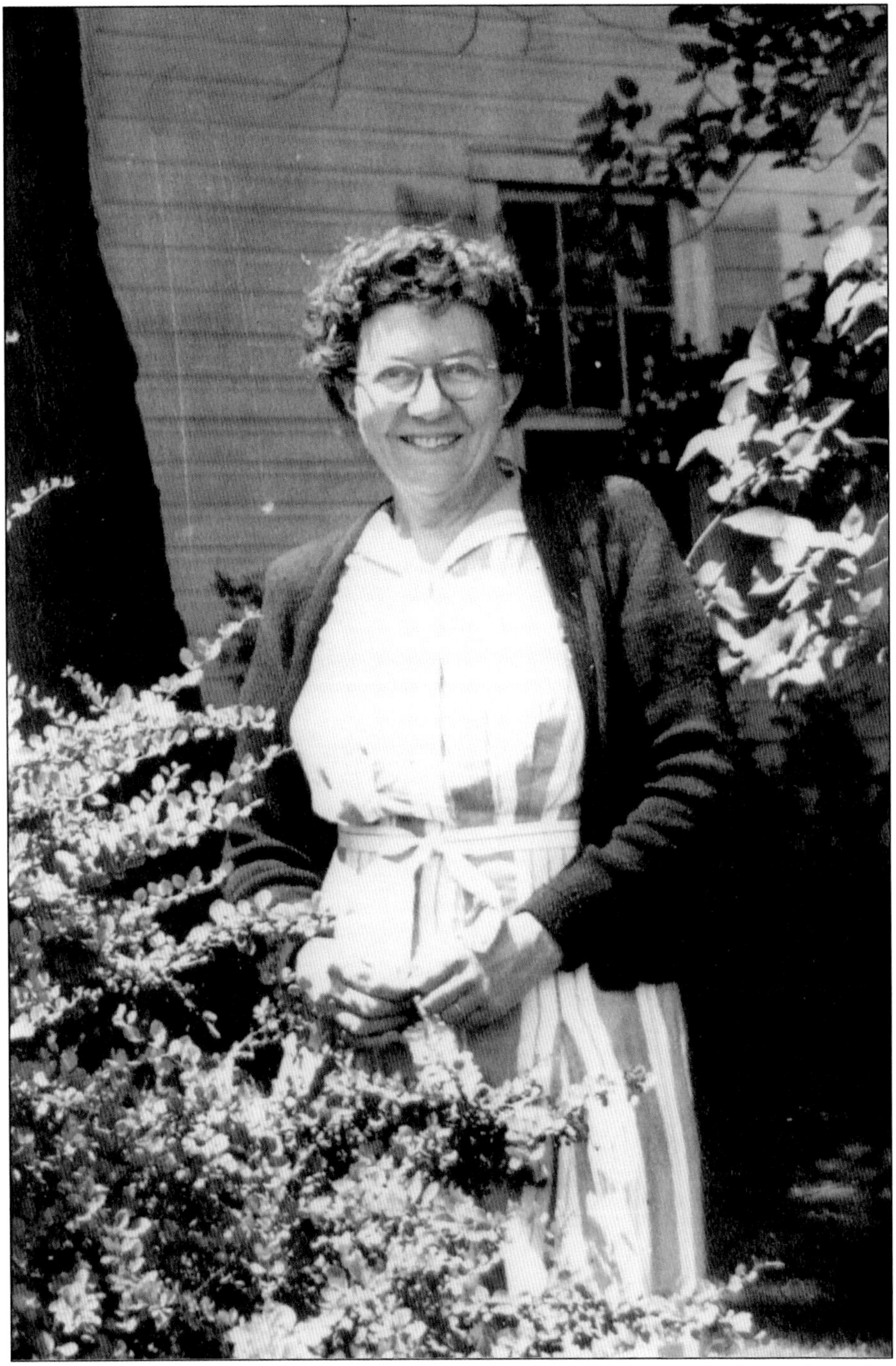

HELEN GAYMAN, C. 1960. Helen Gayman was a local artist who worked in oils and taught art for many years. Her scenes captured the rural landscape and often included her husband, George. The beauty of the area brought an influx of new residents, including many artists, writers, and actors drawn to the region by the historic sites and unspoiled landscape. Gayman is, perhaps, best known as a dedicated public school teacher, working in the old Plumstead Township school system for 30 years.

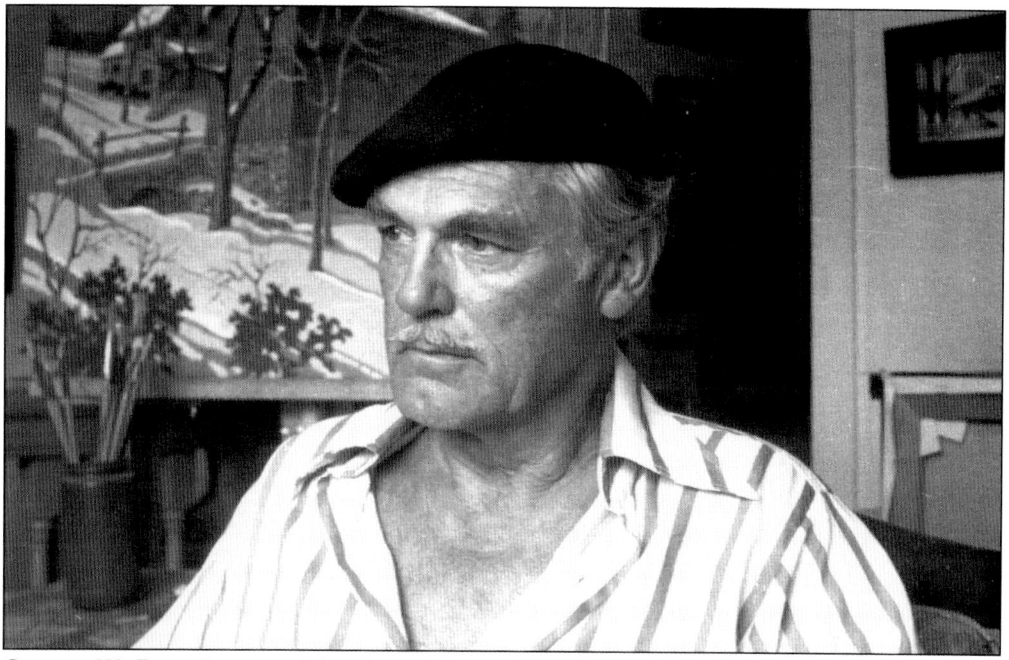

George W. Booz Jr., c. 1960. George Booz was among the many second-generation Bucks County painters. These artists followed earlier Bucks County artists, including Edward Redfield and Daniel Garber. Booz spent most of his life in Gardenville, where he resided in the old Brown residence on Durham Road. His paintings are often noted as capturing the natural beauty of the area and a sense of history. Many other artists were associated with Plumstead Township.

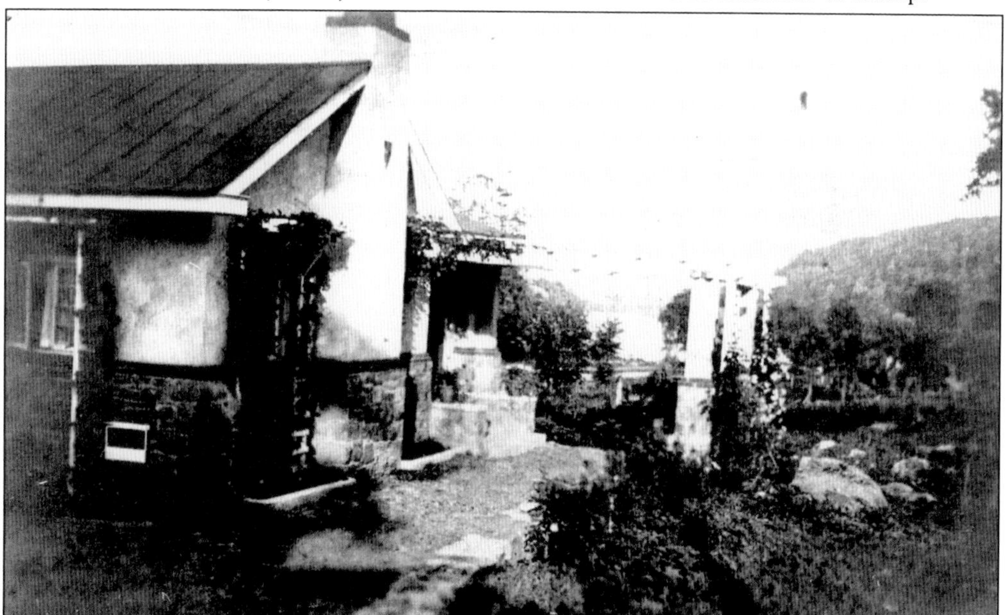

The Brambles, Home of Frank E. English, c. 1912. Frank E. English, a well-known watercolor painter, built this house overlooking the canal and river at Point Pleasant between 1910 and 1912. English resided here until his death in 1922. Many of his paintings depict romantic views of Plumstead landscapes and buildings.

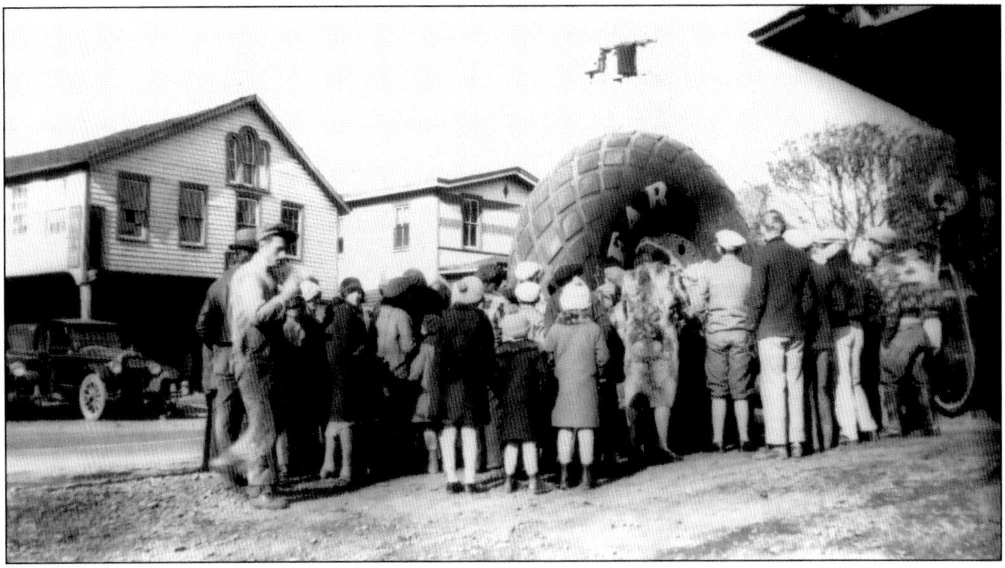

THE WORLD'S LARGEST TIRE VISITS PLUMSTEADVILLE, C. 1930. A Goodyear Tire promotion, "the world's largest tire," traveled to many of the service stations in the area. Here, the entire student body of the Plumsteadville school views the tire at Walter Rush's station at Easton and Stump Roads.

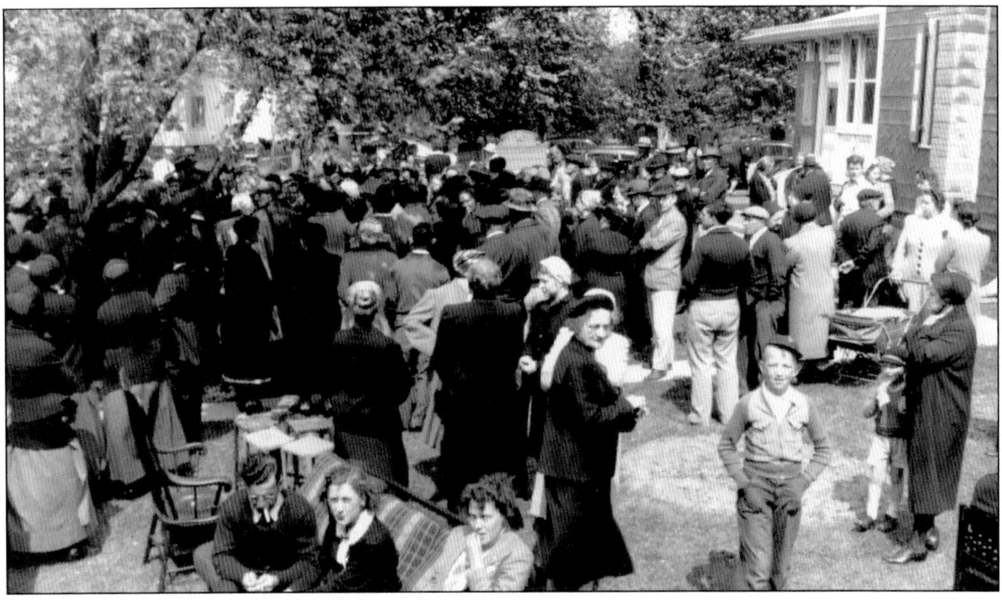

THE COUNTRY AUCTION, C. 1935. Auctions were important community events. Pictured is a large crowd that has gathered for the sale of the Joseph Myers residence in Plumsteadville.

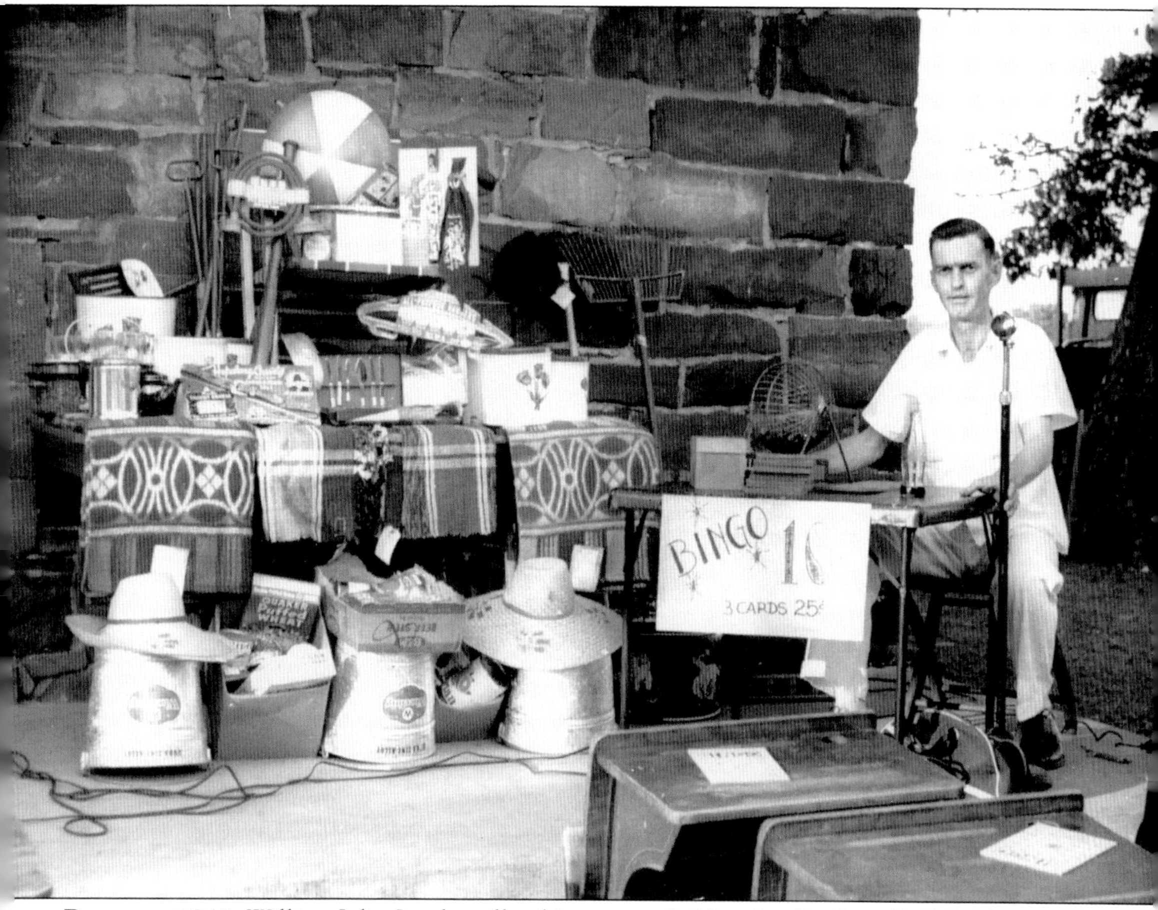

BINGO, C. 1940. William John Jacobs calls a bingo game held at the Gardenville School.

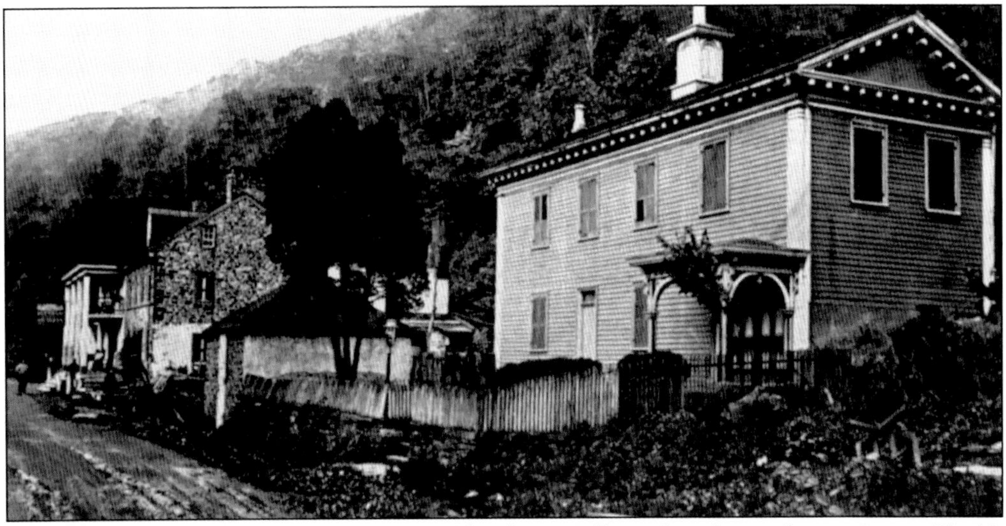

The Odd Fellows Hall, c. 1900. The Odd Fellows Hall was found next door to Lower Black's Eddy Hotel. The hall still stands, although it is no longer used by the Independent Order of Odd Fellows.

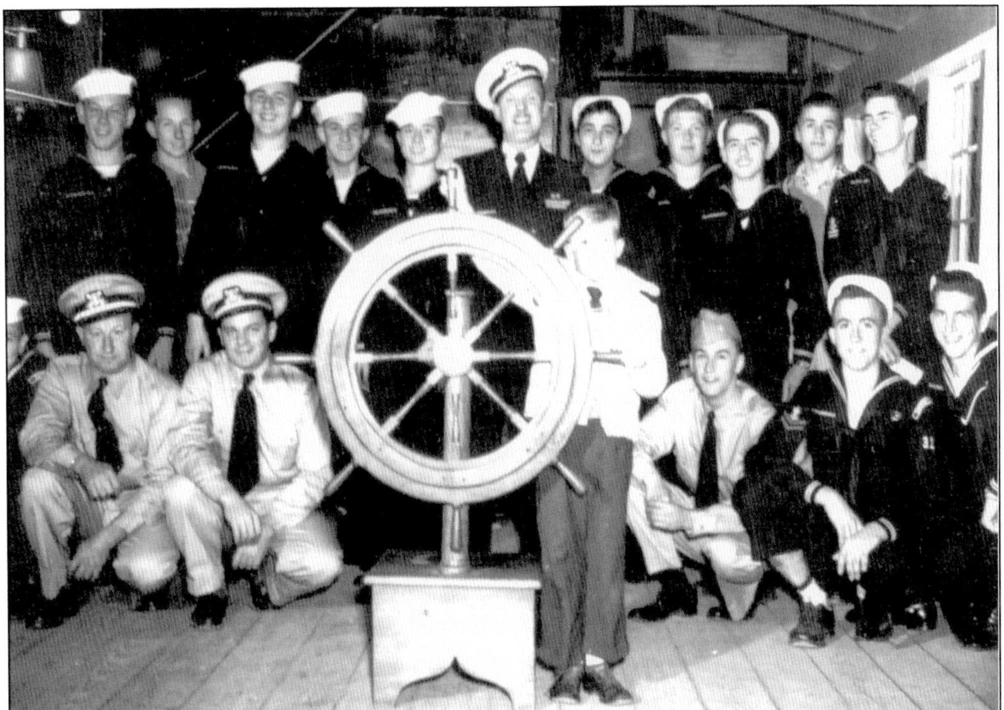

The Sea Scouts Explorer Club, c. 1947. The Sea Scouts were organized by Stewart G. Montgomery, a Point Pleasant resident and veteran. The club met in Clifford Berry's chicken house near Gardenville. The group is shown here in their clubhouse with a ship's wheel constructed by Donald Morris. From left to right are the following: (first row) Edward Kabala, Frank Mullan, unidentified, Clifford Berry, William Hasenauer, and Donald Morris; (second row) Richard Wilson Jr., William Savage, unidentified, Horace Drake, Anthony Siron, Steward Montgomery, Steven Ralph, Robert Wood, two unidentified men, and Frank Kolbe Jr.

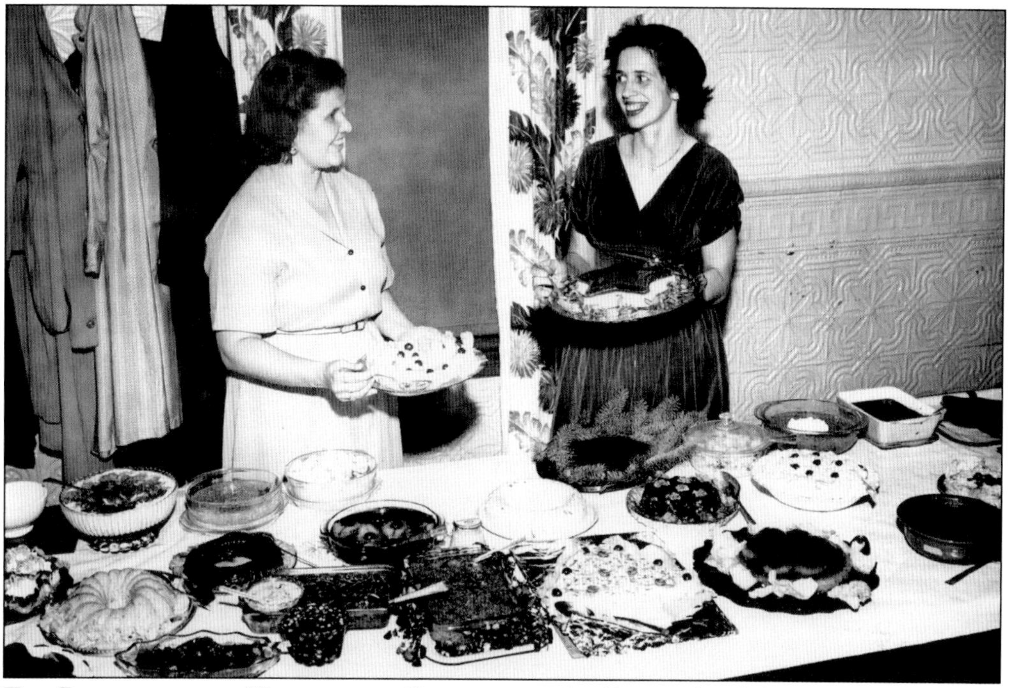

THE PLUMSTEADVILLE HOMEMAKERS GROUP, C. 1960. For much of the early 20th century, women spent most of their social life participating in activities associated with church groups, the Grange, fire company auxiliaries, and homemaking groups. Members of the Plumsteadville homemakers group, under the direction of Frances Vannoy, were taught housekeeping methods and cooking techniques. Shown here are Rachel Gross (left) and Margaret Moyer, preparing for a holiday buffet at the Grange.

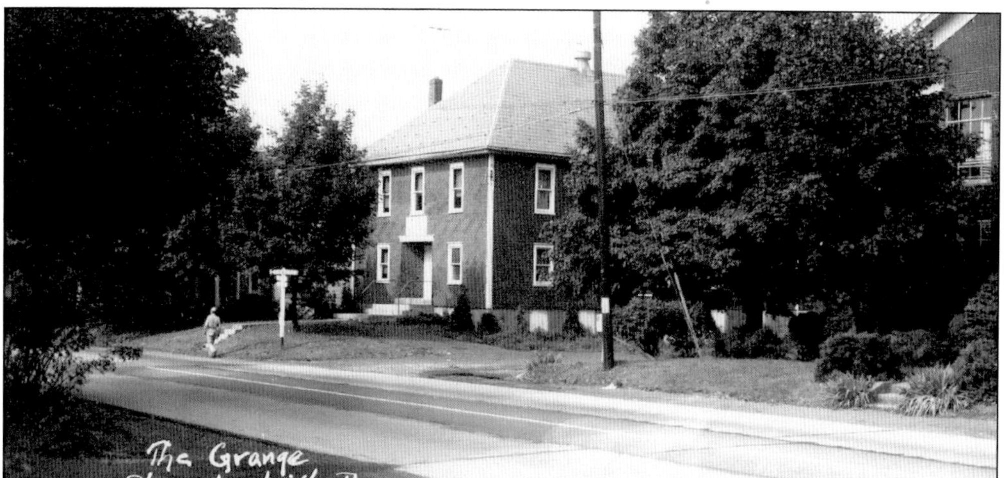

THE GRANGE, C. 1920. The Plumstead Grange was organized in 1917, and the group met on the second floor of the Plumsteadville Hotel. After the closing of the Kratz carriage factory in 1924, the Grange acquired the site of the Kratz wagon shed and constructed the present building. The organization was founded for the benefit of farmers. In its heyday, it boasted more than 200 members. Today, the Plumstead group constitutes one of three remaining Grange halls in Bucks County.

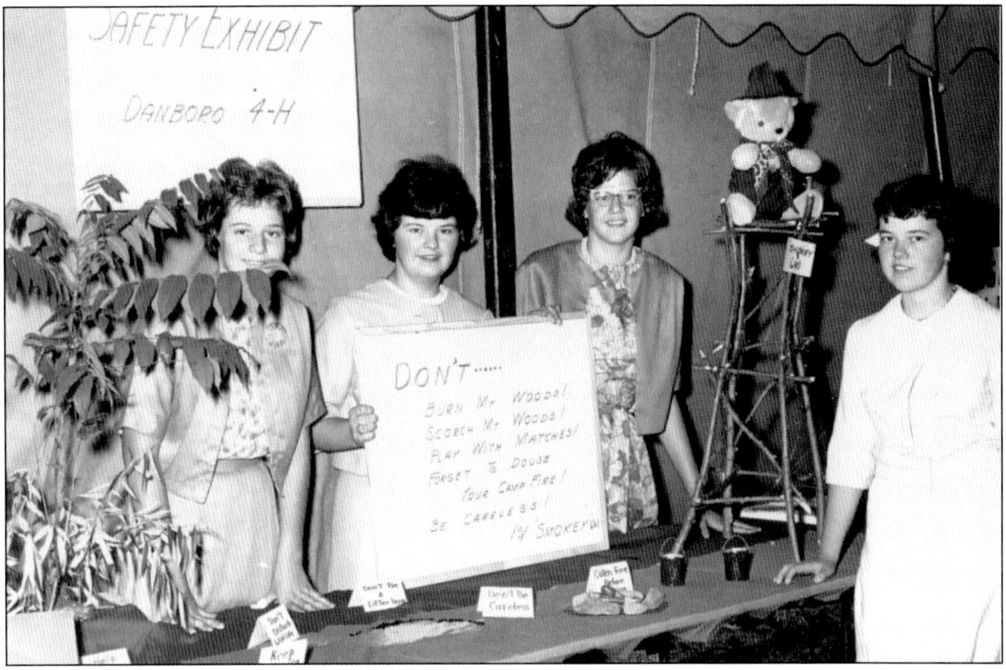

THE DANBORO 4-H CLUB, C. 1962. Presenting a 4-H exhibit on fire safety are, from left to right, Barbara Walton, Sarah Fullam, Susan Walton, and Mary Jane Fullam.

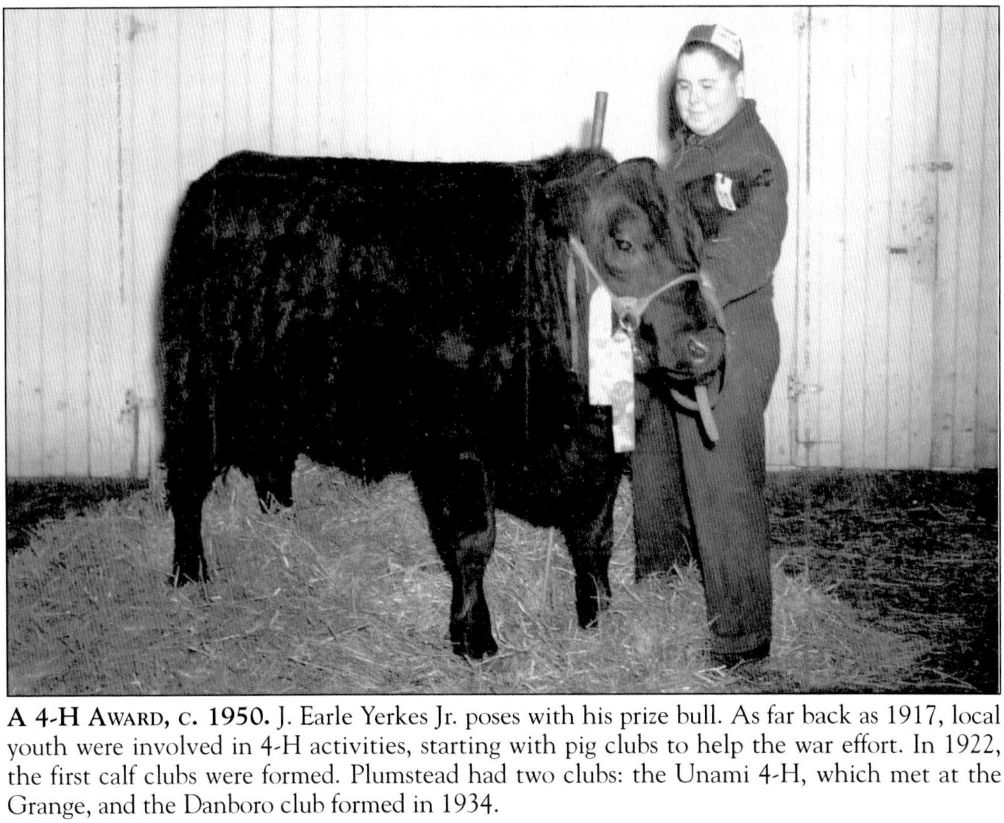

A 4-H AWARD, C. 1950. J. Earle Yerkes Jr. poses with his prize bull. As far back as 1917, local youth were involved in 4-H activities, starting with pig clubs to help the war effort. In 1922, the first calf clubs were formed. Plumstead had two clubs: the Unami 4-H, which met at the Grange, and the Danboro club formed in 1934.

Six

SERVICE

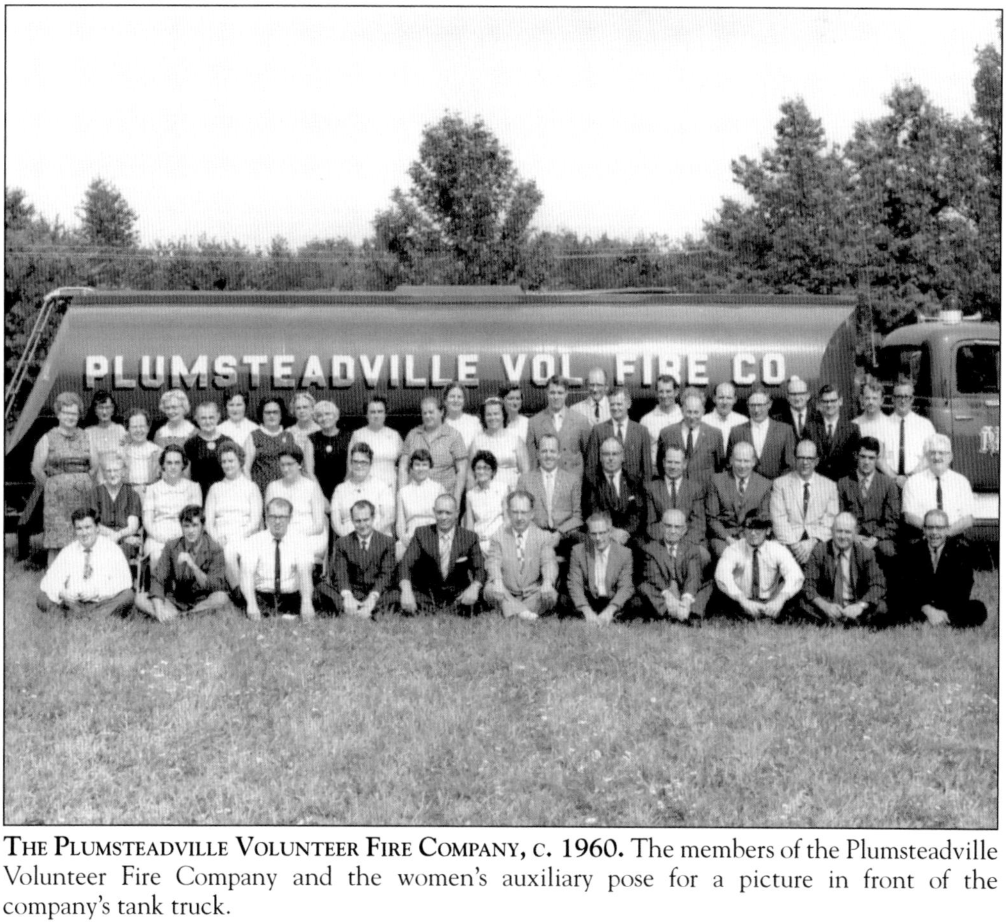

THE PLUMSTEADVILLE VOLUNTEER FIRE COMPANY, C. 1960. The members of the Plumsteadville Volunteer Fire Company and the women's auxiliary pose for a picture in front of the company's tank truck.

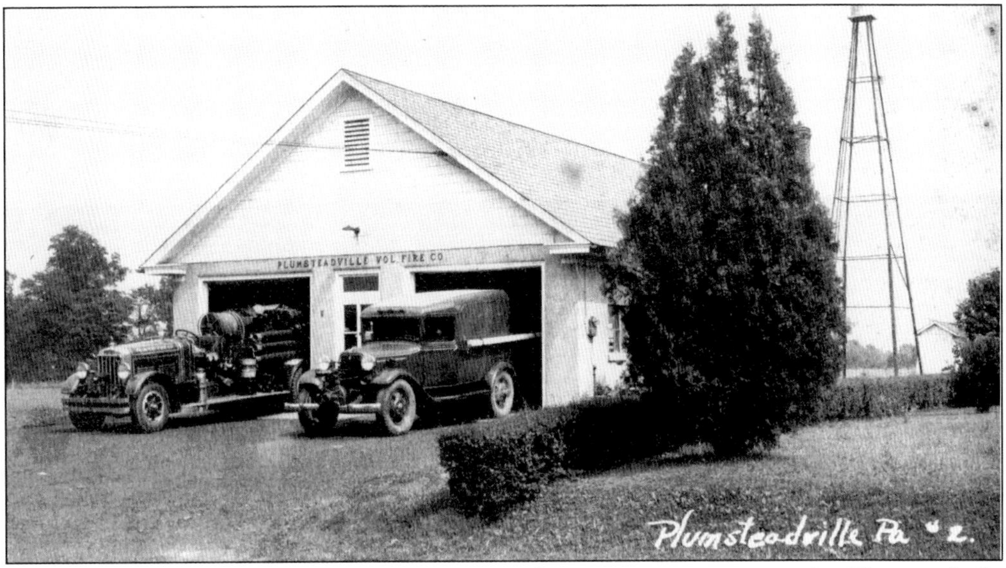

The Plumsteadville Firehouse, c. 1950. A new fire station was constructed at Plumsteadville in 1950 and was enlarged in 1964 and 1986. This picture shows the original fire truck and a 1933 Ford, which was nicknamed "Suicide Wagon" because it was top heavy and had mechanical brakes.

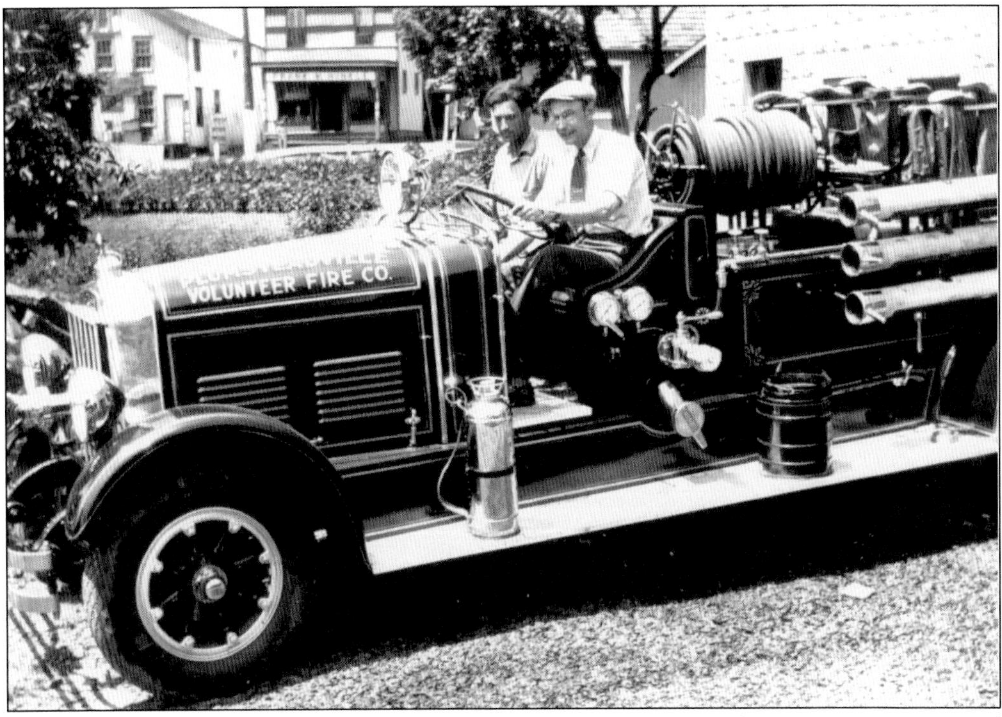

Plumsteadville's First Truck, c. 1931. A barn fire on the Lincoln Kratz property, caused by fireworks on July 4, 1929, was the impetus for the formation of the Plumsteadville Volunteer Fire Company in 1930. The first engine was delivered on May 30, 1931, at a cost of $3,500. The Hahn truck is pictured here, with the first chief, Robert Schleicher, at the wheel and Sam Rice beside him. The first fire station is visible in the background at right.

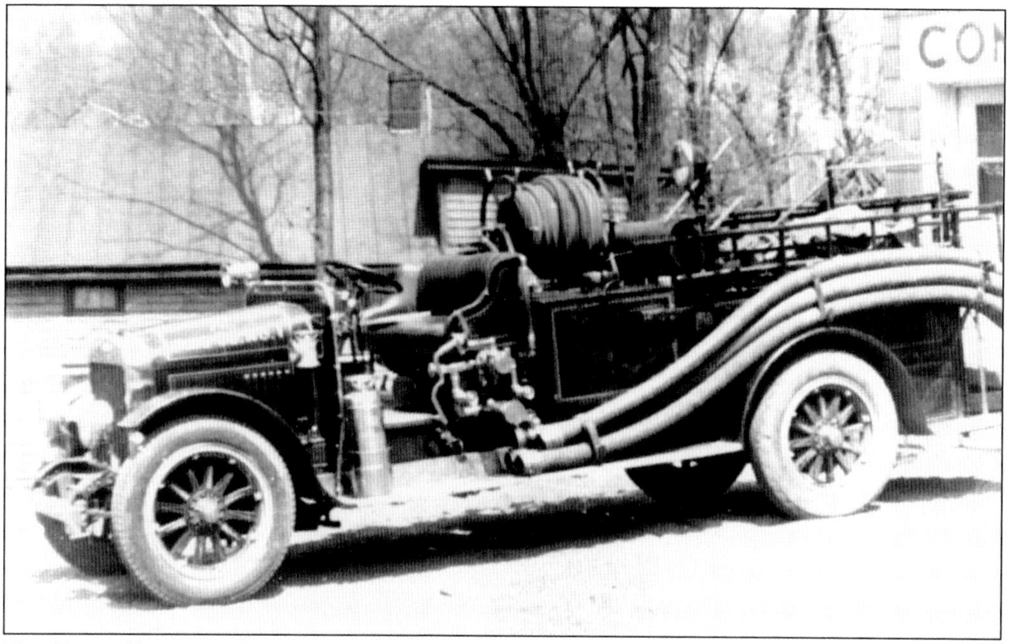

The Point Pleasant Volunteer Fire Company, c. 1930. The Point Pleasant Volunteer Fire Company was formed in 1924 after a fire destroyed Grimm's store in the village. During that same year, the company purchased a 1924 Hahn truck for $4,207. Initially, a temporary structure was built for the fire company, and by 1925, land for the station on River Road was purchased. Also in 1925, the women's auxiliary was formed. The fire station pictured below served the community from 1925 until a new building was constructed outside the village in 1991.

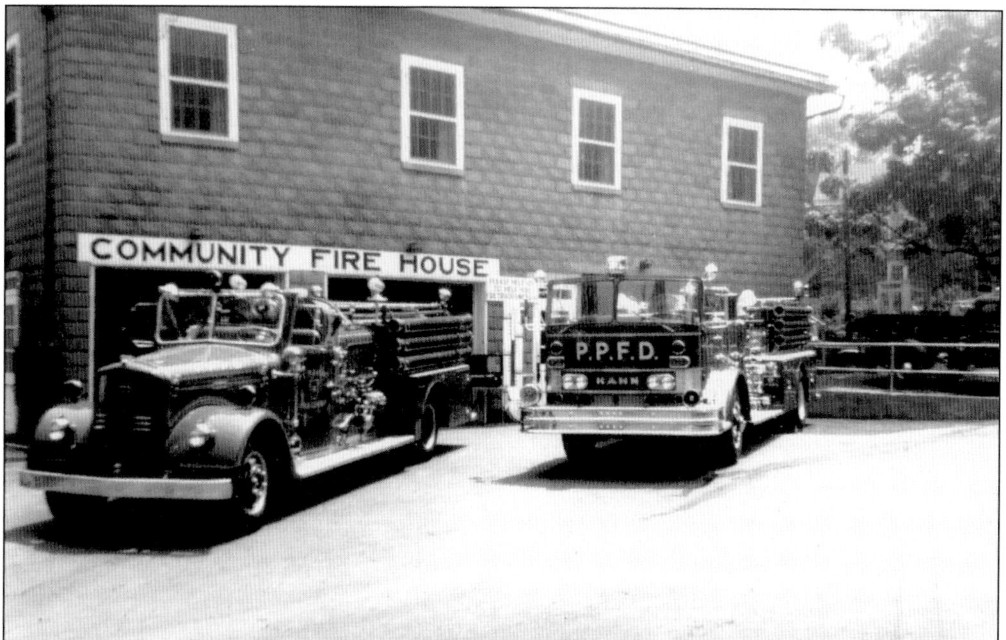

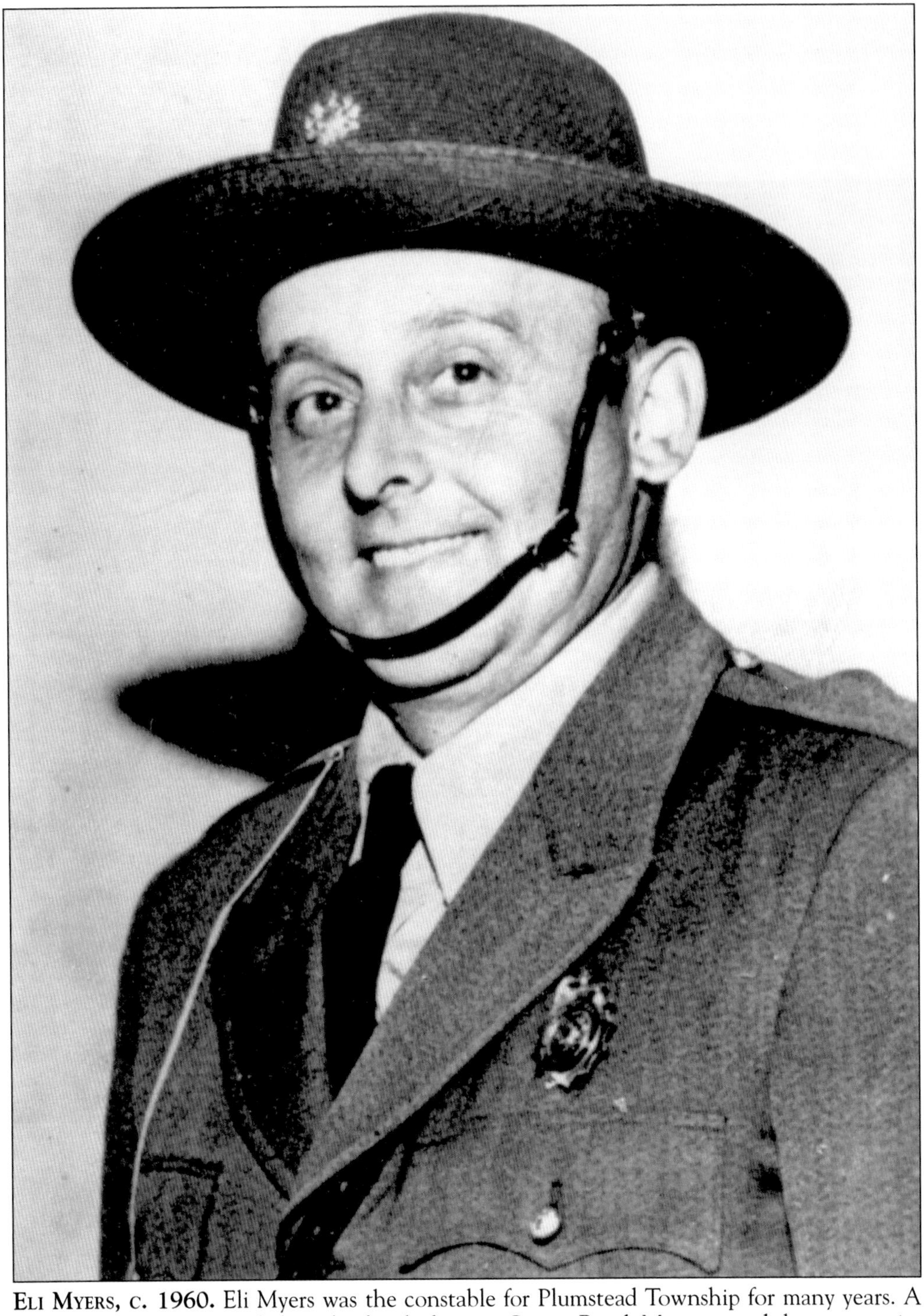

Eli Myers, c. 1960. Eli Myers was the constable for Plumstead Township for many years. A Plumstead native, he resided on the family farm on Stump Road. Myers served the community in many capacities, including as a member of the Plumsteadville Volunteer Fire Company. Many residents remember him as their school bus driver. He died in the line of duty while directing traffic in nearby Dublin.

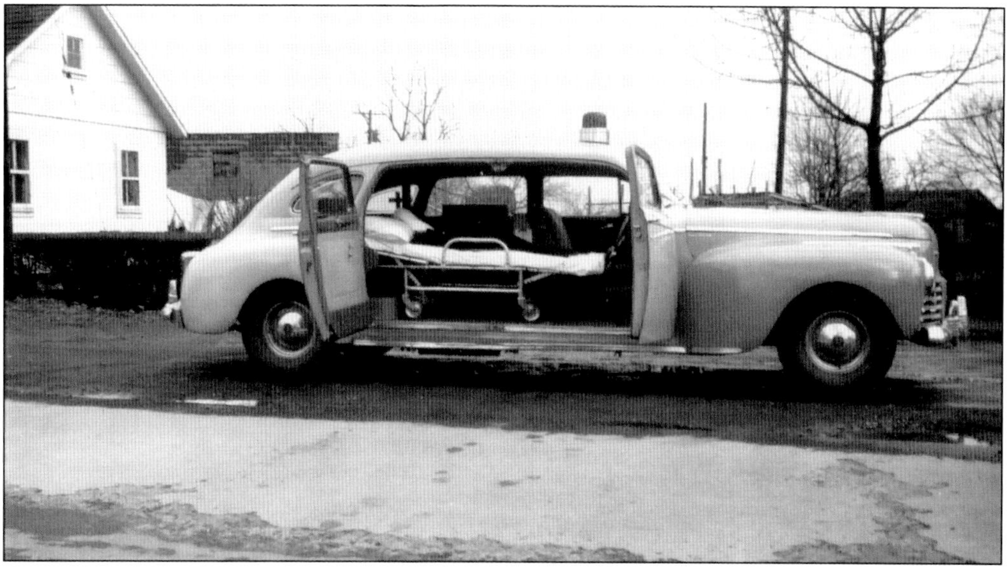

THE PLUMSTEADVILLE AMBULANCE CORPS, C. 1956. The Plumsteadville Volunteer Fire Company ambulance corps was formed in 1956 when it received its first ambulance as a gift from the Dublin Fire Company. The vehicle was a 1941 Chrysler.

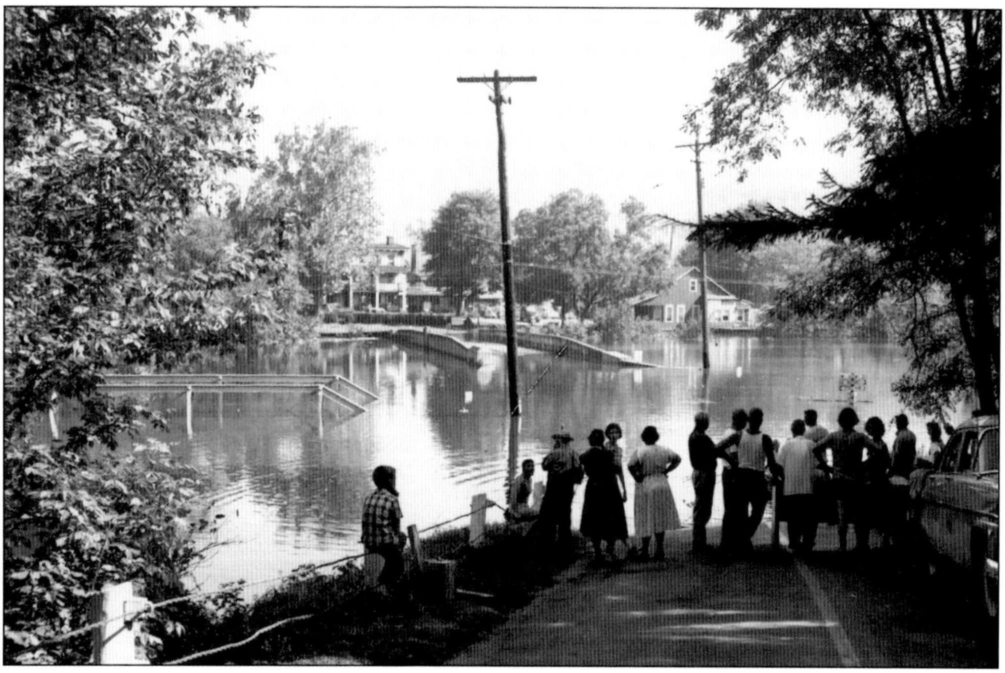

THE FLOOD OF 1955. The flood of 1955 caused destruction along the Delaware River. Most buildings on River Road in Point Pleasant were flooded. This picture shows the Geddes Run Bridge (left center) and Tohickon Creek Bridge in the background, with Point Pleasant Pike in the foreground. The Point Pleasant firehouse became the center for flood relief. A canteen that was operated there by the ladies auxiliary fed people for two weeks.

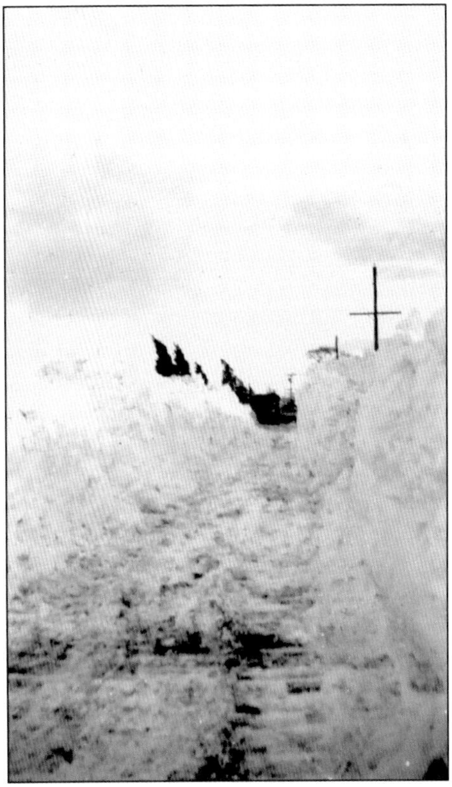

A Snowstorm, February 1947. Heavy snowstorms were common in the 1940s and 1950s. Shown here is a section of Stump Road just east of Wismer. Snow removal was done with a bulldozer and by manual labor—men with shovels. It took 15 hours to clear approximately a quarter mile of roadway after this storm.

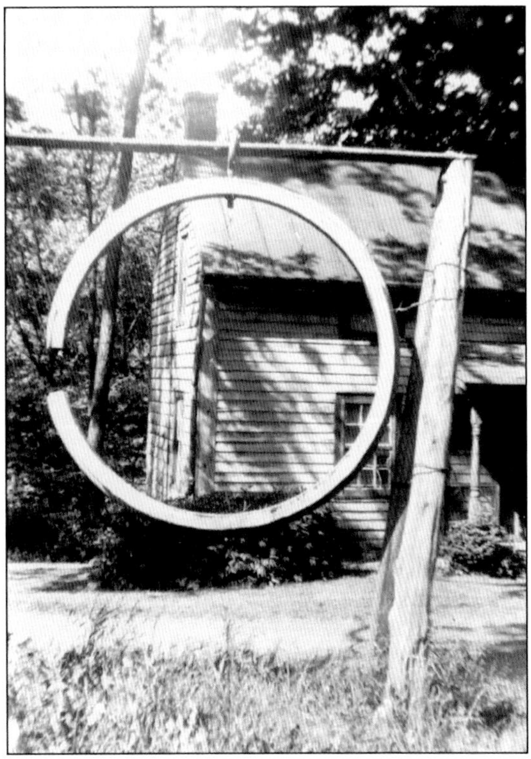

The Point Pleasant Fire Company Gong, c. 1930. Before there were sirens, there was a gong in front of the firehouse that was used to alert firemen and residents during an emergency. The gong was made from a locomotive wheel.

A World War I Sailor, c. 1918. Marshall Yost poses here on the Geddes Run Bridge in his U.S. Navy uniform during World War I. Later in life, Yost was postmaster at Point Pleasant, serving in that capacity until his retirement in 1963.

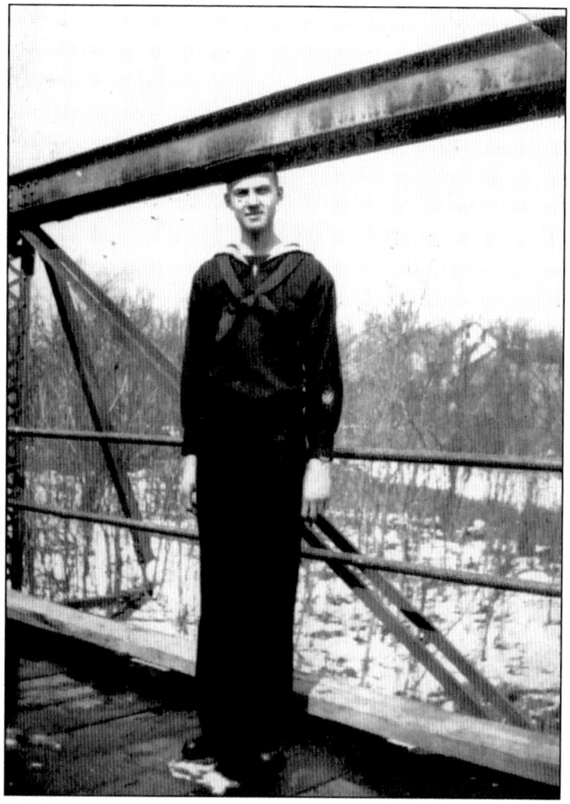

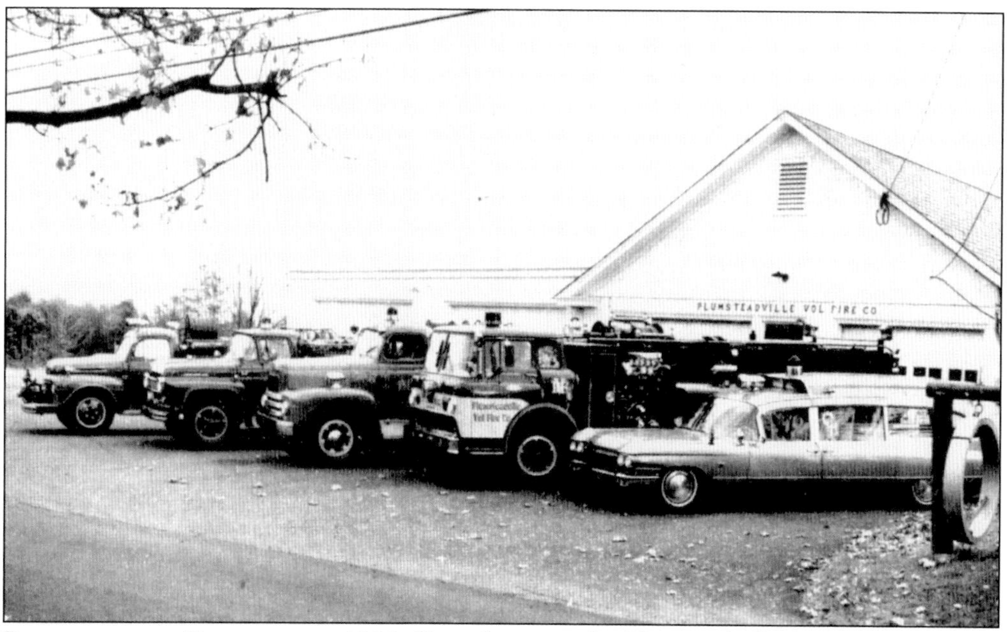

Plumsteadville Firehouse, c. 1960. Over the years, the Plumsteadville firehouse has grown. By the early 1960s, it had a new wing and a collection of engines. A new ambulance was among the equipment.

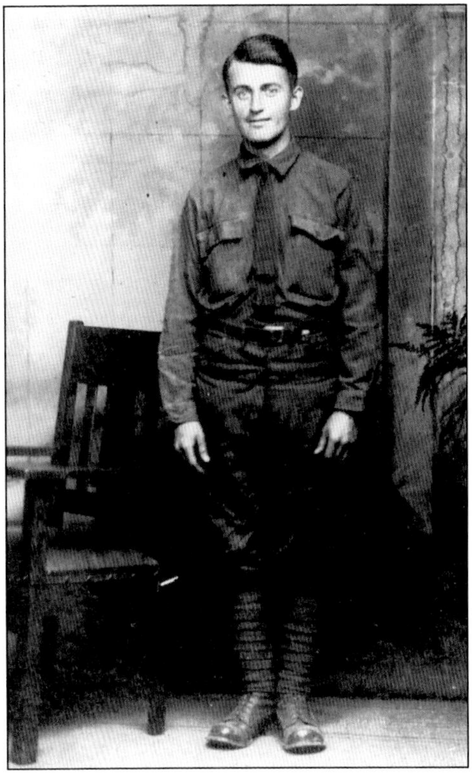

LLOYD AND MARY SMITH, C. 1918. Young men throughout the township served their country during World War I. At left, Lloyd Smith, a Plumstead native, poses in his uniform. Soon after the war, he married Mary Magdalena Mergenthaler, pictured below, of Stump Road. The couple walked in deep snow from Wismer to Tinicum Township to get married.

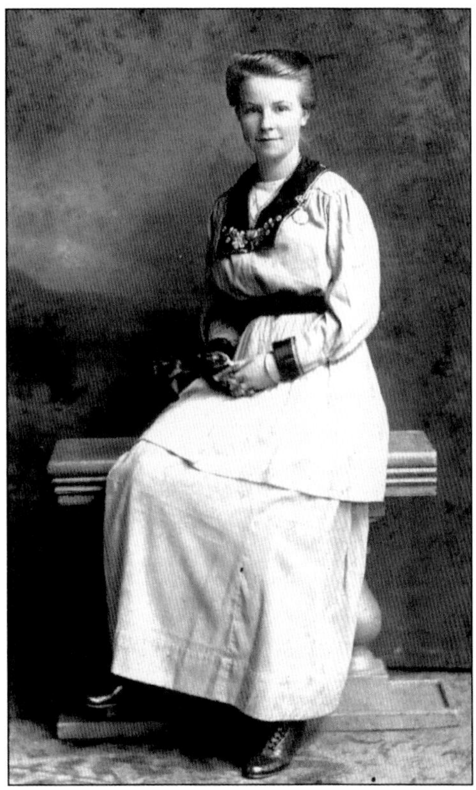

A SAILOR READY FOR WAR, C. 1943. Norman Lear of Gardenville poses for the camera at the corner of Point Pleasant Pike and Durham Road.

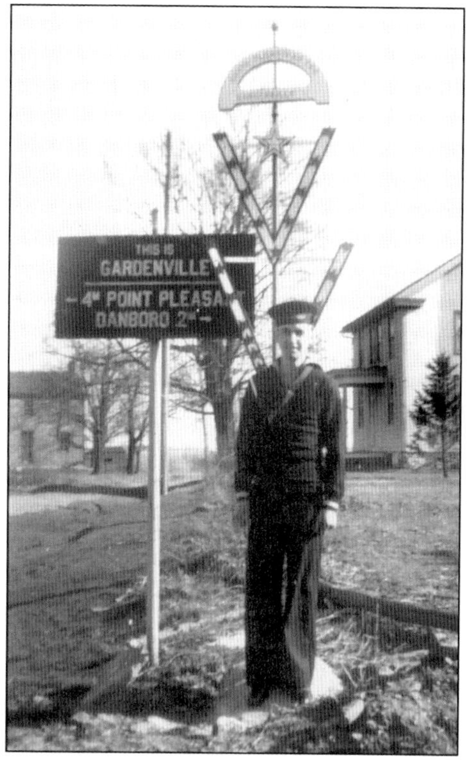

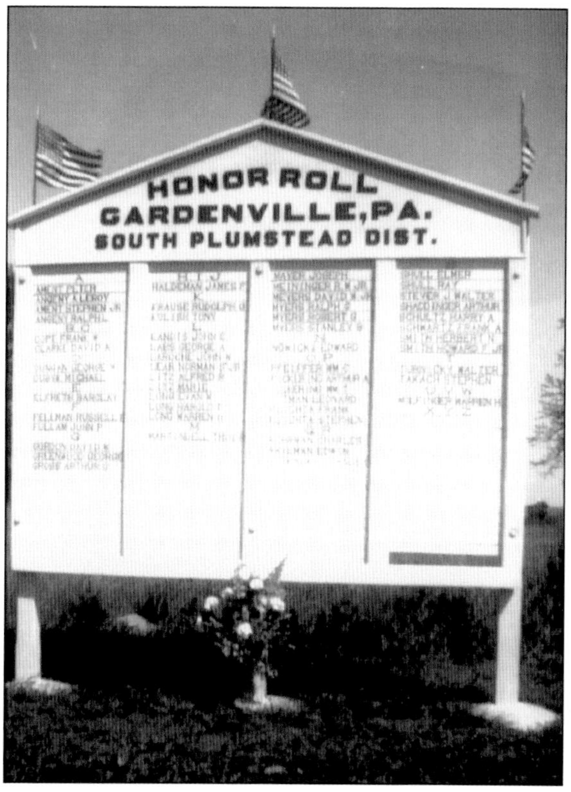

GARDENVILLE HONOR ROLL, C. 1945. Plaques bearing the names of residents who were serving their country during World War II were common sights in many towns. Point Pleasant and Plumsteadville had similar honor rolls.

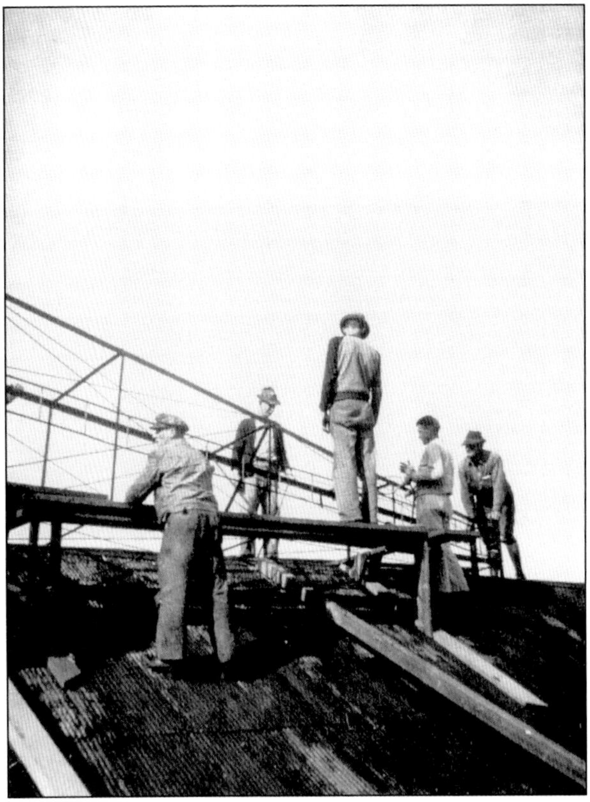

An Air Raid Tower, c. 1941. Air raid sirens and towers were constructed in various locations in the township during World War II in order to signal residents of possible danger. This tower was constructed at the Angeny property in Danboro and was later rebuilt at the Plumsteadville Fire Company.

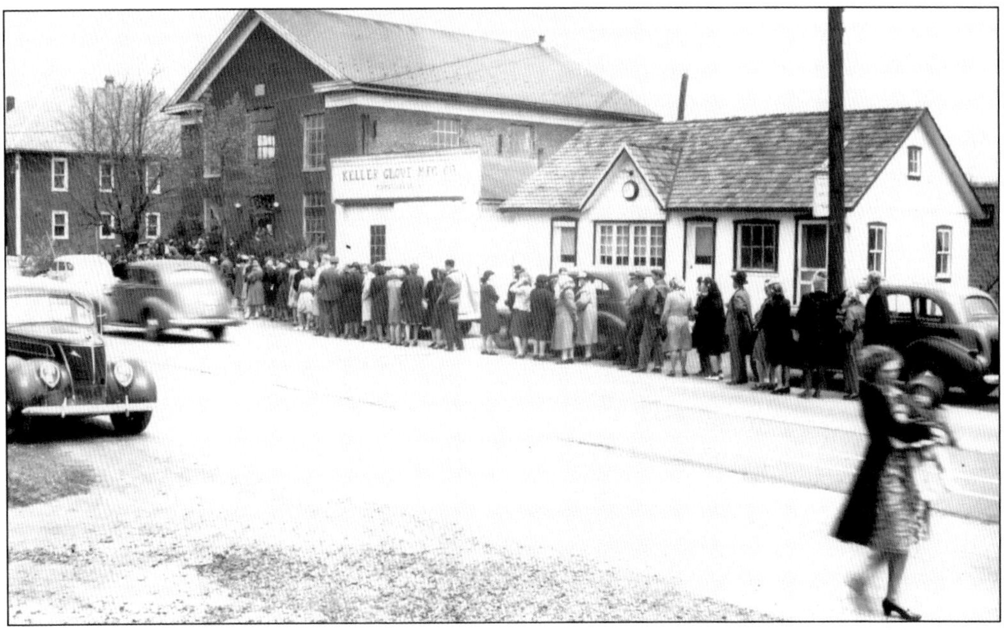

Lining up for Nylons, c. 1945. Nylons were in short supply during World War II. Once the war was over, nylons were put on sale at the Keller Glove Factory, and lines of customers formed outside.

Seven

CHANGING TIMES

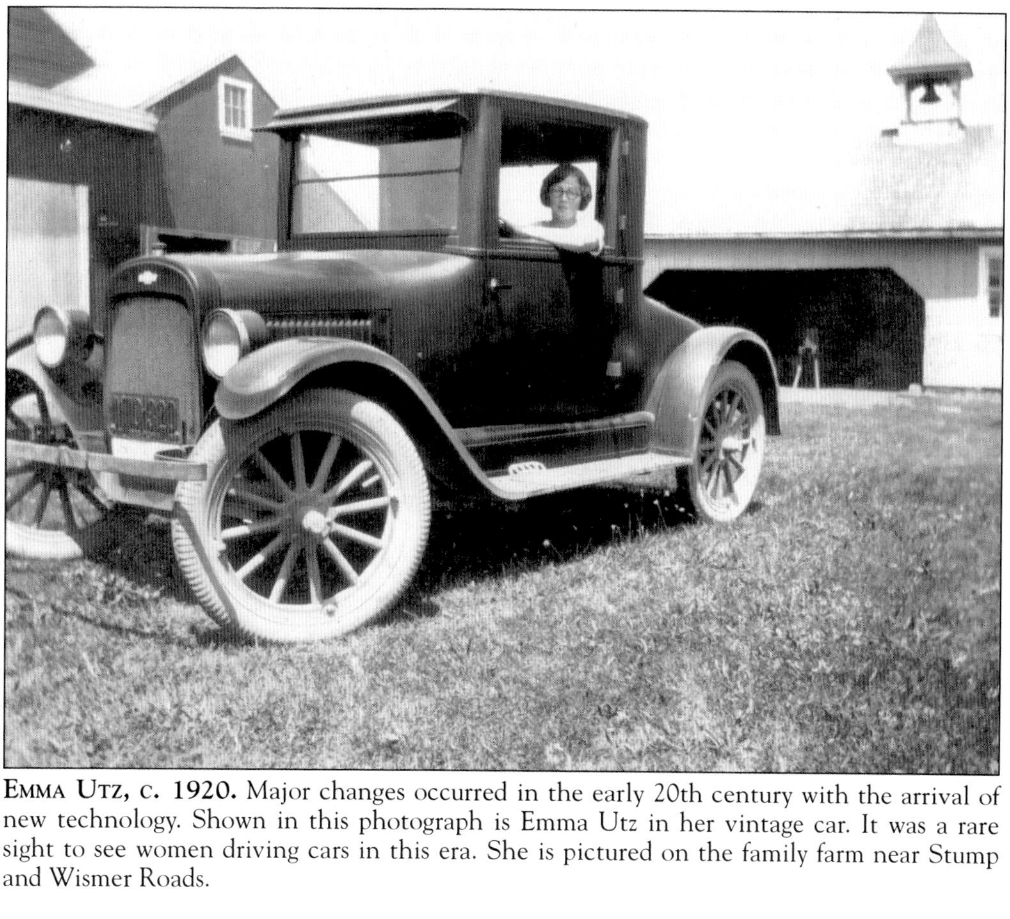

EMMA UTZ, C. 1920. Major changes occurred in the early 20th century with the arrival of new technology. Shown in this photograph is Emma Utz in her vintage car. It was a rare sight to see women driving cars in this era. She is pictured on the family farm near Stump and Wismer Roads.

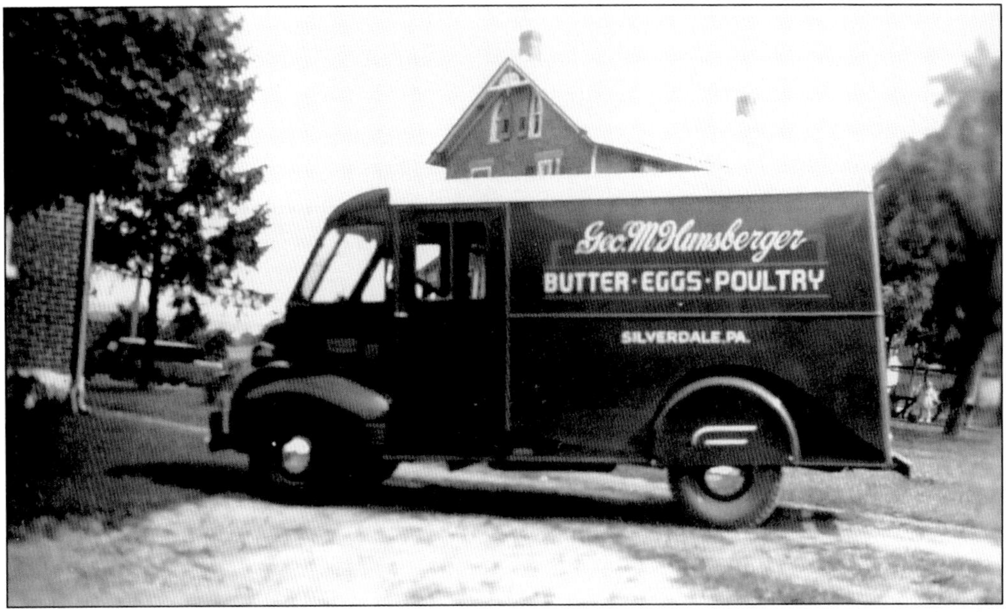

PRODUCT DELIVERY, C. 1940. Delivery trucks replaced the old horse-and-wagon peddlers by the mid-20th century. This truck is parked in front of the Hunsberger Farm on Stump Road.

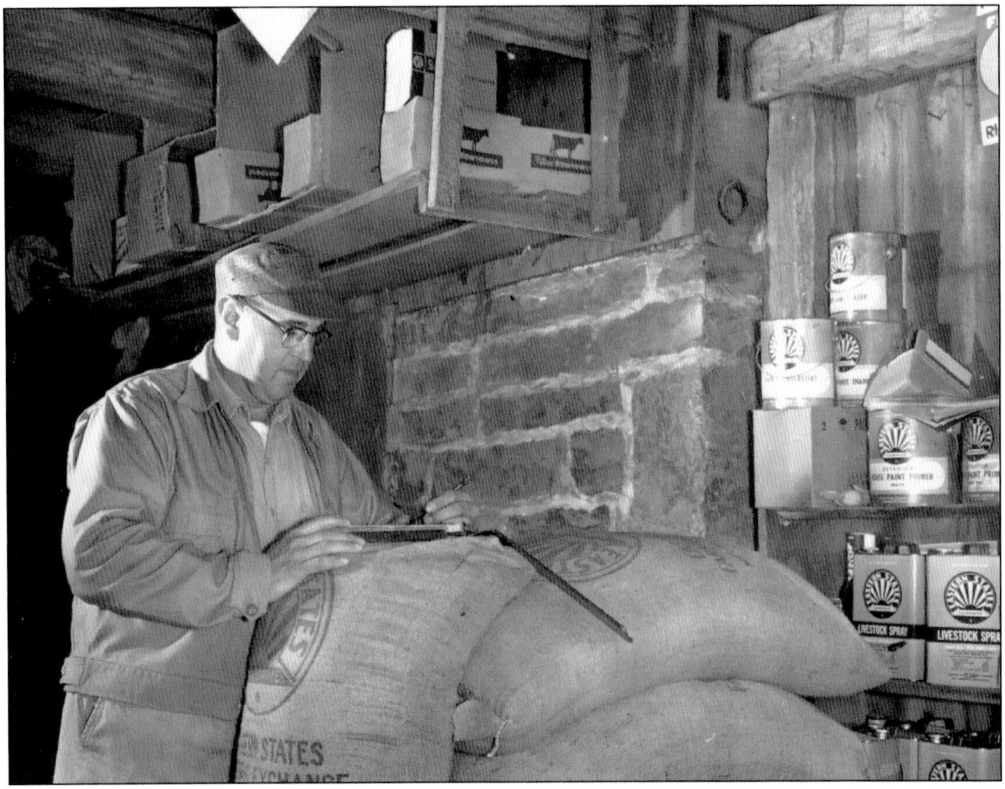

FARMING SUPPLIES, C. 1947. George Hunsberger is pictured here, going over his inventory. Besides working as a farmer, Hunsberger was a local distributor of farming supplies. His store was located in the barn that is still on the property.

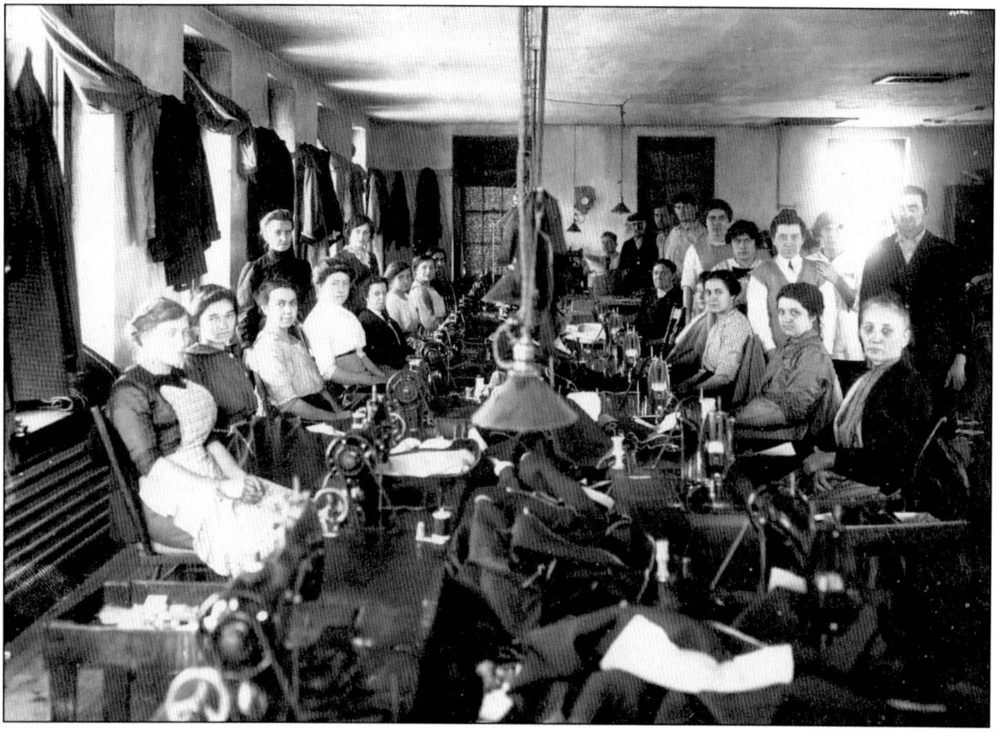

The Fretz Pants Factory, c. 1920. In nearby Pipersville, a pants factory opened in the early 1900s. Many of its employees were women from Plumstead Township.

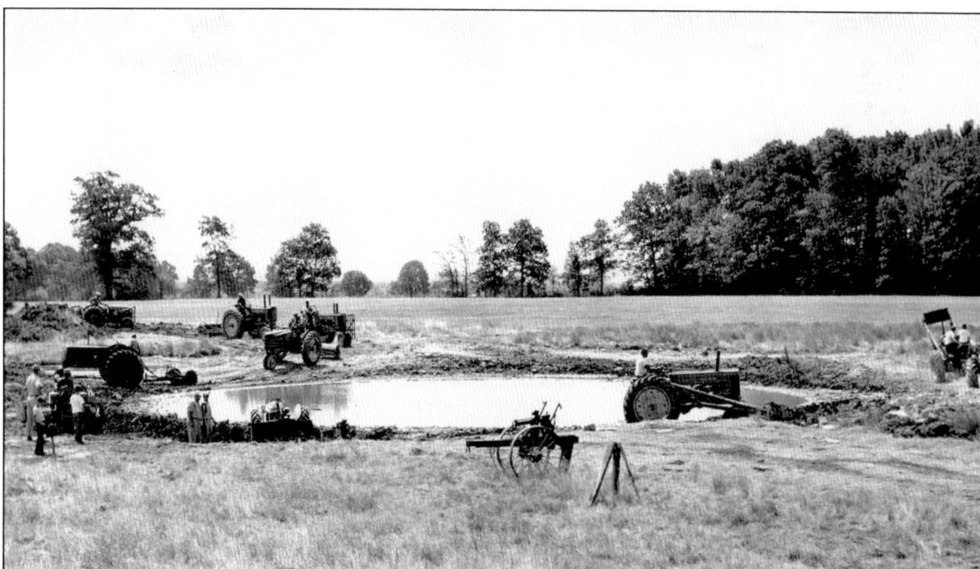

Pond Construction, c. 1945. Neighbors assist in enlarging a pond at the Gross Farm along Stump Road.

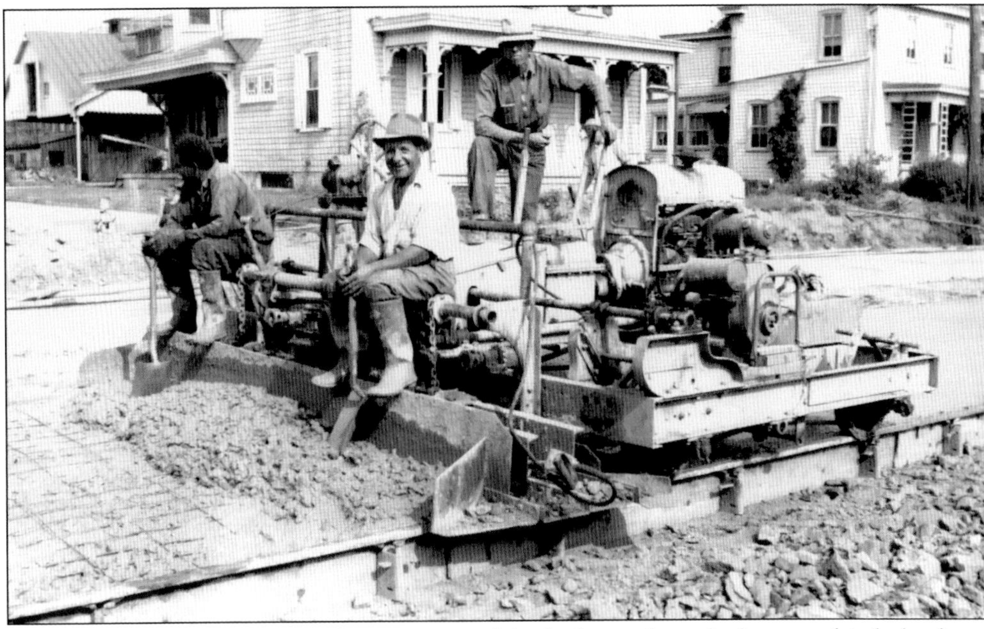

Paving Route 611, c. 1939. Construction of the highway through the township helped spur commercial construction, especially along a stretch of the new roadway west of Danboro. Here, workers take a break from paving in Plumsteadville.

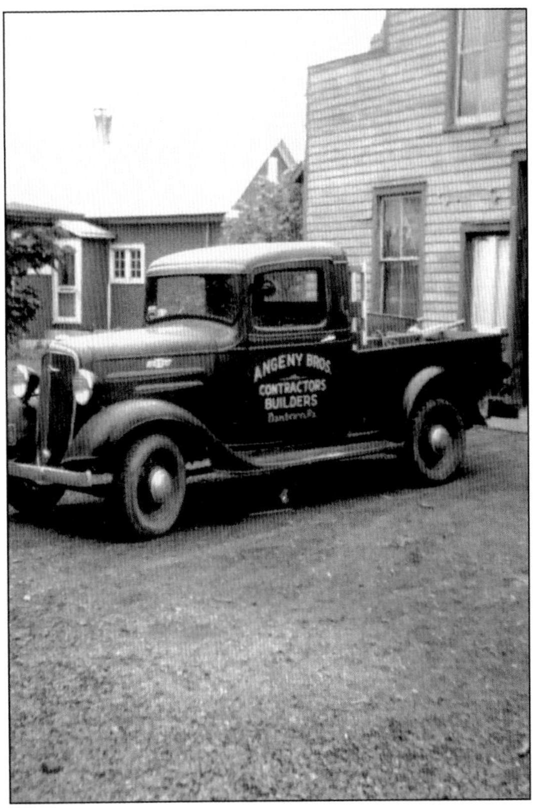

Angeny Brothers, 1940. Construction and development after World War II began to change the appearance of the community. The Angeny brothers of Danboro were local carpenters who worked on old and new homes.

A Stonemason at Work, c. 1940. The building industry was a booming business by the mid-20th century, due to the expansion of roadways and influx of new residents. Here, E. Howard Hinkle, a local stonemason, repairs a chimney on Potters Lane.

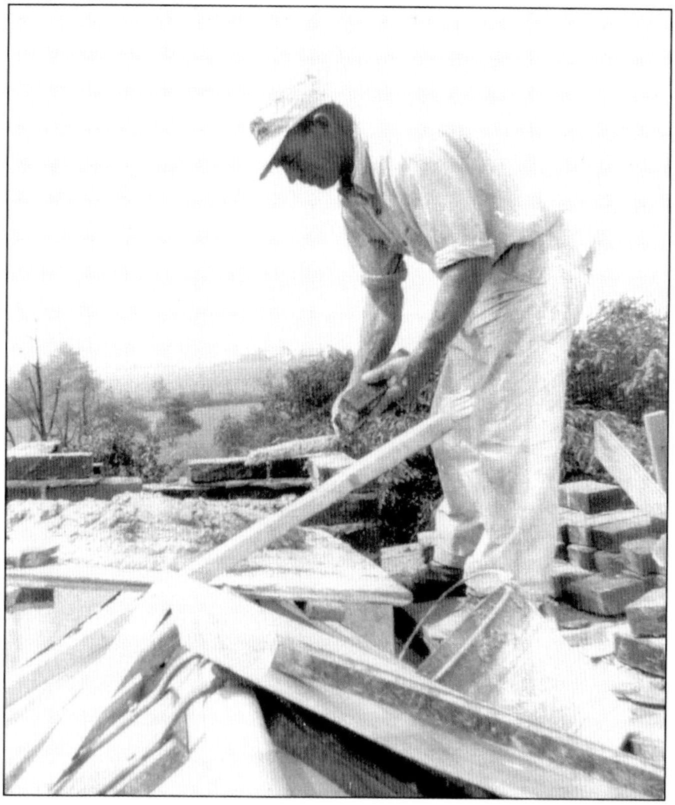

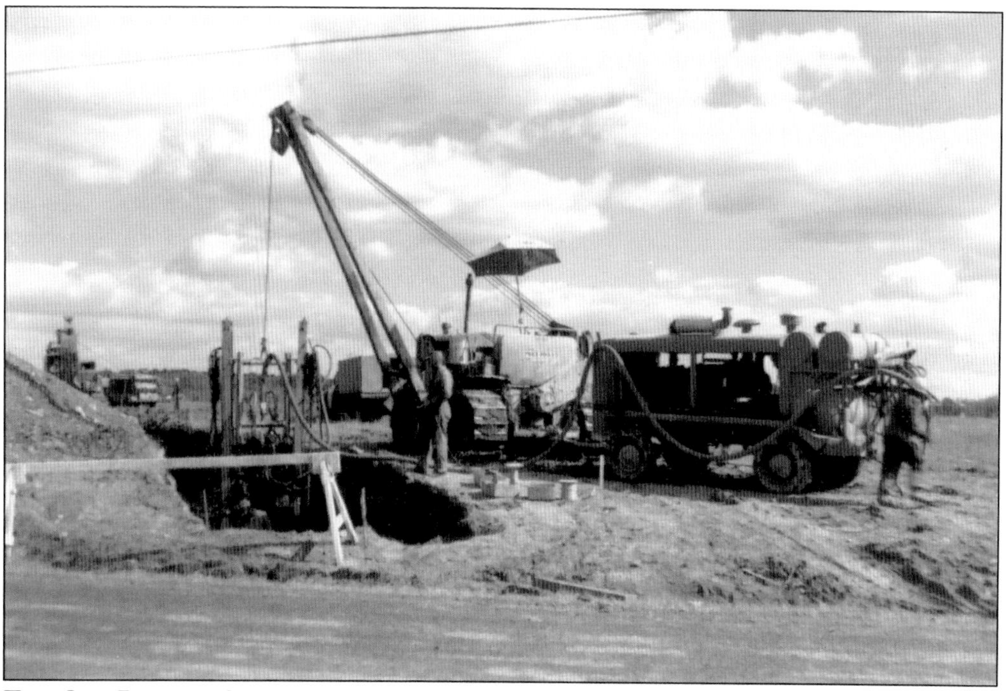

The Gas Pipeline Construction, c. 1958. A gas pipeline was constructed through the township in the mid-1950s.

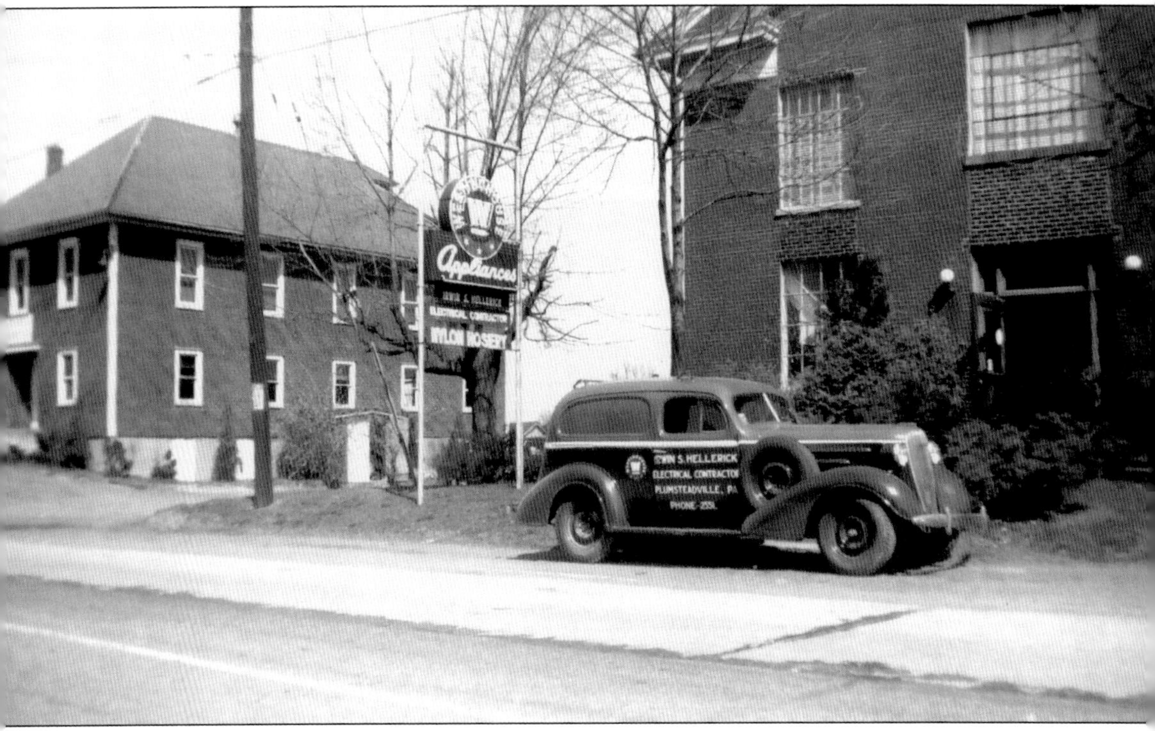

HELLERICK'S ELECTRICAL COMPANY, C. 1950. The old Presbyterian church was converted into the Keller Glove Factory in the early 1900s. The building became the site of Irv Hellerick's electrical company (on right) when the factory moved south of the village. Hellerick was an electrician and also sold electrical appliances. A large sign was installed out front to advertise the business, and Hellerick's truck also displayed advertising for the company.

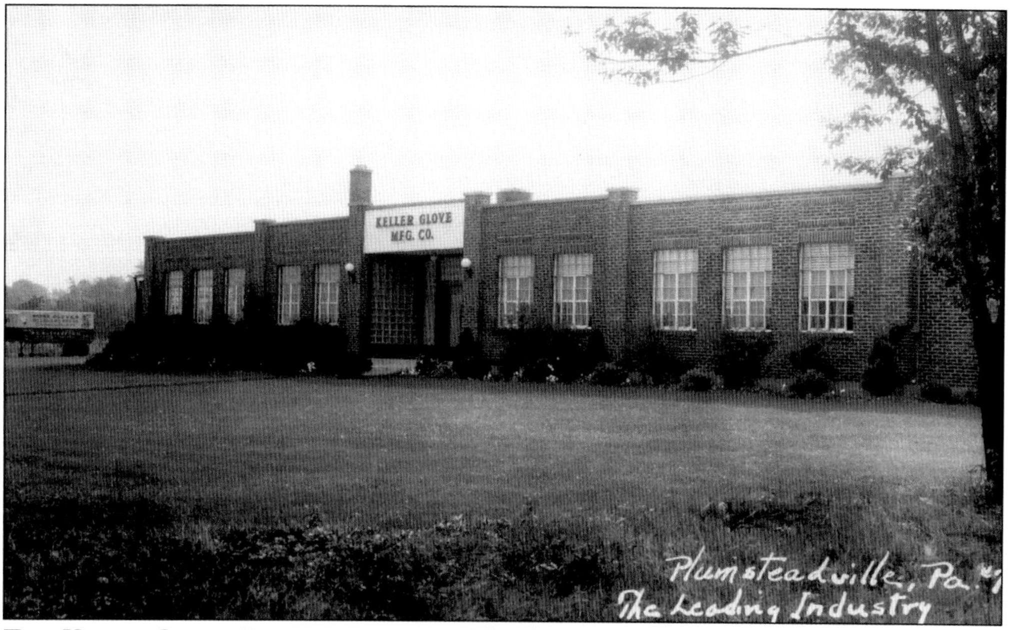

The Keller Glove Factory, c. 1950. The factory moved to a new location south of Plumsteadville, along the new highway. The new building was constructed of brick, and by the mid-20th century the glove factory was the leading industry in the township. The building has been expanded over the years and is now occupied by Malmark Bells. Below, Bob Schleicher (left) and Irv Hellerick pose inside the new Keller Glove Factory.

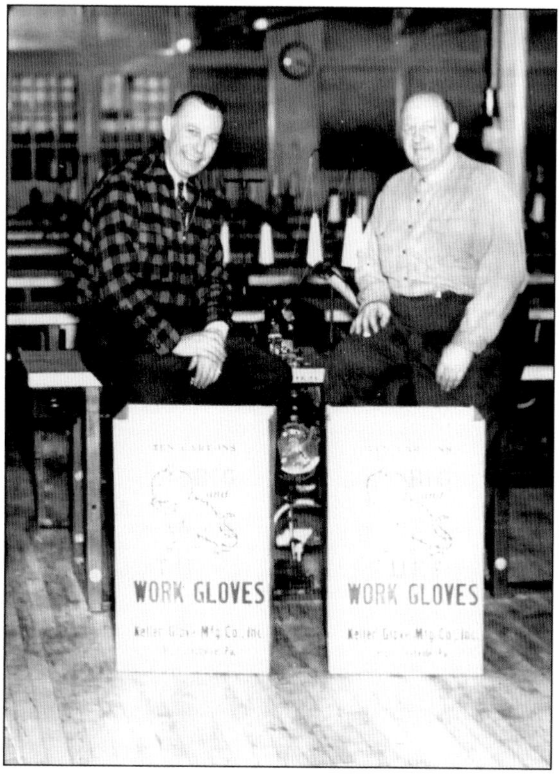

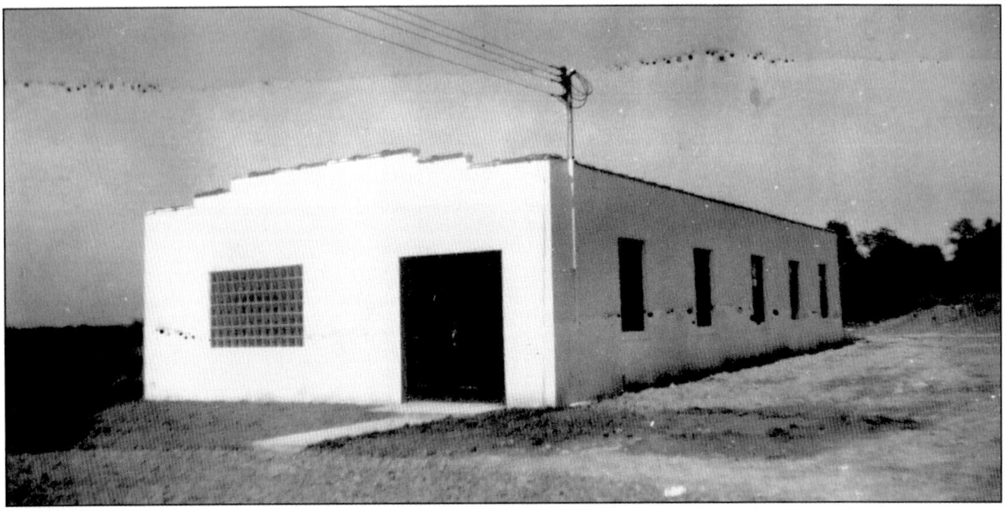

THE RONNETTE HOSIERY MILL, C. 1947. The Ronnette Hosiery Mill of Danboro, operated by Adam and Cathryn Sabath, opened along the new Route 611 highway in 1947. In Bucks County, production of hosiery and stockings was a major industry. Plumstead Township had three mills at this time. The building was expanded over the years and today is incorporated as part of a small shopping center near Silo Hill Road.

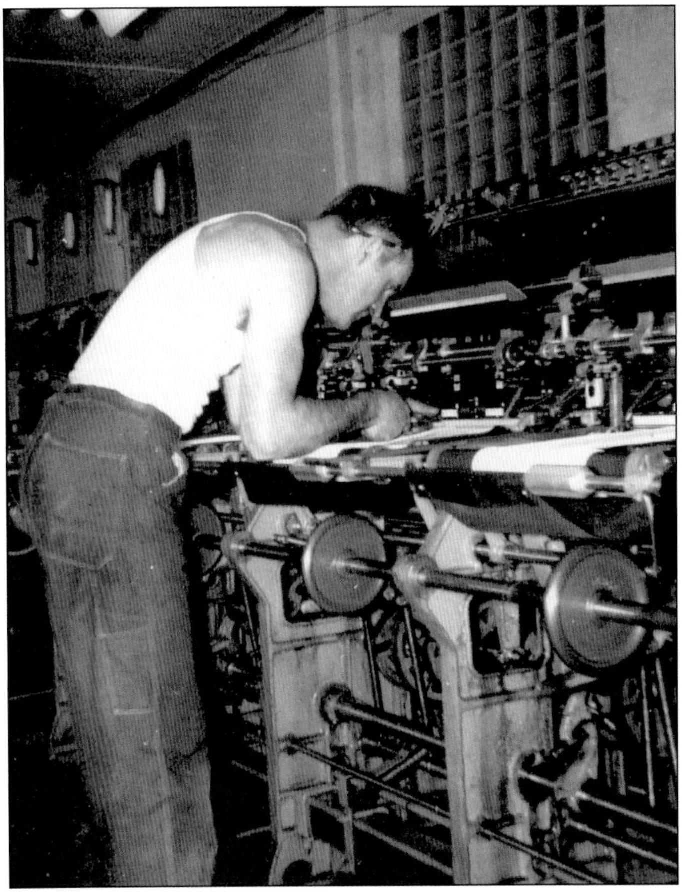

ADAM SABATH IN THE HOSIERY MILL, C. 1952. Adam Sabath, owner of the mill, is seen here tending to the operation of the hosiery machines.

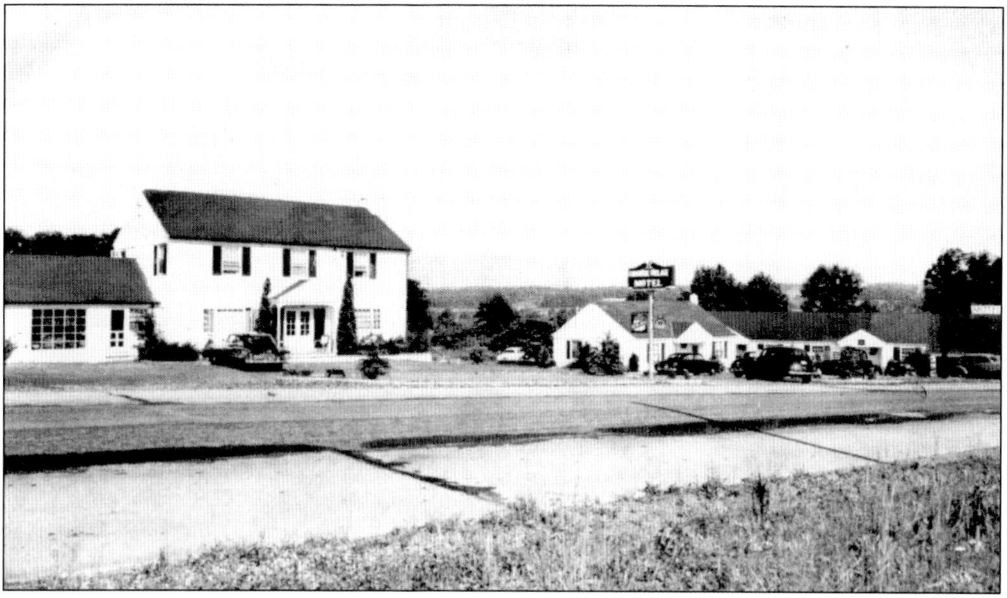

The Colonial Village Motel, c. 1950. A new motel was constructed along the new highway to serve motorists. For many years, the motel also housed the local state police station.

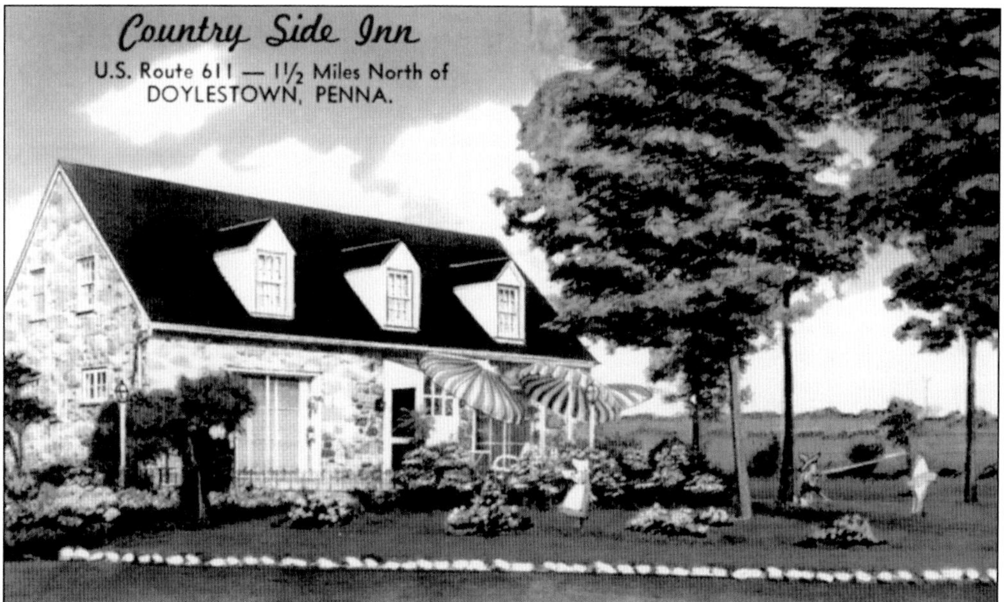

The Country Side Inn, c. 1950. Roadside restaurants, such as the Country Side Inn (above), were also built for motorists traveling the new highway. This inn was found on the east side of the new road, near Cross Keys.

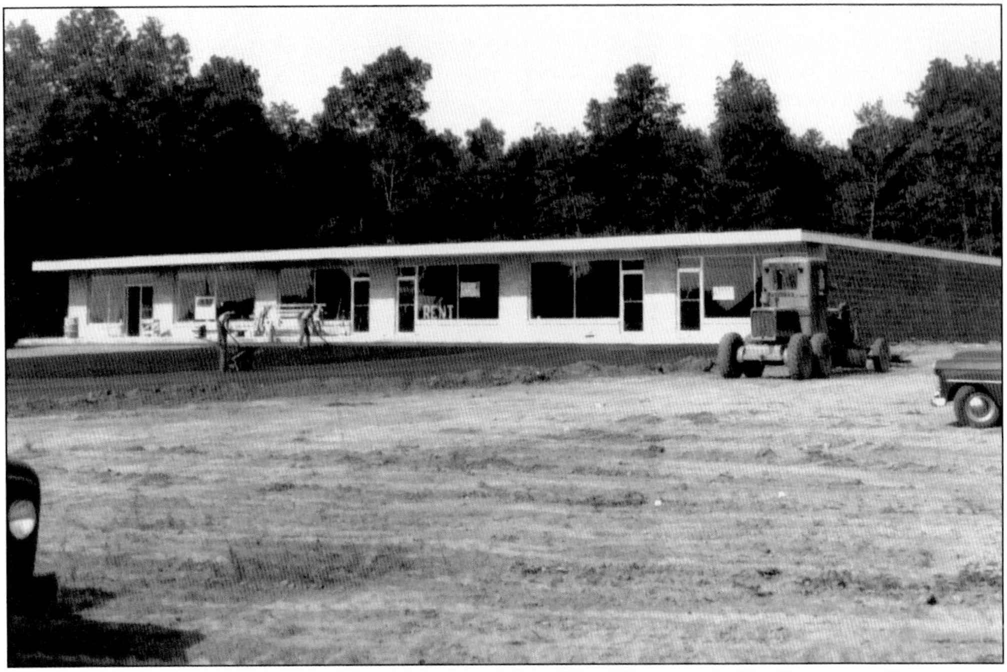

THE PLUMSTEADVILLE SHOPPING CENTER, c. 1962. The Plumsteadville Shopping Center was opened in 1963, just south of the village, along the highway. Only five stores were originally constructed; one was used for the post office.

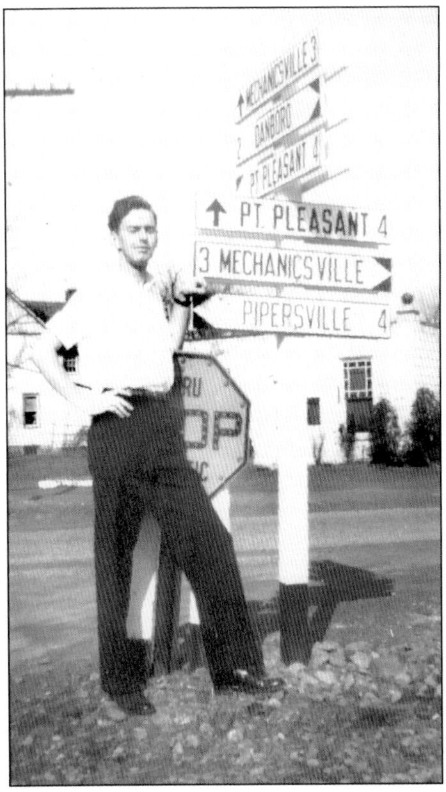

THE GARDENVILLE CROSSROADS, c. 1943. William J. Jacobs Jr. stands in front of the old crossroads sign at Point Pleasant Pike and Durham Road.